Haydenville

The Company Owned Ohio Town that Outlived the Company

A Memoir

Larry A. Horn, Sr.

Monday Creek Publishing
Ohio USA

Certain photos courtesy of Mark Howell, Author and Historian

Cover Design by Gina McKnight

ISBN: 0692937307
ISBN-13: 978-0692937303

To the History of Haydenville

Special thanks to those who helped preserve these bits of Haydenville's past. Without your help, some of Haydenville's history would have been lost forever.

Thanks to those who contributed their stories, photographs, and support, including Patty Carr, Mark Howell, and Addison Paige Fuchs.

Table of Contents

Preface

Thanks to those who helped preserve these bits of Haydenville's past. Without your help, some of Haydenville's history would have been lost forever.

Thank you for trusting me to print your life experiences and precious memories of Haydenville, your families and friends, in the culture and slang exactly as you told me.

To the readers of these memoirs, yes you may find flaws and errors, but it was not my intent to make this book perfect, but to honor the trust given to me by the contributors "to tells it like it was in days gone by."

Prologue

Many historic events have been part of Haydenville's past since its humble beginning in the early 1800's when the Hocking Valley Iron Furnace Co. smelting furnace was producing vast quantities of iron. By the time the demand for iron was beginning to decline, the coal mines, brick and terra cotta clay products factories were in full production. All under the ownership of Hayden Mining & Mfg. Co. (H M & M Co.), who also founded the company owned town of Haydenville.

Transportation has always played a major role in the growth of Haydenville and its factories. The stagecoach and horse-drawn wagon gave way to the canal boats. The railroad, with its mighty steam powered engines, replaced the canal boats, and in later years large trucks traveling on modern highways replaced the railroad.

1959 ushered in *the end of an era* for Haydenville, the industrial clay manufacturing and mining giant, with its hundreds of manual laborers and steam powered machinery, would close its doors forever.

Most of the original company built and owned homes still stand today, a lasting tribute and memorial to the men and factories of days gone by.

The 2008 annals of the town will note that the town did not die; it installed its first ever streetlights, concrete sidewalks, and replaced an old abandon school building with a community park.

Haydenville holds the distinguished honor of:
The last company owned town in Ohio
The town that out lived the Company

Chapter 1: Timeline

Haydenville, Ohio
(Previously known as)
Hocking Furnace
Hocking Valley Iron Company
S.E, 1/4 of Section 13 Green Township, Hocking County, Ohio

The little town of Haydenville is located approximately 50 miles South of Columbus, Ohio via of U.S. Route 33. It is a picturesque little town, truly a one of a kind in architecture design and was exception to the rule of company owned towns.

Its beginning goes back to early settlers who were farmers and trappers, amongst them was Christopher Wolfe,(Chris) & his consort Ronda. They brought their family to Southeastern, Ohio from Pennsylvania around1790. Early 1800's Chris moved his family from, what is presently known as Athens, County to the 2,000 plus acres of land he had acquired in Green, Ward, Starr Township, Hocking County.

Chris and Ronda both passed away in 1845 and are buried in the Wolfe family private cemetery at the East edge of Haydenville (on the hill that overlooked the Stiers farm and the Hocking River Valley.) Their 10 children married into local families and kept parts of the original Wolfe homestead for themselves.

By 1830 investors had started developing the mineral recourses of South-eastern, Ohio. The mineral resources in Hocking County attracted Peter Hayden, a young entrepreneur from Columbus, Ohio, who was seeking his fortune in banking, foundry, tool manufacturing, and transportation, including canal boats.

Peter Hayden purchased several hundred acres of adjoining land in Green, Starr, and Ward Townships in Hocking County, Ohio. Peter began his mining venture as Hayden Mining Company in Section #7 Green Township, a few years later the area would be known as Hopperville. Peter placed James Overton

Reamey in charge of the mining operation and shortly thereafter James married Peter's daughter, Alice De Forrest Hayden. James managed the mining operations until his death in 1872.

1832-1842: The Hocking Canal was opened from Athens to Carroll near Columbus. The Hocking Canal served as a feeder for the Ohio Canal which started at Cleveland and continued South to the Ohio River at Portsmouth, Ohio. Prior 1850 Green Township plat map identifies Hocking Valley Iron Company and the S.S. Mills stone quarry. The close proximity of the stone quarry would have been the deciding factor of the Iron Ore Smelting furnace being erected at what is now Haydenville, Ohio.

1850: August 14th, Hocking County deed records Book L Page 184; show George Crawford and wife Mariah by her "mark" (X) of Hocking County, Ohio for $1.00 deeded .94 acres to the Trustee of Methodist Episcopal Church of the United States of America. "The said trustee or successor in trust ' Shall' erect and build or cause to be erected a House or Place of Worship for member of the Methodist Episcopal Church in the United States of America".

1851: September 13th, Hocking County deed record Book L Page 219-220 Joseph D. Clark and his wife Mary Clark, To Israel Dille, John W. Brice and William M. Moore constituting the firm of Dillie, Brice, and Moore of Licking County Ohio being part of Lots 771 and 772 premises and appuntinenas, in Hocking County being part of the Ohio Company Purchase

1851: October 20th, Hocking County deed records Book N Page 169-170 Robert Wright and wife Almina Wright to Dillie, Brice and Moore part of Lot 773and774 premises with appuntinenas, in Hocking County being part of the Ohio Company Purchase.

1854: June 30th, Hocking County deed records Book N Page 191-192 Dillie, Brice and Moore for the sum of $50,000 dollars paid to them by Hocking Iron Company(Peter Hayden) sells all their interest in the land and appuntinenas included in the deed from Robert Wright and wife Almina together with all building, machinery, and fixtures belonging or appertaining to the "Furnace" situated on said land. Peter changed its name to Hocking Furnace and named his nephew Hallack Hayden manager of the furnace. The furnace had been erected at the foot of the hill (now Haydenville, Ohio) some of the furnace remnants are visible from Frog Hollow Road.

1861-1883: Peter Hayden had purchased over 2,000 plus acres of land, minerals and timber in Green, Ward and Starr Township, Hocking County, Ohio. Ref. page 12.

1866: Peter Hayden issued bonds for the construction of the Mineral Railroad (later known as Columbus and Hocking Valley Railroad (C & HVR R), the railroad was completed in 1871, this opened up new market for "coal". Hayden was its first president and one of the railroad's major customers, earnings from coal exceeded combined receipts of passenger and other freight.

1867: October-27 Hocking County Records of Deeds Book 40 page 167 Wilford Stiers granted a right of way, through his property, to the Mineral Railroad. In consideration that a Railroad Depot to be constructed on the J.D. Wolfe property near the Canal Lock known as the "Wolfe Lock." (Now Laurel Run Road Cty. Rd. #26).

1869: Peter Hayden hired William Wolfe Jr. to construct a private standard gauge railroad spur from the main line at Wolfe Locke of the C & HVRR to his coal hoppers. The area around the coal hoppers became known as Hopperville. Rail shipment from Hayden coal mines increased steadily from 45,235 tons in 1871 to 70,291 tons in 1872. Employees at the Hayden mines increased from 100 men in 1869 to 150 men in March 1871.

1869: The Hocking Iron Company iron ore smelting furnace shut down. This furnace had been erected at what is now Haydenville, Ohio A few years later the massive furnace blocks would be a part of the foundation for, the H M & M Co. office/store complex.

1869: Report of the area by Levi Davis, a local registered surveyor, shows the existence of a Church close to the (now) Haydenville Cemetery. This was "prior" to the 1871 recorded date Peter Hayden and his second wife, Sarah, deeded this property to trustees of The Methodist Episcopal Church.

1871: August 1st, Hocking County records Book "Z" page 184; show Peter Hayden and wife Sarah S. Hayden of the City and County of New York for $25.00 deeded 1.34 acres to; The trustee of The Methodist Episcopal Church. Local residence referred to this Church as the "Little Church on the hill."

1871: The railroad's receipts by its first president, Peter Hayden, showed earnings from "coal" exceeded receipts of passengers and other freight. Thus expansion of the railroad during that time period knew no bounds. Two new industries were then born in rural Southern Ohio, “king coal” and railroad transportation.

1877: Peter Hayden and his wife hosted a Christmas party for the local residence and his employees. This became an annual Company tradition until the factories close in late 1950’s.

1878: The C&HVRR railroad receipts showed; rolling stock of 31 locomotives and 1,220 freight cars and averaged over 1,000,000 tons of freight and 138,472 passengers per year.

1882: Peter Hayden seized upon the 1870 discovery of marketable fire-clay under the coal seams in his mines. He began building a large factory (Plant #1) between the canal and railroad, the factory was completed in 1886. Factory (Plant #2) was added on a few years later. The factories were steamed powered and employed a large work-force of manual labors that turned out immense quantities of fire proof building tile, terra cotta clay products, red brick and red clay tile roofing.

1883: Peter Hayden formed The Haydenville Mining and Manufacturing Company (H M & M CO), Peter Hayden, President, Charles H. Hayden,(Peter's son) Vice-President, John W. Jones, General Manger. J.W. Jones, C.E. Bowen, and August Magoon all of Logan, each had a share in the company. The balance of the outstanding shares of the company was held by the Hayden family.

1883: June 4th, Hocking County deeds record Book 10 Page 56-57Peter Hayden president of The Hocking Iron Company, by Quit Claim Deed, all real estate and appuntinenas in Hocking County, Ohio to H.M.M. Co.

1883: June 4th, Hocking County deeds record Book 10 page 57 Peter Hayden and his wife Sarah L. Hayden by Warranty Deed for the sum of $263,000Dollars all real-estate and appuntinenas in Hocking County, Ohio to H.M.M. Co.

1883: H M & M Co developed a village around the factories. Peter named it “Haydenville” in honor of the family village of Haydenville, Massachusetts, which had received its name from the manufacturing activities of two of Peter’s brothers Joel and Josiah.

1884: October 7th, a patent #306,251 was issued to by the US Patten Office on Hayden Paving Brick. This patent protect the surface designs of circles, dimples, raised bar and punched 3 ½" x 3 ½" x square cavity 2 ½" on the back side of the brick before the brick were salt glazed. The brick were originally manufactured by *Hocking Clay Manufacturing Co. (HCMCo.) Peter Hayden factory in Logan, Ohio. Several few years later the salting glazing process became a standard molding process to the tile and brick at his plant in Haydenville.

*Logan Clay Products Co. presently has a clay drain tile manufacturing factory at this location(2020).

1887: On the North side of the canal and facing the factory #1, H M & M Co, built a large red brick two-story office/company store, ice plant. The complex and was occupied January 14, 1888. The original company office was on the opposite side of the canal, west of this complex. The company built using Red Brick; a two-story eight unit boarding house, a one and one half story house, five two-story houses and five one and one half story houses, these last five houses have salt glazed brick and tile decor from HCM Co. Logan, Ohio. All houses were built exclusive for the comfort of company employees and to display the company finished products.

1888: The present Methodist Church was started and completed 1893. H M & M CO. paid 90% of the cost and the community paying 10% via way of 'voluntary' pay roll deduction from company employee. At the same time, the Church was being built the company provided the land and materials for a school, to be built on the adjoining lot (now the church parking lot).

1888: Peter Hayden passed away at age of 82, and is buried in Greenlawn Cemetery in Columbus, Ohio. Peter Hayden never lived in the town that bore his name and spent most of his time in New York City, leaving local management of his businesses to relatives. Upon Peter Hayden death his son Charles Hayden became president of H M & M Co. Several of Peter's employees and their families boarded the passenger train to Columbus, as a token, of respect and gratitude. Peter Hayden took great care in providing for his employees, many of them felt it was an honor and privilege to work for him.

1889: August 17th, The Hocking Valley Canal closed. Porter Alexander was captain of the canal boat "Frances" and the honor of being the last canal boat to pass through Haydenville. Coal had been loaded in a canal boat in Nelsonville, and was destine to the Logan banker, Mr. C.E. Bowen.

1893: The "Little Church on the Hill" history notes it was being use as a one room school, when it was destroyed by fire. Student were schooled in Company houses until a new school was built on a vacant lot west of the church (now the community park).

1902: Charles Hayden sold the company's assets, including landholding, mines, factories and town of Haydenville to National Fire Proofing Company of Pittsburg for $75,000 Dollars The new company had been organized in 1889 and was recognized as an authority on hollow tile construction specializing in fireproof building material. The acquisition of the Haydenville factories, brought their total of clay manufacturing plants to twenty three in the United States and one in Canada. In later years, the company changed its name to NATCO. (National Automatic Tool Company).

1903: The present glazed brick train depot (demolished in 2020) was built to strict Railroad standards. The red tile roof is a clay terra cotta products of the original Haydenville factories The first station master of the new depot was John Dougherty the grandfather of kill farman (kiln fire man) Jack Dougherty; Ed Amos of Haydenville was the last station master. The original wooden depot building was East of the present depot and had been converted to a home; its last resident was Paul (Hope) (nick name) Fielder's family.

1907: National Fire Proofing changed its name to National Automatic Tool Company (NATCO).

1907-1914: In keeping with Peter Hayden tradition of caring for his employees, National Fireproofing/Natco built several houses using Peter's basic design except instead of using red brick of yester years, they used the National Fire Proofing/Natco salt glazed brick and hollow leaf face design building tile.

1911: T.D. Brown assumed the general manager position of the factories, the mines, and the town.

1912-1918: *"Silo tile" were made and shipped to the farm lands in the North-East and Mid-West, to make grain 'Silo's and large water drains. Natco constructed seventeen "Silo" (round houses) and converted them into employee residents. *One Silo (round house) still stands and is the home of a Haydenville resident at the east end of Haydenville.

1917: A narrow gauge railroad from the mines to the factories was built and a tunnel (the tunnel) was dug through the hill by the cemetery (the entrance is still visible).

1919: A large wooden building was constructed for community events, close to the overhead trestle, an odd fellow lodge building was on the opposite side of the old brick road. I remember paying five cents to set on hard wooden bleachers, in the community building, to watch the movie Butch Cassidy as the Sundance kid.

1919: The present highway was constructed through Haydenville along the edge of the old canal and part of Wolfe Basin was filled-in to accommodate the new highway. The original brick road went along the canal and at the East end of town it was up on the hill side above the canal, "at Wolfe Canal Lock", it went over the locks, an crossed the river, turned left and followed the river to what is now State Route 278.

1922: The Haydenville factories were producing about 5,000 tons of clay products a month and burning 1,000 tons of coal per month.

1922: The first High School building, burned and a new one was built at the same location, which is now the location of the community park.

1930: A study of the company's coal reserves revealed that the coal was being depleted and that the factories would have to purchase coal from local area mine.

1931: Mr. Clarence (C.S.) Matheny replaced T.D. Brown as general manager of the (factories) plants, the mines and town. Mr. Matheny held that position until the plants closed, he help negotiate the sale of the home to the Natco employees.

1933: Haydenville High School last graduating class had 12 students. The following year High School age students were bused to Logan or Union Furnace High School. The building was then converted to a 8 room grade school until it closed in 1951 (now the site of the community park).

1934: The Haydenville coal mines closed, due to lack of coal. The mines continued to supply clay to the factories via of the1917 narrow gauge railroad.

1939: The Great Depression hit the clay industry hard, the company had to lay off workers, and sold its surface land holdings, to the Federal Government.

“Except” the mineral rights, which the company reserved for its self, and “Except” the town of Haydenville and 20 acres of land surrounding town.

1940: During the war there was a serious short of able bodied men. To offset this shortage, several of the local women, when to work as general labor at the factories.

1950: The economic recovery in the early 50's brought temporary relief to the factories, business was good and the plants work Saturday morning. The plants and mine were still manually labor originated; labor cost was a major factor in a now highly completive industry.

1951: Grades one through eight were moved from the old High/Grade School Building in Haydenville to the newly constructed grade school building close to the intersection of U.S. 33 and 595.The old school building was closed and eventually demolished, Haydenville became part of the Green School District. The Community Park now sets on the vacant lot where the old school buildings sat.

1955: Several major customers including Western Electric were lost during a labor strike by the United Brick workers union in the early 1950's. Haydenville clay products were not available during the labor strike and its customers had no other alternative but to purchase a product made elsewhere. The Haydenville factories were becoming a losing investment for their owners, business was declining, but the investors were still required to pay over $96,000 dollars a year in real-estate taxes to Hocking County.

1957: The company’s clay mines were closed and abandon. The eighty plus years of mining had exhausted the supply of clay. The company was required to purchase clay and coal form local mines. Thus creating a never before financial burden.

1957: Plant #1 (factory) closed resulting in 150 manual labors out of work.

1961: Plant # 2 (factory) closed, plants #1 and #2 (factories) were sold for scrap, the buildings and kilns and smoke stacks were demolished and hauled away. The clay manufacturing giant, and mines, of Haydenville are now a part of history. The legacy of the God fearing, hard working men and women who made the company town, that out lived the company, lives on yet today!

It should be noted here that the Government benefit of today did not exist during this time period. The men and woman worked wherever and at whatever to make money to provide for their families.

1961: January, Natco sold the town of Haydenville to John M. Maschetta, a Real estate investor and attorney, from Washington Pennsylvania for $100,000 dollars.

1963: Peter Hayden had laid Haydenville out as a company owned town, it was not platted in the official record of Hocking County. Therefore before the sale could be finalized to Mr. Maschetta, each lot, streets and alleys ways had to be surveyed and platted for official records. *Mr. C. S. Matheny worked with Mr. Maschetta who offer the homes on land contract to the former employee/renters. The price for a house and lot ranged from $2,400 to$5,000 dollars with a10% down payment, terms of 6% simple interest calculated every 6 month. Mary Jane Martin a former Natco office worker was in charge of the paperwork for the sale of each house. Over half of the houses were purchased by former employees/renters, the balance were offered at public sale and all sold but two.
* Mr. Matheny in keeping with the tradition, "that Haydenville takes care of its own."

1973: Haydenville's 120 properties and the 20 acres that encompass the town were placed on the National Registry of Historic places.

1982: The first Old Haydenville School Reunion was held on October 3, 1982, with 150 people in attendance at Rising Park, in Lancaster Ohio. .

1988: A museum was opened to the public, to display historical artifact of Haydenville. A small segment of first ever-concrete public sidewalk was constructed.

1993: The Old Straitsville Water Association, a rural water system serving areas in Hocking County, extended a waterline into Haydenville; line tap fee was $350.00

2008: Thanks To Larry Horn, street light now glow where only darkness once prevailed, a total of 17 were installed, the first one turned on March 8, 2008 (never before were there an street lights in town). Green Township Trustee pay the monthly service fee for these 17 streel lights. The land where both old schools sat was purchased April 8, 2008, at a cost of $40,000, for the future site of the first ever Community Park The town held a ground breaking for the Community Park on September 1, 2008.

2009: Emergency automatic activated weather siren was installed in the Community Park. A Shelter House with aluminum picnic tables became a welcome addition to Community Park.

2010: Haydenville had its first ever candidate for Hocking County Commissioner and another "first": a woman (Patty Horn). Regretfully she lost to the two-term incumbent by 47 votes.

2010: Concrete basketball court and a chain link fence was installed at the Community Park.

2011: April 18th, Patty Horn formed Haydenville Improvement Committee Inc. A 501 (c) (3) Nonprofit organization to "Rejuvenating the Last Company Owned Town in Ohio."

2011: The life of the little community of Haydenville spans over 100 years. It has witnessed and lived through the good times and the bad, the boom and bust, but it's still very much alive. The Community spirit is alive and strong, it has (3) Non-Profit organizations: Haydenville Improvement Committee, headed by Patty Horn, Haydenville Youth Group, headed by Bonnie Seymour and Haydenville Preservation Committee, headed by Nyla Vollmer.

2011: The Post Office is scheduled to close at the end of this year.

2012: The Haydenville Museum closed May 1st, 2012. The post office remains open for business with limited hours. Mel and Kim Myers opened a carryout in the former Frances (Sparks) Grocery Store.

2013: February 1st Haydenville Improvement Committee entered into a lease agreement with the Hocking Valley Scenic Railroad for the Haydenville Train Depot.

2014: June 1st the Green Township Trustee's approved a petition of the local residents. Haydenville became an ATV Friendly Community.

2014: Haydenville Tunnel, the entrance by the cemetery, was partly closed due to its unsafe interior structural conditions. This tunnel was for the narrow gauge railroad, that came from the mines to the factory.

2013: A porch using only Haydenville brick was laid up at 16866 Haydenville Road, as a lasting tribute to the men and women who worked at the Haydenville Factories. Thanks to Phillip Blackford of Carbon Hill, Ohio, for designing and laying up the unique bricks for this special project. A Haydenville time capsule was buried in the porch to preserve the history and way of life, photos of the unique homes, and pictures from the past, which will be enjoyed by those who open the time capsule (50 years from now) August 17, 2064.

2014: Haydenville Youth Group closes down due to lack of membership.

2014: Post Office will be open two hours per day, the lobby is open 24 hours a day for local residents to receive mail from their mail boxes.

2015: Larry Horn completed research on Haydenville Cemetery and has documented the names from the headstones, when legible, and names of those in unmarked graves.

2015: Haydenville Improvement Committee Inc. (Patty Horn) entered into a lease agreement with a local real-estate investor to acquire the house at 16876 Haydenville Road. Haydenville, Ohio which will become the new Haydenville Church Parsonage.

2015: Pastor David Sherman and his wife Becky moved into the new Parsonage.

2016: National Association of Professional Woman inducted Patty M. Horn into our VIP woman of the year circle: for excellence, leadership and commitment to her profession, while encouraging the achievement of Professional Woman.

2017: October Another memory was added to Haydenville's past; the last Haydenville Annual Reunion "The town had out lived it's old school class mates and families of yester years."

2020: Wayne National Forest agreed to recognize Hopperville as a historical site and will allow the installation of a marker at the site.

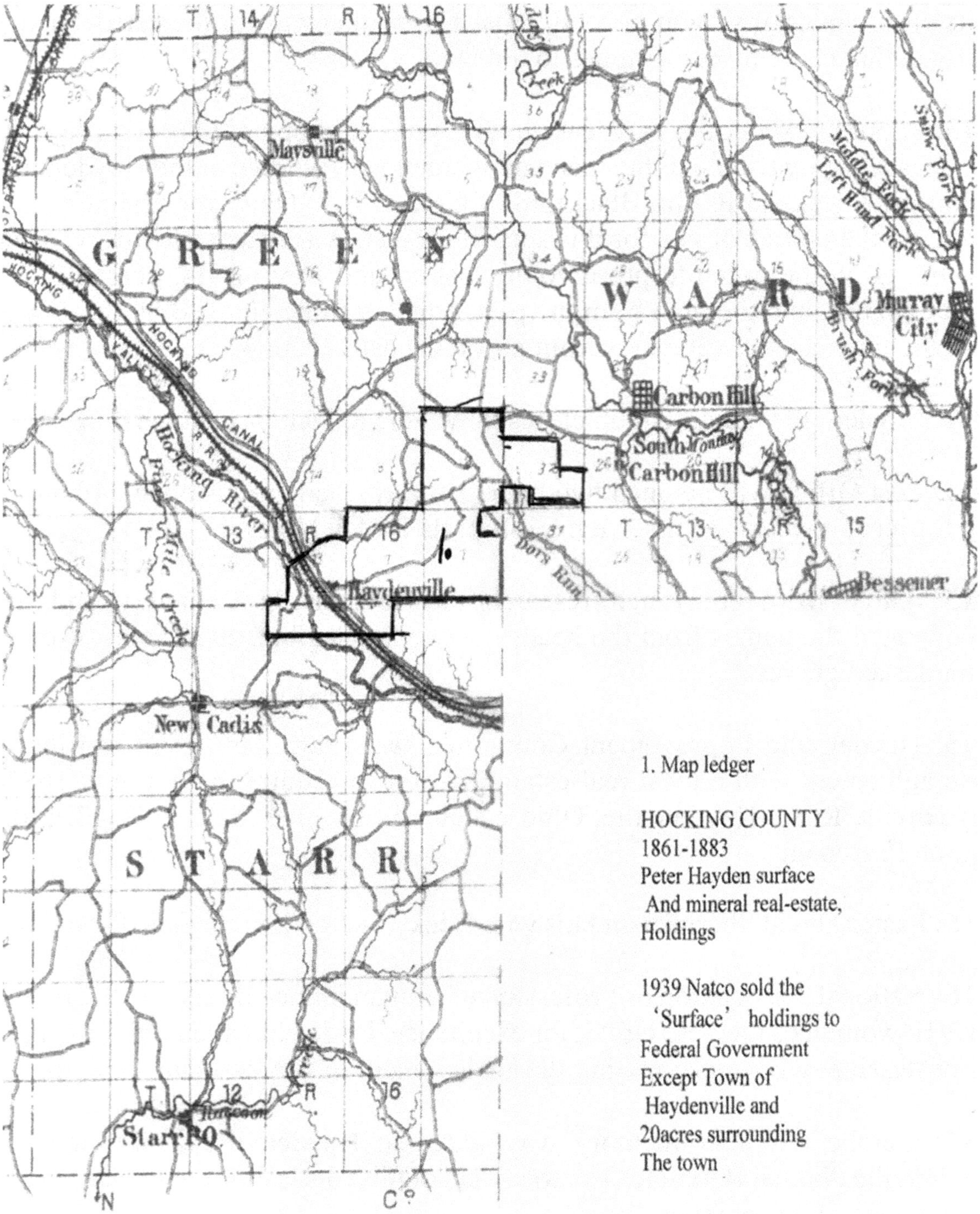

Figure 1 Hocking County Map 1861-1883, 1939.

Chapter 2: Iron Ore Smelting Furnace

Figure 2 Iron Ore Furnace

Hocking County is a part of the Hanging Rocks Iron Ore Region which extends from Greenup County, Kentucky to Southern Hocking County. The iron ore in many areas of Hocking County is over a foot thick and crops out of the hillsides. The limestone and sand necessary to smelt the iron ore were provided by the local S.S. Mills stone quarry. Charcoal was produced locally from the timber cut from the surrounding hillsides.

Prior to 1850 plat map identifies one of S. S. Mills stone quarries approximately one mile North of the smelting furnace of Hocking Valley Iron Company

Mid 1800's the coal, iron ore, clay and lime stone of Southeastern, Ohio were being exploited. These mineral resources in Hocking County attracted Peter Hayden, a young entrepreneur from Columbus. Peter purchase several hundred acres of adjoining land in Green, Starr and Ward Township, Hocking County ref. map pg. and began mining coal in Green Township. The coal was transported via his canal boats, which was one of, the various business enterprises he owned or controlled in Columbus.

1851-September13 Hocking County deeds of records book L page 219-20 John D. Clark and wife Mary Clark to Israel Dillie, John W. Brice and William M. Moore constituting the firm of Dillie. Brice. and Moore of Licking County, Ohio being part of lot 771 and 772 premises and appurtenances in Hocking County and part of the Ohio Company Purchase

1851- October 20 Hocking County deeds of records book N page 169-70 Robert Wright and wife Almina Wright to Dillie, Brice, and Moore part of lots 773 and774 premises and appurtenances in Hocking County being part of the Ohio Land Purchase

1854-June 30 Hocking County deeds of records book N page 191-92 Dille, Moore, and Brice partnership for $50,000 dollars sells to Hocking Iron Company their land and appurtenances included in the deed from Robert Wright and wife Almina, Hocking County deeds of records ref. pgs.? Book N page169-70 together with all buildings, machinery and fixtures belonging or appertaining to the Furnace situated on said land. Peter Hayden changed the name Hocking Valley Iron Company to "Hocking Furnace" and placed his son William Halleck in charge of the operation of the furnace.

These recorded documents support the fact that an Iron Ore Smelting Furnace had been erected several years before Peter Hayden purchased real-estate in Green, Starr, and Ward Township, Hocking County.

The furnace had been erected along the banks of the canal and part of the bridge house for the furnace is visible on the bluff that overlooks Frog Hollow Road. The furnace stack was 32 feet high with a 9 foot bosh (opening at the top). It was one of the13 furnace operating in this area doing that time period. After the furnace stopped producing iron ore, its Hugh stones became the foundation for the office/company store complex and factory buildings. The furnace's iron manufacturing rooms became the work shop for Company house maintenance crew.

Making Iron Ore

Miners dug large shallow pits and extracted the Iron Ore and cut limestone from the local stone quarry. Horse and/or oxen drawn wagons hauled this raw materials to the furnace site stock pile until needed.

Woodcutters cut and split native hard wood though out the winter, the split wood was used to make charcoal in the spring, summer and fall.

Charcoal was made in pits measuring thirty to forty feet in diameter, about thirty to fifty cords of fire wood was stacked in this pit(a cord of wood is a stack of split logs, four feet wide eight feet long and four feet high). The mound of split logs was then covered with leaves and dirt, a smoldering fire was started in the center of the mound. The Collier . ("Colliers" man operating the charcoal pit.) carefully tended the charcoal pits twenty four hours a day for up to fourteen days, while living in primitive huts near the pits during the charcoal making process. Optimum temperature for the charcoal pit was 700-800 degrees, Fahrenheit, but the wood could reach a temperature of up to 2000 degrees Fahrenheit in some places. The two-weeks of smoldering released the trapped moisture and nutrients and "coaled" the wood.

With all the raw material in place the "Founder" (furnace supervisor) would direct "charging of the blast" carts and wheelbarrows full of iron ore, limestone and charcoal were dumped in a specific order into the top of the furnace. A water wheels was used to operate a pair of blowing tubes that worked like giant bellows to force air into the furnace and raise the temperature inside the furnace to 2,500 to 3,000 degrees Fahrenheit. When the iron ore became a molten liquid it was drained from the bottom of the furnace into a long shallow ditch joined with several smaller ditches. Thus the name "pig iron" was born. The ditches resembled a mother pig nursing her baby pigs.

After the iron had cool enough to handle by hand, the "pigs" were loaded onto canal boats and shipped to processing mills in Columbus.
Finished products include cast iron pots pans and skillets and numerous other cast iron products.

The pig iron was melted down again to remove all the impurities and processed into steel products of various sizes and designs.

DEED BOOK N, Page 169-170

Robert Wright & wife
To
Israel Dellia
John W. Brice
William M. Moore

Deed

Know all men by these presents that we Robert Wright and Almira Wright his wife of the County of Hocking in the state of Ohio in consideration of the sum of one hundred an sixty two and 58 dollars in hand paid and secured to be paid by Israel Dellia John W. Brice William M. Moore of Licking County Ohio have bargained and sold

170

and do hereby grant bargain sell and convey unto the said Dellia Brice & Moore & their heirs and assigns forever the following real estate situate in the County of Hocking in the State of Ohio and in Green Township and described as follows to wit " Part of Lots No. 773 & 774 in section No 13 Township No 13 Range No 16 Ohio companies purchase beginning at the intersection of the centre of the Hocking valley Canal with the East boundry line of said lot No 773 thence North by said line 12.41 chs to a post thence south 64° West 10.91 chs to the centre of the Hocking valley Canal thence by the centre of said Canal south 28° East 180 chs thence south 56° East 10.82 chs to the place of beginning containing 6.54 acres more or less as surveyed by Lewis Davis County surveyor June 16, 1851

To have and to hold said premises with appurtenances unto the said Dellia Brice & Moore and their heirs and assigns forever and the said Robert Wright for himself and heirs doth hereby covenant with said Dellia Brice & Moore & their heirs and assigns that he is lawfully seized of the Premises aforesaid that the premises are free and clear from all incumbrances whatever and that he will forever warrant and defend the same with the appurtenances unto the said Dellia Brice & Moore & their their heirs and assigns against the lawfull claims of all persons

In testimony whereof the said Robert Wright & Almira Wright his wife hereunto set their hands and seals this 20th day of October A.D. 1851

Executed in presence of
H. Case
A. White

Robert Wright (Seal)
Almira Wright (Seal)

The State of Ohio Hocking County ss

Before me Alexander White a Justice of the peace in and for said County personally appeared the said Robert Wright and Almira Wright his wife and acknowledged the siging and sealing of the foregoing deed of conveyance to be their voluntary act and deed and the said Almira Wright wife of the said Robert Wright being by me examined separate and apart from her said husband and the contents of said Deed fully made known to her by me she did then acknowledge and declare that she did voluntarily sign seal and acknowledge the same and that she is still satisfied therewith this 20th day of October 1851

A. White J.P.

Received June 28th 1854
Recorded July 25. 1854
James R. Geoghan Rec.

DEED BOOK L Page 219 – 220

J. D. Clark & wife To Dille Brice & Moore DEED 25.95 Acres
Know all men by these presents that we Joseph D Clark and Mary Clark his wife of the County of Hocking in consideration of three hundred and Twenty four dollars in hand paid by Israel Dille John W Brice and Wm M Moore constituting the firm of Dille Brice and Moore of Licking County Ohio have bargained and sold and do hereby grant barg

bargain sell and convey unto the said Dille Brice and Moore and their heirs and assign forever the following real Estate situate in the County of Hocking and State of Ohio and described as follows viz twenty five 95/100 acres off of the South End of Lots Numbers 771 & 772 in Section No 13 Township No 13 Range No 16 Ohio Company's Purchase Beginning at the south corner of Section No/ Lot No. 771 thence North 22.40 chains to a White Oak 9 inches in Diameter on the East Boundary line of said Lot, thence South 67° West 14.40 Chs to a post on the West boundary line of Lot No 772 – thence South 16.78 chs To the South west corner of sd Lot – thence East 13.25 to the place of beginning as Surveyed by Levi Davis County Surveyor of Hocking County – June 16 1854 and if said lines do not include the said quantity of 25.95 acres these presents hereby authorize and the said grantors hereby grant and sell to the said Grantees sufficient to make said quantity by running far enough North of said North line parallel thereto to include the said quantity of 25.95 acres. To have and To hold said premises with the appurtenances unto the said Dille Brice and Moore their heirs and assigns forever, and the said Joseph D Clark for himself and heirs doth hereby covenant with said Dille Brice and Moore and their heirs and assigns that he is lawfully seized of the premises aforesa and that the premises are free and clear from all incumbrances whatsoever and that he will forever Warrant and defend the same with the appurtenances unto the said Dille Brice & Moore and their heirs and assigns against against the lawful claims of all persons whomsoever. In testimony whereof the said the said Joseph D Clark and Mary Clark his wife have unto set their hands and seals this 13th day of September AD 1851

Executed in the presence of us   Joseph D Clark (Seal)
R Wright   Mary x Clark (Seal)
David Beagle   The State of Ohio Hocking County SS.
Before me R Wright an associate Judge in and for said County personally appeared the said Joseph D Clark and Mary Clark his wife the grantors in the foregoing deed of Conveyance and acknowledged the signing and sealing of the foregoing deed of Conveyance to be their voluntary act and deed and the said Mary Clark wife of the said Joseph D Clark being by me Examined seperate and apart from her said husband and the contents of said Deed fully made known to her by me she then declared that that she did ~~voluntary~~ they acknowledge and declare ~~that~~ she did voluntarily sign seal and acknowledge the same and that she is still satisfied therewith this thirteenth day of September AD 1851,
Rec'd Sept 25th 1851.   Robert Wright Associate
Recorded Sept 26th 1851   Judge
J W Wyman Recorder H Co

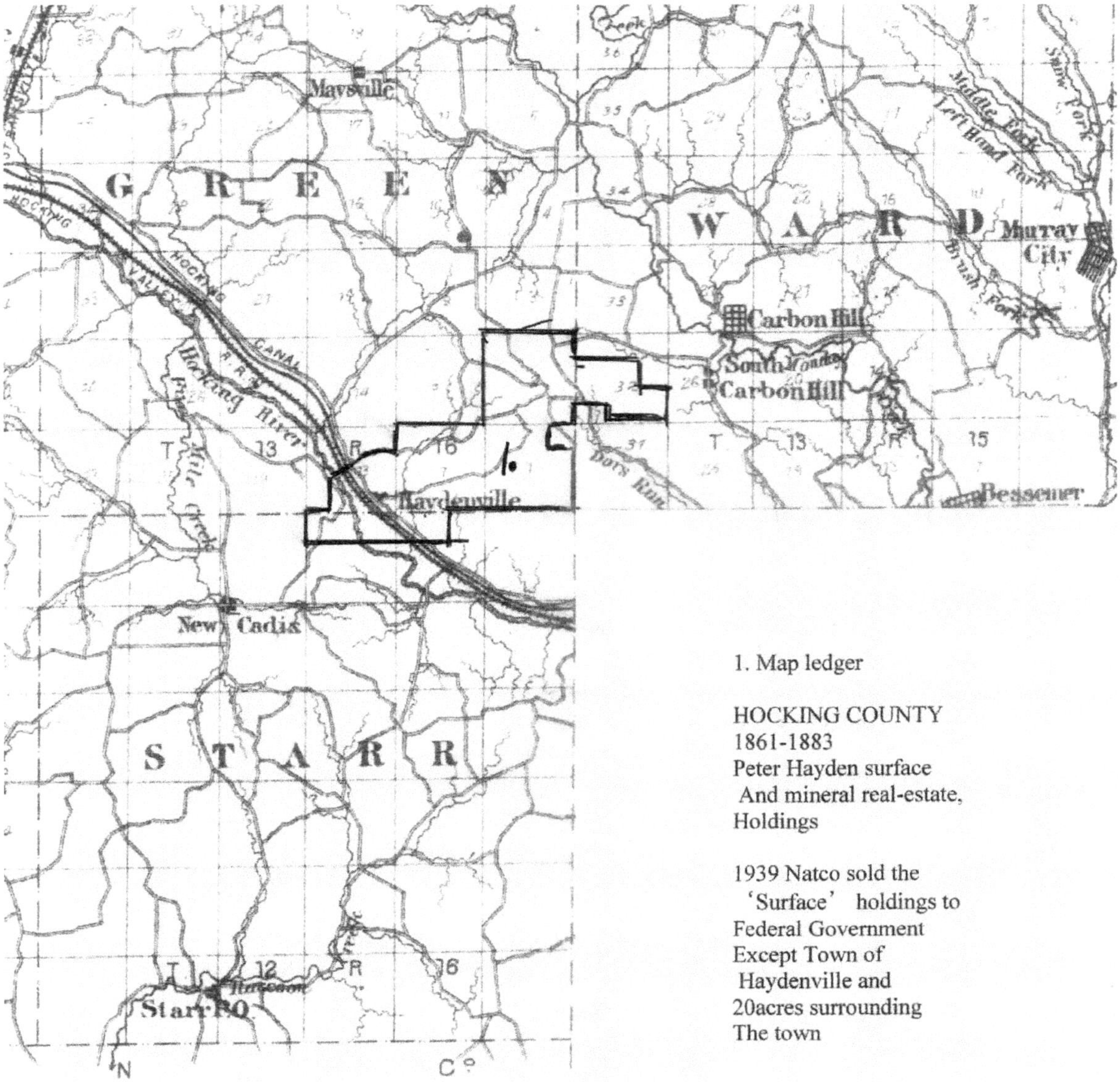

1. Map ledger

HOCKING COUNTY
1861-1883
Peter Hayden surface
And mineral real-estate,
Holdings

1939 Natco sold the
'Surface' holdings to
Federal Government
Except Town of
Haydenville and
20acres surrounding
The town

DEED BOOK N, Page 191-192

Dille Brice & Moore
To
Hocking Iron Company
Deed

Know all men by these presents that whereas the late firm of Dille Brice and Moore for the consideration of fifty thousand dollars to said firm paid by the Hocking Iron Company a body corporate organized under a general corporation law of the State of Ohio for the manufacture of Iron in the County of Hocking did sell to the said Hocking Iron Company certain lands and tenements a part whereof is hereinafter described and did agree to convey the same in fee simple therefore we Israel Dille and Sophronia his wife John W. Brice and Fanny his wife and William M. Moore and Emiline his wife of the County

BOOK N PAGE 192

192

of Licking in the State of Ohio (the said Israel Dille John W. Brice
and William M. Moore having composed the said firm of Dille Brice
and Moore) for the consideration aforesaid have bargained and sold
and do now hereby grant and convey unto the said the Hocking
Iron Company and its assigns forever all the lands and tenements
herein described and situate in the said County of Hocking and
bounded and described as follows: to wit: Twenty five and 98/100 acres
off of the South end of lots numbers seven hundred and seventy one
seven hundred and seventy two (771 & 772) in section (13) thirteen
Township thirteen (13) Range sixteen (16) of the Ohio Companies purchase
beginning at the South east corner of lot 771 thence North 22,40
chains to a white oak tree 9 inch diameter on the east boundary
line of said lot thence south 67° west 14.40 chains to a post on
the west boundary line of lot 772 thence South 16,78 chains to
the south west corner of said lot thence east 13.25 chains to the
place of beginning as surveyed by Levi Davis June 16, 1881 and
if the aforesaid boundaries do not contain 25.98 acres then the
said North boundary line is to be removed so far North that
the quantity of 25.98 shall be included and being the same
tract conveyed to the said Dille Brice and Moore by Joseph
D. Clark and wife by deed of Septem 15, 1881 Recorded in Book
"L" page 219 & 220. Also another tract in the same Range
Township and section and parts of Lots 773 and 774 bounded
as follows: beginning and beginning at the intersection of the centre
of the Hocking Valley Canal with the East boundary line of said
Lot 775 thence North by said line 12,41 chains to a post thence
South sixty four 64° west 10.91 chains to the centre of the Hocking
Valley Canal thence by the centre of said Canal south 28° east
6.80 chains thence south 56° east 10.82 chains to the place of
beginning containing 6 84/100 acres more or less as surveyed
by Levi Davis County surveyor June 16, 1881 and conveyed
to said Dille Brice and Moore by deed of Oct 20' 1881 made
by Robert Wright and wife together with all the buildings
machinery and fixtures belonging or appertaining to the Furnace
situate on said land to have and to hold the same unto the
said The Hocking Iron Co and assigns forever and we
the said Isreal Dille John W. Brice and William M. Moore
for ourselves and heirs do hereby covenant with the said The
Hocking ~~Furnace~~ Iron Company and to its assigns that the said
lands and tenements are free and clear of and from all
incumbrances and that we do and our heirs executors and
administrators shall forever warrant and defend the same unto
the said the Hocking Iron Company and its assigns against
the lawful claims of all persons whomsoever
In testimony whereof we have hereunto set our hands and
seals this 30th day of June A.D. 1884

I. Dille (seal)
S. Dille (seal)
John W. Brice (seal)
Yrainy Brice (seal)
Wm. M. Moore (seal)
Evaline Moore (seal)

Signed sealed and delivered in presence of us
Francis Muller Kate Darlington
B. F. Bancroft as to I. Dille & wife
John Lunceford as to all

Chapter 3: Hocking Canal

About 1840 the Hocking Canal was completed through, what is now called Haydenville. It was a major economic boom to the community and the Hocking Valley. Prior to the arrival of the canal the only means of transportation and moving goods out of the valley was stage coach, horse and wagon or a flat bottom boat on the Hocking River.

The canal opened new and accessible markets to the North, mainly, Columbus, Ohio. Shipments to Columbus were slow, taking approximate 7 days, but much safer than the pirate infested Hocking River by flat bottom boat.

Remnants of an old canal lock # 17 Wright Locks , and aqueduct are visible in the small public park at junction of Route 33 and 595 'Wright Lock' was so named after the original land owner C. Wright.

Figure 3 Aqueduct over 3-Mile Creek was part of lock #17 Wright Locks. The tow mule walking on the bridle path pulling the canal boat. The aqueduct served as a creek crossing.

Canal locks had large wooden gates at each end that had to be manually opened. When one was opened the other one was still closed thus the canal boat was raised or lowered to the level of the waterway it was traveling on.

Figure 4 Remnants of canal lock #17 at junction of US State Route 595 and 33 adjacent to 3-mile creek aqueduct

In later years the railroad would paralleled the canal and sections of the canal were filled and leveled to make a location for Haydenville factories and house close to the railroad.

The 0ctober 27, 1867 Hocking County Records of Deeds Book 40 page 167, make reference to the "Wolf Lock". Local resident Bill Evans Sr. recalls the locks being located where Laurel Run Road crosses the railroad tracks. These locks controlled the water in what was commonly referred to, by local residents, as Wolf Basin. It was one of many, large ponds of water that was used as a reserve to regulate the depth of the canal water. The most prominent is Buckeye Lake which was originally constructed for the same purpose.

The original 'brick' road that circumvents Wolf Basin, stopped at the Diamon clay brick factory. It was a branch from the road that went over Wolfe Locks and the Hocking River, then parallels the river to what is now State Route 278. When the present highway was built, Wolfe Locks became the foundation for the present county road "Laurel Run". Part of Wolfe Basin pond was filled-in and the highway built on top of that fill. The brick road surrounding the basin was renamed Karnes Road.

My father told me the story of catching snapping turtles in Wolf Basin. He said the turtles were as large as a #2 wash tub. He caught them while fishing off the back porch of my Aunt house at the intersection of Karnes Road and County Road #25.

Mr. Leroy Mace told me he lived across the road from the canal and "recalls going down 13 steps from the edge of the road to the water in the old canal which was about 4 feet deep."

My Grandfather Harry Mills told me many time the story of "walking along the railroad track and throwing rocks at the snakes in the old canal."

My Aunt Betty Linnaberry told me that as a young girl, she lived in Nelsonville with her parents James Horn, she would "dump the ashes from the family coal stoves into the canal." This part of the canal eventually became Canal Street and is presently the major thru-a-fair through the town.

Ernest "Ernie" Lehman lived on US Route 595 a short distance from his father Jacob, known as Jake. Ernie was a well-respected resident of Hocking County and a Green Township Trustee for many years.

He was seventy years old when he told his daughter this story of his father's life beginning in a canal boat on the Hocking Canal. Two of the Lehman brothers John and Warner earned their living by hauling freight up and down the Hocking Canal in their canal boats, which would hold about 60 to 80 tons of coal, other types of freight and passengers were welcome. Passengers paid a cent and a half per mile, per person to ride on the canal boat. Their canal boats traveled at about four miles per hour, the normal speed of the tow mules, walking along the bridle (tow) path, pulling the loaded canal boat. The brothers seldom had a day off, so their families lived with them on their canal boats. John and Warner had tied their boats up in the basin at the upper end of Lock Number #17 (Wright Locks) close to the proposed town of Pattonville (junction of Route33 and 595). Warmer's wife was expecting the birth of a child very soon; as was the custom of those days most babies were born at home. Jacob (Jake) Wilbert Lehman, was no exception, his life began at home, in his father (John's) canal boat. Jacob 'Jake', who had begun his life on a canal boat, was fifty years old when his youngest son Ernest was born.

Local history notes that in 1863 the Confederate General John Hunt Morgan, the infamous Morgan's Raiders, invaded Nelsonville and before they left burned a covered bridge crossing the Hocking River and eleven canal boats. One canal boats, which was home to a family, was spared while the others were torched to prevent them from being used to support the Union army efforts.

Some of the older citizens recall the last canal boat named "Frances" passing through Haydenville on August 1, 1889, loaded with coal for C.E. Bowen a local banker in Logan. The captain of the "Francis" was Porter Alexander, a colorful local fellow who had a wide acquaintance along the canal.

In the 1870s the railroad was becoming the sole means of public transportation and freight carrier. Rumors were that five trains a day, loaded with coal, passed through Haydenville from the rich Appalachian coal fields on their way north to Columbus and beyond.

The canal had achieved its purpose. It opened the Hocking Valley to the outside world. The end of an 'ERA' was fast approaching. Mother Nature was slowly reclaiming her Own. The 1874 floods of the Hocking River did irreparable damage to the canal and locks between Nelsonville and Athens. The canal water became stagnant and plaque infested, that section of the canal was permanently closed and abandon. The 1894 floods of the Hocking River did extensive damage to the remaining canal system and marked the end of the canal in the Hocking Valley.

Chapter 4: Hopperville

Green Township Section 7
Green Township Road 2226
Hocking County, Ohio

Over the hill and up the valley toward the now closed Haydenville mines was the long forgotten town of Hopperville. Little is known about this now forgotten little mining town, whose existence was the breath of life for the Community of Haydenville as we know it today. Knowledge of the town's existence solves many puzzling questions:

What caused the ruts of an old dirt road from the top of the hill, and through the cemetery? The road continued down the hill (this is before the overhead railroad trestle was built) and up to the iron ore smelting furnace where the ore was processed and shipped North by canal boat.

Why was a Chapel built at the curve of the road 200 feet below the Haydenville Cemetery some its foundation brick are still visible?

It is safe to assume that the 104+ unmarked graves in the Haydenville Cemetery is the final resting place for many of those God-fearing, men, women and children of Hopperville and the surrounding area.

1830 Peter Hayden purchased large adjoining tracks of land in Green, Starr and Ward Township , Hocking County. Peter then formed Hayden Mining Company and appointed James Overton Ramey manager of the mining operation, the position he held until his death in 1872.

The raw materials from the mines was hauled by horse and/or oxen drawn wagons, on the dirt road that crossed the valley to the top of the hill overlooking the Hocking River, then the road when through what is now Haydenville Cemetery and continued to a curve on the flat section of the hill. A Chapel was built on the left side of this curve in the road, some of the foundation is still visible. The road continued down the hill and up to the iron ore smelting furnace of the Hocking Valley Iron Company.

1867 Hocking County Deeds of Records Book 40 Page 6 "refers" to a Canal lock knows as Wolfe Locks and the construction of a railroad depot.

Which would serve the railroad spur going to the coal hoppers at Hopperville. This depot was the first one in what is now known as Haydenville, in later years it was converted in to a residents. Paul (Hope) Fielder's family live in this old depot building until it was torn down.

J.D. Wolf Heirs homestead was built on high ground overlooking several hundred acres of land parallel to the Hocking Canal and C & H V R R , and the new railroad depot. The house is presently (2019) the family residents of James Colvin, county house number #17046 Demolishing of this house began late 2020.

1869 Green Township Map William Wolf Jr. Born 11-3-1838 exercised his construction skills, he had learned as foreman for the Columbus & Hocking Valley Railroad C& H V R R for .50 cents a day and dinner. Peter Hayden hired him to build a standard gauge railroad spur, from the main track of the Columbus & Hocking Valley Railroad, at Wolfe Locks to his coal hopper and mines (Hopperville). William continued to work for Peter Hayden for ten-plus more years, before health problems forced him to quit.

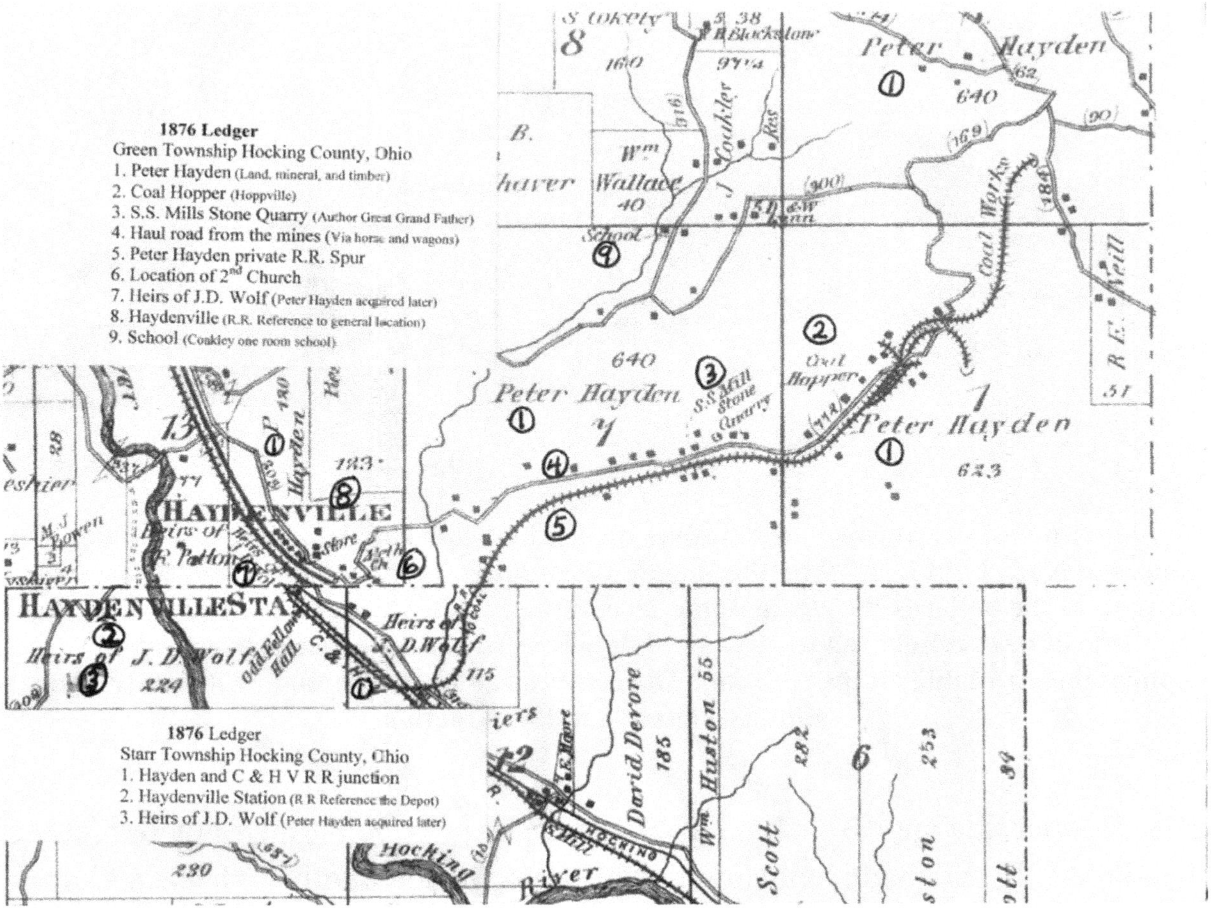

Figure 5 1876 Green Township Hocking County Ohio

As part of this railroad spur project, a coal tipple (hopper) was a built near the entrance to the underground mines. The coal hoppers processed the coal from Hayden's and surrounding deep mines and shipped it via of this railroad spur to the main railroad of C. &. H.V. R.R. at Wolfe the locks from there to Haydenville and customers all over the world.

The area surrounding the hoppers became populated with labors from the mines, thus the area became known as "Hopperville."

Peter Hayden had these two locomotive specially build to move the railroad cars back and forth from the coal hopper, via of his private railroad spur, to a junction on the main C.& H. V. R. R. track.

Figure 6 One of two early locomotives owned by Peter Hayden. Here is a builder's photo of No.2, built in 1879 by the Rogers Locomotive Works of Paterson, New Jersey. On top of the boiler is the steam dome seen in the middle then two sand domes on each side of it. It Is believed the two sand domes were ordered special because of no turntable available on the railroad. The engines ran back and forth without turning and used lots of sand for traction.

The Hopperville spur is a slight decline from the hoppers to the junction at the C& H V R R line. Sand being applied between the locomotive wheels and track provided the extra traction necessary to move the railroad cars to and from the hoppers.

- 1873 Peter Hayden transfer John Dougherty from one of his Columbus, Ohio companies to Haydenville, Ohio be the telegraph operator and company bookkeeper. The position he held for 67 years.
- Peter Hayden constructed a wooden (40'x 70') three story boarding house and several other house at Hopperville, for his employee and their families.
- 1880 U S Census list the following as probable residents of that boarding house: Charles Miller & Wife and 5 children (miner), G. Stoddard (bookkeeper) Matilda (wife & housekeeper), Callie (servant), Mary (servant), James Ferguson (assist bookkeeper), Samuel (clerk), Duke Scaff (clerk), F. Warren (manager), W.W. Wickham (operator) Mary (wife & housekeeper), Peter Bass (fill fuses /explosives for the mines) Delila(wife & housekeeper and one child), George Duloy (border). Elaine Hutchinson approached me with a picture of her mother Jennette Walker sitting in a chair on the porch at this boarding house, and the desire to preserve the history of Hopperville. Lois and her Red Row & Hopperville Remembrance Group have work tirelessly to preserve the history of Hopperville, and the area surrounding. A major accomplishment is that Wayne National Forest Service has agreed to recognize the area as a "historic site" and issued the group a permit to erect a monument at the site of the old boarding house.
- 1920 U S Census Green Township Hocking County shows 150 families living in the vicinity of the coal mines and Hopperville. Including Lois, Grandmother Jessie A. Jeffery Grandfather Robert H. Walker, her uncles Emmette Jeffery who married Leona Nichols, and Wayne Rolland who died in his father arms, of the fever when he was 10 years old and laid to rest in the Haydenville Cemetery.
- Jim Moore and Don Keels both life residents of Haydenville provided me these names of a "few" of the families they remember that lived in Hopperville; Jesse Van Bibber, Cecil Dowler, Joe Lehman, Paul Lehman, Arthur Bond, Marion Mace, Albert Sparks, Albert Sparks' (Dad), Don Bowerstock, Clearance Bowerstock, Arthur Crane, Gerald

Miller, Marie Moore, Sam Patton, Charlie Rieder, Fred Chrisman, Bill Milstead, Ed. Oliver Willis Gastin, Teddy Six, Virgil Woodson, Luther Burch, Levi (Doc) Wade. Nance Devol , Pearle McGathey many families are now forgotten history.

- Fannie (Mc Fadden) Horn in her memoirs tell the story of moving to the "Hoppers" when she was two years old. She was the second child of Winfield and Mary (Wolfe) McFadden, Fannie Horn, born November 26, 1881, tells the story that when she was about two years old, her family moved to the Hoppers, where coal from the underground mines was dumped into Hoppers to be processed and then into large railroad cars to go to Haydenville. Her dad operated the small tow motor that went down into the underground mines and pulled the coal laden cars out to the Hoppers. She tells the story of walking in the snow from Hopperville to the one room Coakley School, the road she traveled would have been, part of the stage coach road that past in front of the Company boarding house at Hopperville. The road exits on to Purdum road, Wayne National Forestry has installed an iron gate to keep vehicle out. The Coakley School was about one half mile back in the woods from this gate.
- Fannie's neighbors were Kate and Will Fisher, Clara and Nellie, Ed Lehman and wife; they had four boys, Emett, John, Ramey, and Noel, John Reider and family. Her Uncle John and Aunt Maria McSherry had three children – Mabel, Bernice, and Freda.
- 1871 August 1 Hocking County Deeds of Records Book Z Page 184 Peter Hayden and his second wife Sarah L. Hayden for $25.00 deeded 1.34 acres to the trustee of Methodist Episcopal Chapel. This Church was in the bend of the road past the present Haydenville Cemetery. An old dirt road winds past the Chapel in an Easterly direction to the Wolf Cemetery.
- The Green/Starr Township Map, Section 13, Hocking County, Ohio, identifies the location of S.S. Mills Stone Quarry in the vicinity of Coal Hoppers (Hopperville).
- Ruth Mae (Mills) Horn is my mother and a brother to Raymond Mills. So it is safe to assume that S. S. Mills is my great grandfather.

- Jim Moore told me (Larry Horn) many time that my Uncle Raymond Mills said, "his grandfather and other Mills family members are buried in the woods behind Buss Walkers house on Route 595." Numerous attempts to locate these grave has been unsuccessful.
- 1877 Peter Hayden hosted a Christmas party for his employees. * This became a Hayden company tradition that continued until the factories closed in late 1950's.
- 1917 The standard gauge railroads spur to Hopperville was taken up. A narrow gauge railroad spur was built, following the original old dirt haul road to the bottom of the hill. A 1000 foot long tunnel was dug through the hill and came out at the Haydenville factories. This railroad insured that the factories received needed raw materials regardless of weather conditions.

Figure 7 Tunnel entrance for the narrow gauge railroad that went through the hill from the mines to the Haydenville clay factories.

- 1930 A study showed the coal reserves in the mines were being depleted and would not be able to supply enough coal to maintain the Haydenville factories, thus requiring the factories to purchase coal from other suppliers. Charlie Vaughn of Logan was one of the main suppliers of coal to the factories.
- 1934 The coal mines closed, and the coal hopper, was dismantled. The dismantling of the coal hopper was the end of an era. Hopperville soon

joined the rank and file of forgotten mining towns of days gone by. The legacy of Hopperville lives on yet today "as the town that breathed the breath of life into Haydenville."

1-Coal Hopper

2-Stone Quarry

3- Dirt Haul Road to Haydenville before present tunnel and narrow gauge rail road was built to Haydenville factories

4-Standard Gauge Rail road from Hopperville to C & H.V. R.R. (Columbus & Hocking Valley RR.)

5-Company Store

6-2nd. Church

7-Houses

8-1st Church & Cemetery

9-1st R.R. Depot

10-1st Odd Fellows Hall

11- [illegible] Mill

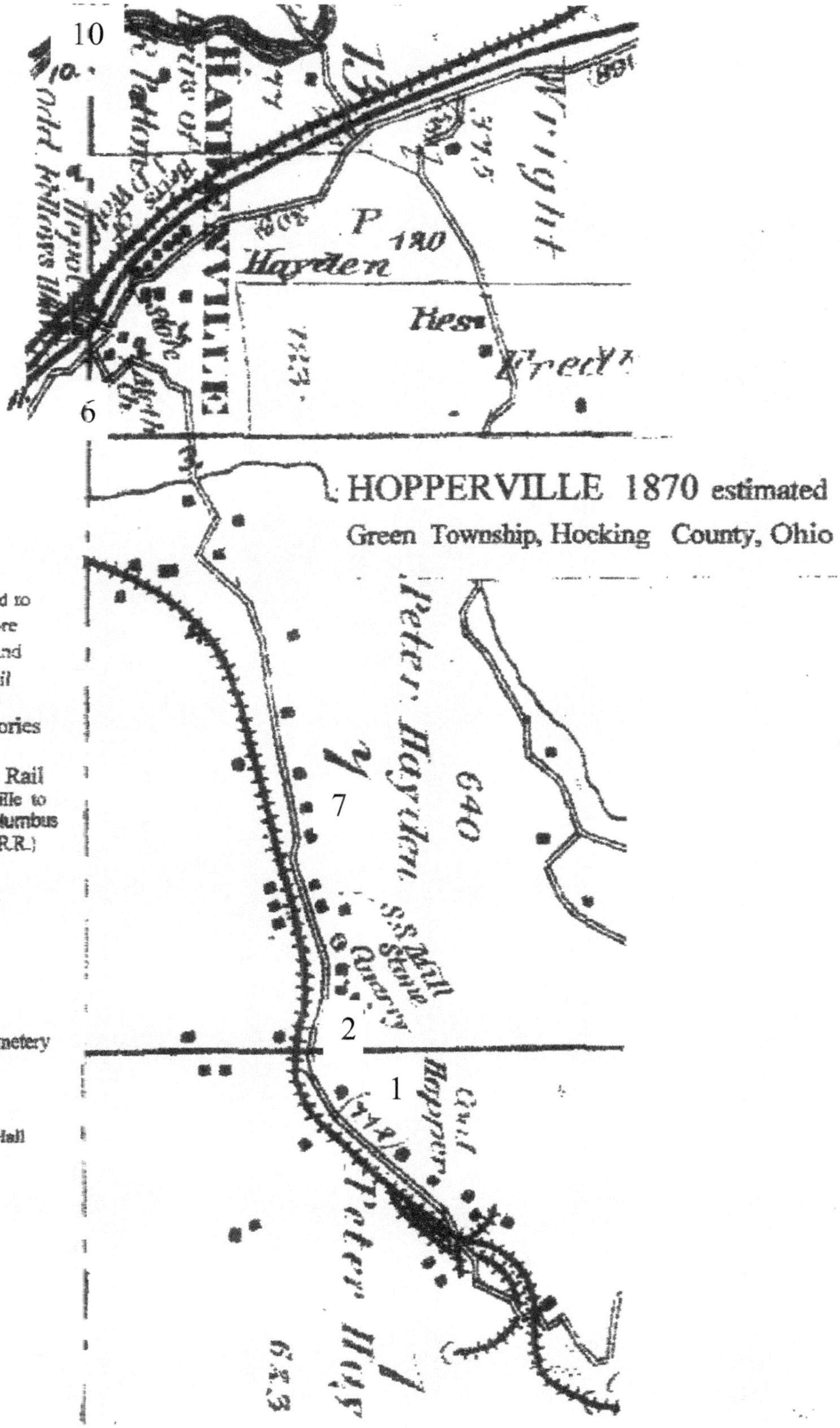

Chapter 5: Peter Hayden

Figure 3 September 15, 1806 - April 6, 1888

Peter was born September 15, 1806, in the Oneida Indian Village, Madison County, New York. Peter was the seventh generation of his immigrant ancestor, John Hayden and the seventh child of his missionary parents, Josiah Hayden and Esther Hallock. “Philanthropes” is Peter’s baptismal name, one of the U.S.

Census reports listed him as Philip and his nephews knew him as "Uncle Phylan" but throughout his adult and business life he was known as Peter.

In 1809 his parents returned to Williamsburg, Massachusetts and then a few years later to Cummington. As a young boy he helped his parents in their Cummington Cotton Manufacturing Company (a small cotton mill).

The 1830 U.S. Census for Cummington, Massachusetts shows Hayden family members but there is no reference to Peter Hayden.

Peter and his older brother, Cotton, became contractors for prison labors in Auburn, New York. Cotton moved to Nunda, New York, and died there at the young age of 34. Peter, continued to operate the company with prison laborers.

In 1830 Peter purchased several tracts of land in Green, Ward and Starr Townships, Hocking County and formed the Haydenville Mining Company. Peter appointed James Overton Ramey as manager of mining operations, who a short time later married Peter's daughter Alice De Forrest Hayden. James held the manager's position until his death in 1872.

In 1835 Peter's prior business experience was tested when he negotiated a five year prison labor contract, with the State of Ohio, to employ fifty to one hundred convicts from the newly completed Ohio Penitentiary. This business venture was basically an expansion of his Auburn, New York, company's plating and manufacturing of saddlery and harness trimmings business.

In 1835, Peter became a manufacturer and seller of ironware produced in his factory "Columbus Iron Works, Rolling Mill and Wire Mill." The factory produced a wide variety of iron and steel products including, fine wire cloth, railroad rails and related railroad products. He established mercantile house outlets and distributor partnerships in St. Louis, Chicago, Galveston, and San Francisco all to absorb the output of his expanding business ventures.

In 1835 Peter met and married his first wife Alice Booth she was approximately 25 years old and Peter was 29. Their first child Charles Hallock was born July 17th, 1837, in Auburn, New York. William, Alice, Adelaide, and Harriet were born on Columbus, Ohio as per 1850 U S Census 2nd Ward page 359 and 678.

In a 1840 September 8th a Columbus newspaper refers to the P. Hayden & Co. as a manufacturer and dealer in carriages. The vehicles were advertised as the most approved and fashionable styles and offered for sale at a very low price for cash or approved credit.

In 1844 Peter was the principal partner in Hayden, Morrison & Co. wool buyers and manufacturers of carpet at the Ohio State Penitentiary.

In 1845 Peter set up a saddlery hardware business at 79 Beckman Street, New York City. Peter appointed his brother's son, Thomas Smith Hayden as an associate to operate the business.

1845 newspaper advertisement Peter Hayden saddlery and hardware at 112W. Broad Street Columbus, Ohio; Brick testing machinery, Kiln bands, Hayden clay and rock crushers, Dry and wet pans(used to prepare clay for brick and tile manufacturing)

1847 the Hayden Chain Factory was put into production in Columbus, Ohio.

In 1847 Peter constructed a large factory on his State Avenue, property along the East bank of the Scioto River. By today's standards this project would be considered an enormous undertaking by one man. The building was 196 feet long, consisting of a center building 46 feet wide, four stories high with two wings 75 feet long, all constructed of limestone. The North side housed a one 100 horsepower engine to supplied power to the factory. Joining the engine house was a mill for rolling scrap iron into bars and rods, the mill was capable of producing eight tons of bar iron and three tons of rods daily. In the North yard there was a blacksmith shop 115 feet long and 32 feet wide for making chains, etc. In the South yard there was a 80 by 30 foot three story leather tannery. The first floor of the center building was designed primarily for the manufacture of saddlery hardware and drawing of wire to customer specifications. The North wing of this 3 building complex housed machinery on the first floor for making buckles and rivets, the two upper floors were used for filing, plating and finishing iron and brass work. The factory employed 100 to 150 men and was referred to by local residents as the Birmingham Iron Works.

In 1852 Peter was president and W. Hallack Hayden was the manager of the Hocking Iron Company iron ore smelting furnace in, Green Township, Hocking County, Ohio.

In 1854 Peter purchased all the assets of Hocking Iron Company and changed its name to Hocking Furnace

In the Spring of 1854, Peter bought the successful Ridgeway Foundry in Columbus, Ohio, from the surviving nephew of Joseph Ridgeway Sr. The business was formed in 1822 by Joseph Ridgeway Sr. to manufacture Jethro Woods patent plows. With the advent of Joseph Sr. son Joseph Jr. the business expanded to manufacturing of stream engines, stoves and various metal products. The company employed 50 to 60 employees.

In 1858 Peter served on the Board of Directors of The Ohio Tool Company. The company employed over 200 employees. Its chief product consisted of excellent quality carpenter wood planes and numerous other carpentry tools. The factory was known by local residents as the plane factory.

In 1862 Peter purchased from I. Dille, J. Brice and W. Moore all of their real-estate interest and smelting furnace in Green Township, Hocking County, Ohio.

From 1862 to 1883 Peter made several land purchases in Green, Starr, and Ward Township, Hocking County, Ohio, giving him a combined total of over 3,000 + acres of land in one continuous block.

On January 1, 1866, Peter established the private banking house P. Hayden & Co. at 9 South High Street, Columbus, Ohio. Peter's second son, William, was co-partner.

In 1866 Peter was a director of the National Park Bank in New York. Peter issued bonds for the construction of the Mineral Railroad from Columbus, Ohio to Hocking Furnace and other coal mining towns in the Hocking Valley.

In 1869 P. Hayden & Co. built the Hayden Bank building, 20 Broad Street, Columbus, Ohio, and is presently (2020) used for various banking business. The strength of his private banking business was demonstrated when in 1873 there was a money panic with the banks. The Hayden Bank paid checks drawn on its bank in "gold".

In 1923 the Hayden Bank became a part of the present Huntington National Bank of Columbus, Ohio.

1869 the Hocking Furnace iron ore furnace ceased production because a higher quality iron ore became available in the Lake Superior area.

In 1870 an iron and metal furnace was erected at the Columbus Iron Company, Columbus, Ohio. Peter was one of its founding directors.

August 1, 1871, Hocking County records of deeds Book Z Page 184: Peter Hayden and his (second) wife Sara S. Hayden of the city and county of New York for $25.00 dollars deeded 1.34 acres of land to the Trustee of the Methodist Episcopal Church. This acreage is at the curve in the road before the entrance to Haydenville Cemetery. An 1869 report of the area by Levi Davis, a registered surveyor, shows the existence of this 1.34 acres as a Church lot prior to the 1871 recorded deed.

1883 Peter formed the Hayden Mining & Manufacturing Co. (H M & M Co.). Peter Hayden, President; Charles H. Hayden, Vice-President; John W. Jones, General Manager; J.W. Jones, C.E. Bowen, and August Magoon, all of Logan, Ohio, owned a share in the company. The balance of outstanding shares was held by the Hayden family.

1883 June4th Hocking County records of deeds Book 10 Page 56-57 Peter Hayden president of The Hocking Iron Compony for the sum of $263,000 dollars, quit claim all his real estate interest and appuntinenas in Hocking County to The Haydenville Mining and Manufacturing Company (H M & M Co.)

1883 June 4th Hocking County records of deeds Book 10 Page 58 Peter Hayden and his wife Sarah L. Hayden for the sum of $263,000 dollars warranty deed all Their real-estate interest and appuntinenas in Hocking County to The Haydenville Mining & Manufacturing Co. (H M & M Co.)

1883 H M & M Co. founded the company town of Haydenville, Ohio. Peter named the town after the family village of Haydenville, Massachusetts, which had been named after the manufacturing activities of his two brothers Joel and Josiah Hayden.

1883 The abundance of superior quality fire clay and the high quality coal, enticed Peter to construct a brick manufacturing factory in Haydenville, Ohio. The factory employed several hundred manual labors that turnout vast quantities of red brick, and terra cotta clay products. To meet the demand for these clay products a second factory was built.

October 7, 1884, the U.S. Patent Office issued a patent # 306,251for the Hayden paver. These truly unique design and constructed glazed paving and building brick has a 3 ½" x 3 ½" square 2 ½" deep cavity punched in the back. The surface design consisted of several patterns including multiple circles, dimples, and small raised bars.

These bricks were first manufactured at Peter Hayden, Front Street factory in Logan Ohio (Hocking Clay Manufacturing Co.). The company also manufactured the “MINGO” brand name brick with a distinctive chiseled design. The brick was named to honor the Mingo Indian tribe that had occupied Hocking County.

Peter’s properties and assets in Galveston, South Carolina, were confiscated when the Civil War broke out. Peter, as always, was able to turn adversity to his advantage. He converted his machines form making belt buckles to making bullets and turned his foundry operation into making cannon balls for the Union Army. He also engaged in the production of Calvary equipment for the U.S. Government. These new lines of manufacturing offset the losses at the outset of the Civil War.

1888 Peter Hayden passed away unexpectedly at the age of 88 and is buried in Greenlawn Cemetery , Columbus ,Ohio

Peter’s. death, on April 6, 1888, brought sorrow and grief to many hearts in Haydenville; he was renowned for his patriarchal care, his consideration for the comfort and interests, and benevolence to those he employed. Men of all classes deemed it a honor to work for him. He employed none but sober, industrious, and intelligent men, and never permitted a good man to leave his services, if money and considerate treatment were an inducement to remain. As a result, his enterprises were singularly free from all labor complications; and his career affords an example to follow by all those employing large numbers of men.

Peter did as much if not more than most in developing the growth of the Hocking Valley. He was one of the pioneer coal operators and manufacturing entrepreneur who overcame the adversity of the undeveloped Hocking Valley. A dedicated business man whose religious training as a child was a part of his everyday life.

A Columbus Industrialist, who had brought his family from Auburn, New York, to Columbus, Ohio in 1845. Shortly after arriving in town he began investing in and forming several profitable businesses; P. Hayden & Co. (bank), P. Hayden & Sons (foundry & machine works; coal & coke) P. Hayden Hardware Co., a fleet of Canal Boats, and in Green Township, Hocking County, Ohio; Hayden

Mine Co., Haydenville Mining and Manufacturing Co. and the town of Haydenville, Ohio named after his two brothers Joel and Josiah.

1880-Census shows residence New York County, New York

2nd Wife Sarah Barnard (Leverett) married Nov. 15, 1870 (NYC), daughter Kittie (from 1 marriage) son Peter (age 8 months from 2nd marriage) first wife Alice Booth Hayden (B. Aug.11, 1815 D. Nov. 6, 1865)

Herbert Eugene Hayden: B? D. 1857

Josiah Hayden: B? D. 1857

Lillian J. Hayden: B? D. 1857

Charles Halleck Hayden: B. 1837 D. 1920

William Buck Hayden: B. 1839 D. 1916

Harriet Hayden: B. 1850 D. 1850

1905 Peter Hayden's heirs sold Hocking Clay Manufacturing Co. H C M Co. to an Akron, Ohio investment firm. The new owners stopped manufacturing brick. An began the exclusive manufacturer of "salt glazed" sewer pipe and drain tile.

The factory is still in operation **(2020)** an referred to as Logan Clay Products Co. under the management of the Holl family.

1906 Peter Hayden's heirs sold Haydenville Mining & Manufacturing Co. to National Fireproofing Company included in; the sale was the factories, the town of Haydenville, the mines and all assets of the company.

(Specimens.)

W. B. HAYDEN.

PAVING BLOCK.

No. 306,251. Patented Oct. 7, 1884.

Fig. 1

Fig. 2. *Fig. 3.*

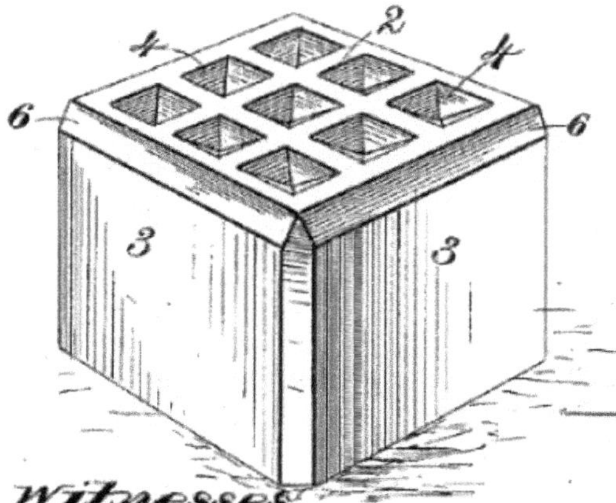

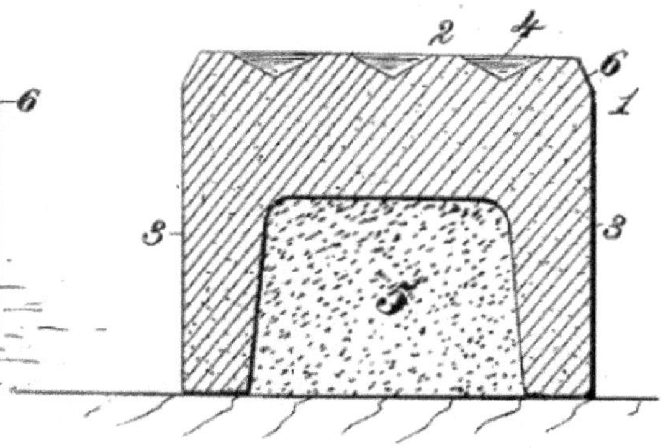

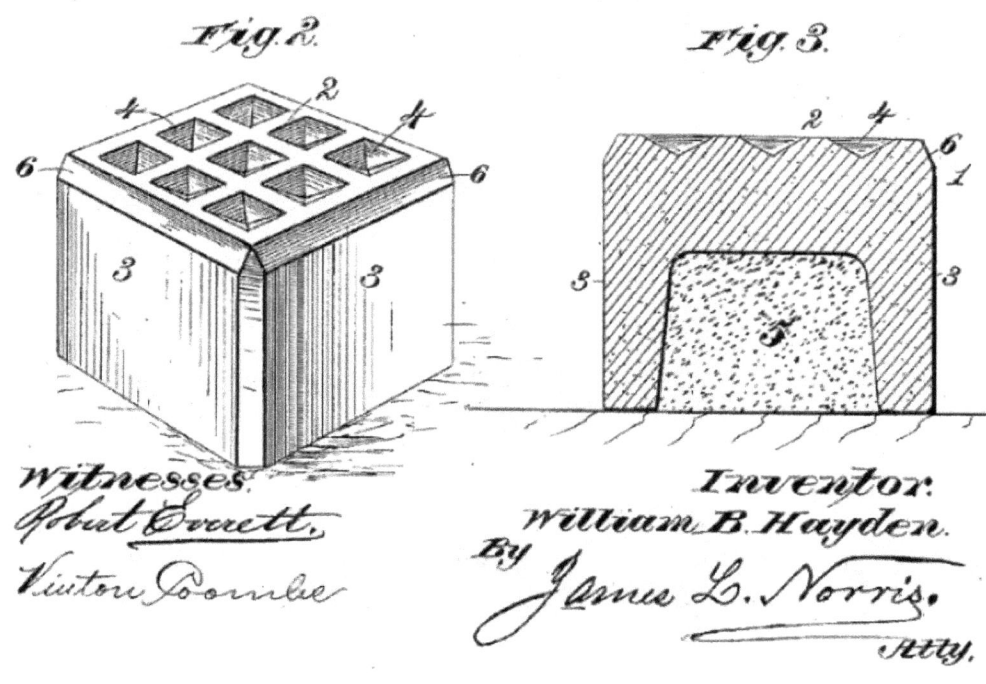

Witnesses.
Robert Everett,
Vinton Coombe

Inventor:
William B. Hayden.
By James L. Norris.
Atty.

N. PETERS, Photo-Lithographer, Washington, D.C.

UNITED STATES PATENT OFFICE.

WILLIAM B. HAYDEN, OF COLUMBUS, OHIO.

PAVING-BLOCK.

SPECIFICATION forming part of Letters Patent No. 306.251, dated October 7, 1884.

Application filed July 10, 1884. (Specimens.)

To all whom it may concern:

Be it known that I, WILLIAM B. HAYDEN, a citizen of the United States, residing at Columbus, Ohio, have invented new and useful Improvements in Paving-Blocks, of which the following is a specification.

This invention relates to improvements in the construction of composition blocks for paving streets, and has for its object to provide an improved method of paving, whereby each paving-block has an imperforate top wall and an interior filling of sand or equivalent material to impart elasticity to the pavement and afford perfect bearing over the entire bottom of each block.

The invention also has for its object to provide a novel construction of paving-block composed of fire-clay or other vitrifiable compound, whereby the block, when baked or burned, will be uniformly vitrified throughout its structure without cracking or overburning any part of the block, as is the case in burning or baking solid blocks of clay or like material, for the reason that the heat destroys the outer surface before properly acting on the center thereof.

The invention also has for its object to provide a hollow burned or baked paving-block which is imperforate and will prevent animals from slipping, while preventing rain or other water or frost from passing through the block to the foundation or ground.

The invention also has for its object to provide a hollow burned or baked paving-block with imperforate walls, which can be filled to form a cushion and render the block elastic when laid on its foundation.

The invention also has for its object to provide burned or baked paving-blocks for producing a more uniform and smooth pavement than ordinary stone, at a much less expense than the latter; to provide a composition paving-block in which the amount of material is lessened to construct the same, and the weight and expense of transportation are reduced to a minimum, and to provide a hollow burned or baked paving-block which will avoid the danger of animals slipping.

These objects I accomplish in the manner and by the means hereinafter described and claimed, reference being had to the accompanying drawings illustrating my invention, in which—

Figure 1 is a perspective view of a portion of a street-pavement embodying my invention; Fig. 2, a perspective view of one of the paving-blocks, and Fig. 3 a vertical central sectional view of the same.

In order to enable others skilled in the art to make and use my invention, I will now proceed to describe the same, referring to the drawings, where the numbers 1 indicate the paving-blocks, shown in Fig. 1 as constituting a street-pavement between the usual sidewalks.

The paving-blocks are composed of a composition of fire-clay or other refractory or vitrifiable material, such as sand and alkaline salts or flint and alkalies, which are formed by molds in a plastic condition into a hollow or chambered body having an imperforate top wall, 2, and vertical side walls, 3, the top wall having a series of indentations, depressions, or cavities, 4, after which the structure is burned or baked until vitrified.

To facilitate the withdrawal from the molds, the chamber in the block is made tapering, the widest portion being at the lower edge.

The construction provides a hollow block the walls of which are of uniform thickness, or approximately so, in such manner that in burning or baking the heat uniformly penetrates and vitrifies the composition to obtain a perfect vitrified exterior wearing-surface.

The blocks so constructed are filled with sand or equivalent material, as at 5, during the process of laying them, whereby each block of the pavement is rendered elastic by the interior cushion of sand, and at the same time perfect bearings over the entire bottoms of the blocks are obtained when they are laid on the foundation, which latter may be the earth or some specially-prepared foundation. The top wall of the block, having indentations or depressions, provides simple and efficient means for preventing animals from slipping, while the top wall being imperforate will prevent rain or other matter or frost from passing therethrough to the foundation of the pavement.

The surrounding upper edges of the blocks are each beveled, as at 6, so that when a series of the blocks are placed together crevices or spaces are provided to receive a filling of sand or like material.

Having thus described my invention, what I claim is—

2 306,251

1. A hollow vitrified paving-block having imperforate side and top walls, and adapted to be filled with sand or equivalent material, to render the block elastic and provide a perfect bearing over its entire bottom portion when laid on the pavement-foundation, substantially as described.

2. A hollow vitrified paving-block having an imperforate top wall formed with depressions, substantially as described.

3. A pavement consisting of hollow vitrified blocks having imperforate top and side walls, and each filled with a cushion of sand or equivalent material, to render the blocks elastic and provide them with perfect bearings over their entire bottom portions, substantially as described.

4. A street-pavement consisting of hollow vitrified blocks having side walls and imperforate top walls formed with depressions, each block containing a filling to render the roadway elastic and provide a perfect bearing over the entire bottom portions of the block, substantially as described.

In testimony whereof I affix my signature in presence of two witnesses.

WM. B. HAYDEN.

Witnesses:
C. H. HAYDEN,
A. C. CORNWALL.

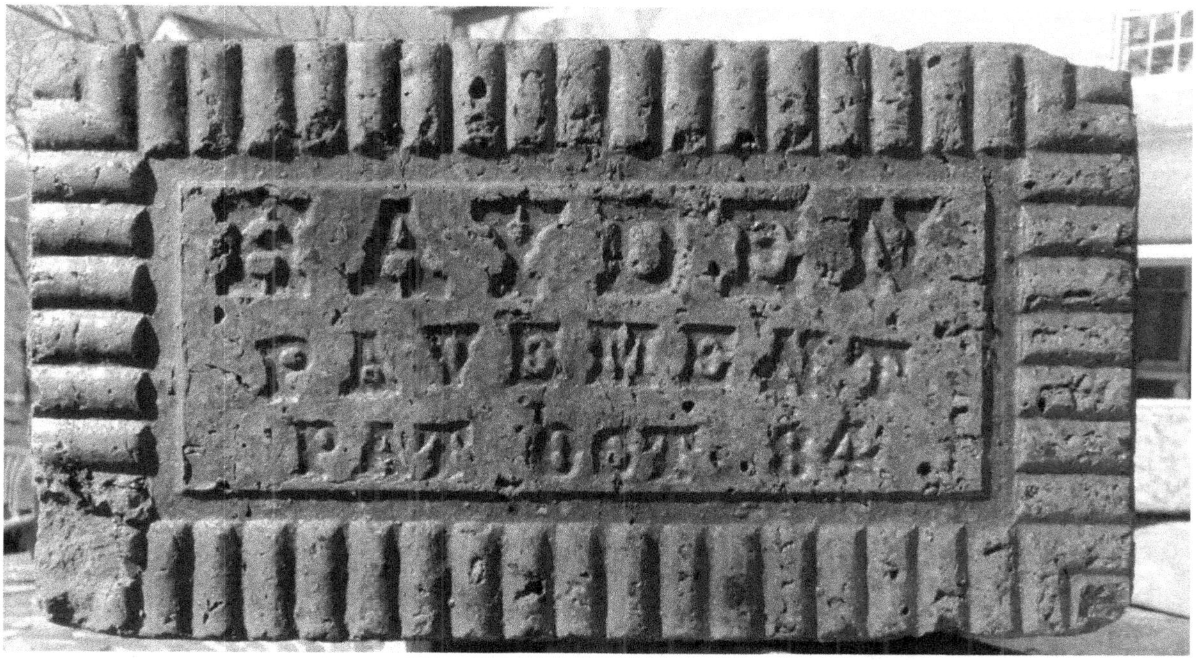

One of several Front design Hayden pavement brick

HAYDEN PAVEMENT BRICK Patent Oct.7, 1884

Back design of all Hayden pavement brick

Chapter 6: H M & M Co. Office & Store Complex

Figure 8 The company store

In the mid 1880's Peter Hayden began construction of a new building which would be the home of the Company Office and Company Store. The new building would replace the current office, provide a modern general store and make space available for the expansion of the factories. This new building would be built on the opposite side of the Canal and present office building but remain close to the present Canal loading docks and the existing Iron Ore Furnace. The Iron Ore Furnace would be dismantled; its' large sand stone blocks would be used as part of the foundation for the new building and factory expansions.

The floor space for the Company Store included ample display space, an ice making plant, and butcher shop, all of which occupied over sixty percent of the total floor space of the buildings first floor. The company offices occupied the balance of the floor space. Several years later years an ice cream parlor and sandwich shop were attached to the side to the building opposite the Company Store. The Company Store was owned and operated exclusively by the company for the benefit of the residents of the town and surrounding areas.

The second floor was the doctor's office and a couple of small hospital rooms. The remainder of the building housed the theater before the motion picture area. In later years it became a storage area for theater props, company and store records.

The operation of the store and notations of a "few" of the many items that were always in stock are from my "Larry Horn's" memories of working in the store and being directly involved with its' day to day operations.

During my High School years, I worked at the company store full time for .35 cents per hour, before and after class, during the week, and all day Saturday, as the only stock boy in the store. Ward Phillips, with the help of his wife, Libby, managed the store and they taught me how to calculate the retail price of the items stocked throughout the store. I can attest to the fact it is a myth "I owe my soul to the Company Store" did not apply to the Haydenville Company Store. An 8% mark-up over wholesale price was added to all items and many time perishable produce was sold at actual cost rather than to have it spoil.

The Company was the financial supporter of the store, Mr. Matheney said, “It has always been the intention of the Company to ensure that the residents of Haydenville would purchase their family needs at a very reasonable price regardless of whether the store showed a profit or not. The store is to provide for those needs and to keep them available at all times.”

Entrance to the store was through a single thick glass door with a wooden frame in the front center of the store. A few feet inside the entrance were two checkout clerks, Bernice “Bea” Carter and Gertrude “Gertie” Achuaer. All charge purchase items were identified and individually hand written in the customer's personnel charge account book. The clerk would total, "hand crank adding machine," up the dollar amount of the purchases and apply State sales tax, if any. Then she placed the company's preapproved charge card into a slot in the cash register, punch in the dollar sales amount, turned the hand crank on the side of the cash register. The cash register recorded that amount on the card. At closing time each day, all charge cards were taken to a clerk in the company office.

The floor throughout the store was wood, a light coat of oil was hand-sprayed on the floor, as need to control the dust. The entire floor of the store was swept, with a push broom, at closing time every night. During the summer months the awning over the front windows was hand cranked down to block out the sun, and the furnace fan was turned on to force cool air from the basement, through the duck work into the store - "air conditioning was unheard of at that time."

At closing time every night, the fresh produce that had been on display was taken to the cooler in the back of the store. There was always ample supply of fresh apples, grapes, onions, potatoes, celery and miscellaneous fresh produce. The bananas were always the large yellow ones, not the green ones you see in the stores today. When the store opened at 7 a.m., I would have to restock the fresh produce display, and started restocking the store shelves as needed.

The shelves against the wall on the company office side of the store held paper products, flour, sugar and baking supplies. The rows of shelves on that side of the store were separated by a set of double wooden doors that opened into the company offices. There was "never" a DO NOT ENTER sign on these doors; everyone knew they were not allowed to go into the company office.

The shelves across the back of the store, were a false wall, behind it was the open aisle to the backdoor of the store. The entrance to the basement and a set of stairs to the second floor was only accessible from this aisle. The part of the shelves visible to the customers was stocked with men's work shoes of various sizes, laundry and house cleaning products, mops, brooms etc. and cooking utensils.

The center of the store had two rows of double-sided shelves that held loaves of white bread, brown wheat bread, a small assortment of store bought cakes, canned goods, boxes of oats, Cheerios, Wheaties, shredded wheat, corn flakes, boxes of grits - the sweeten cereal of today was unheard of. A section at the bottom of one shelf toward the front of the store was for coffee, Bliss brand was .49 cent for a 16 oz. can, regular or decaf, bulk tea or string-less bags, Carnation condensed can milk. Sodapop, frozen items and ice cream were not available in the store.

When you entered the front door, the produce section, was against the left front wall. The row of shelves against the left wall were stocked with hardware supplies. When garden planting time arrived, the floor space in front of the shelves was stocked with various name brands of seed potatoes and onion sets. It took on the appearance of a greenhouse with so many different types of flower and vegetable plants, in addition to the vast selections of package of seeds.

The meat department was in a separate room, for sanitary reasons, entrance was through a glass door beside the produce display. Immediately to your right once inside the meat department was a 12-foot enclosed refrigerated fresh meat display case. The meat display was only accessible by the butcher "meat cutters" John Clouston and Homer Carter. Meat carcasses were purchased by hanging weight, simply meaning a half beef or hog, delivered directly from the slaughter house to the store. There were always two or three carcasses hanging in the walk-in cooler, thus insuring a ready supply of meat for the customers. The "meat cutters" hand cut all meat and ground "scrap trimming" into hamburger, otherwise known as poor man's steak, which sold for .49 cent per pound. Butter, real cow butter, was one pound package of creamery butter, margarine, or oleo, was sold in a one pound block of hard white margarine, similar to the stick margarine we cook with today. Later year's, oleo margarine came in a soft squeeze package with a pill in it; you would work the pill around until it dissolved and turn the oleo yellow. The most popular cuts of meat were those that could use as the bases of a family meal. Poultry was a special order item. Lunchmeat was hand cut to order, a very limited variety was available, except bologna (West Virginia round steak) which was the most inexpensive. Hot dogs were sold bulk weight, all beef was the only kind that existed at that time. My experience in the meat department consisted of slicing, cheese and lunchmeat, grinding meat into hamburger or bulk sausage and cleaning the equipment.

Raising a garden was the accepted rule of survival for the long winter months. The women stored fresh meat by either smoking it or using a hand rub with salt to preserve it. Deep freezers had not been invented yet. Garden vegetables, local fruits and berries were preserved, cold packed in glass jars, also known as “canning.” It was common practice to have over 100 glass jars of preserved food in storage for the coming winter months.

So in reality it was common knowledge to everyone in town what you feed your family. If you had a question about how to prepare a food product a neighbor was always willing to help solve the problem.

A door in the customers section of the meat department open to a passage way to the gasoline station and later year the gasoline station closed and an ice cream parlor and sandwich open in its place.

Figure 9 This sign was mounted in front of the gas station, circa 1940.

Willard Seels "Shorty" operated the gasoline station, the brand name of gasoline was "Silver Flash." In later years Shorty open his own Sohio Station at Pattonville, junction of State Route 595 & 33. It was directly across Rt. 595 from the 5 mile inn, operated by Opera Sharb family (the building had been the Pattonville one room school house). Haydenville was a dry town so everyone who wanted to drink alcohol beverage went to the 5 mile inn.

Deb Smith remembers very vividly the gasoline station before it became an ice cream parlor. It had a wooden ramp beside it to drive your car up to a large wooden platform. You parked your car on the platform and went down several large wooden steps and waited in the station while the service station attended worked on your car.

The ramp and platform were one of the places Deb liked to play. The platform was built on large post that extended several feet above ground level, it was large enough to walk around to get to the steps.

Deb remembers climbing up the steps, then jumping down the steps one at a time . One day he was jumping down the steps as he had done hundreds of times, the step broke and a long spike nail punctured the calf of his leg. It was a serious wound that left the 3" scar (he showed me) on his leg, and a vivid reminder of his child hood days.

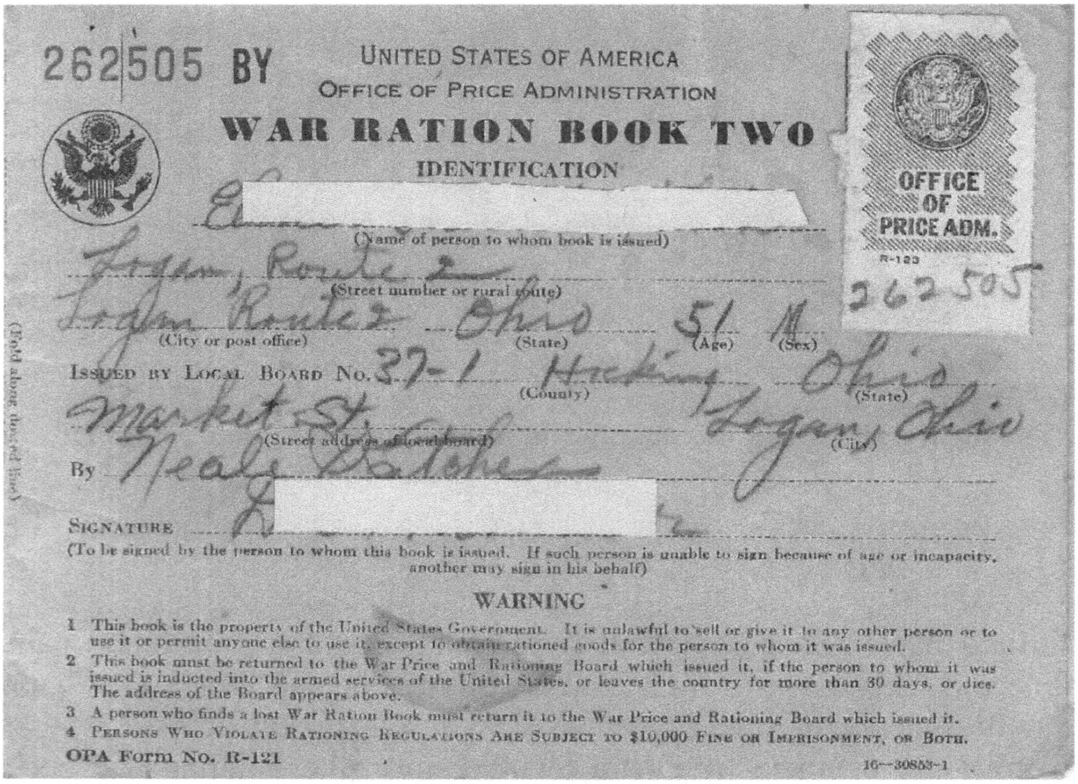

262505 BY

UNITED STATES OF AMERICA

OFFICE OF PRICE ADMINISTRATION

WAR RATION BOOK TWO

IDENTIFICATION

(Name of person to whom book is issued)

Logan, Route 2

(Street number or rural route)

Logan Route 2 Ohio 51 M

(City or post office) (State) (Age) (Sex)

ISSUED BY LOCAL BOARD NO. 37-1 Hocking Ohio

(County) (State)

Market St. Logan, Ohio

(Street address of local board) (City)

By Neale Datcher

SIGNATURE

(To be signed by the person to whom this book is issued. If such person is unable to sign because of age or incapacity, another may sign in his behalf)

OFFICE OF PRICE ADM.

R-123

262505

(Fold above dotted line)

WARNING

1 This book is the property of the United States Government. It is unlawful to sell or give it to any other person or to use it or permit anyone else to use it, except to obtain rationed goods for the person to whom it was issued.

2 This book must be returned to the War Price and Rationing Board which issued it, if the person to whom it was issued is inducted into the armed services of the United States, or leaves the country for more than 30 days, or dies. The address of the Board appears above.

3 A person who finds a lost War Ration Book must return it to the War Price and Rationing Board which issued it.

4 PERSONS WHO VIOLATE RATIONING REGULATIONS ARE SUBJECT TO $10,000 FINE OR IMPRISONMENT, OR BOTH.

OPA Form No. R-121

16--30853-1

Figure 10 War Ration Book

WWII was a difficult time for the civilian population. All able-bodied men were screened for possible military service, which created a shortage of working-class men. Women began filling the unemployment void. The country assumed the attitude of *whatever it takes to keep this country free we will do it together*. Our men in uniform were the number one priority. We accepted government food rationing as a necessary way of life. Our boys in uniform came first.

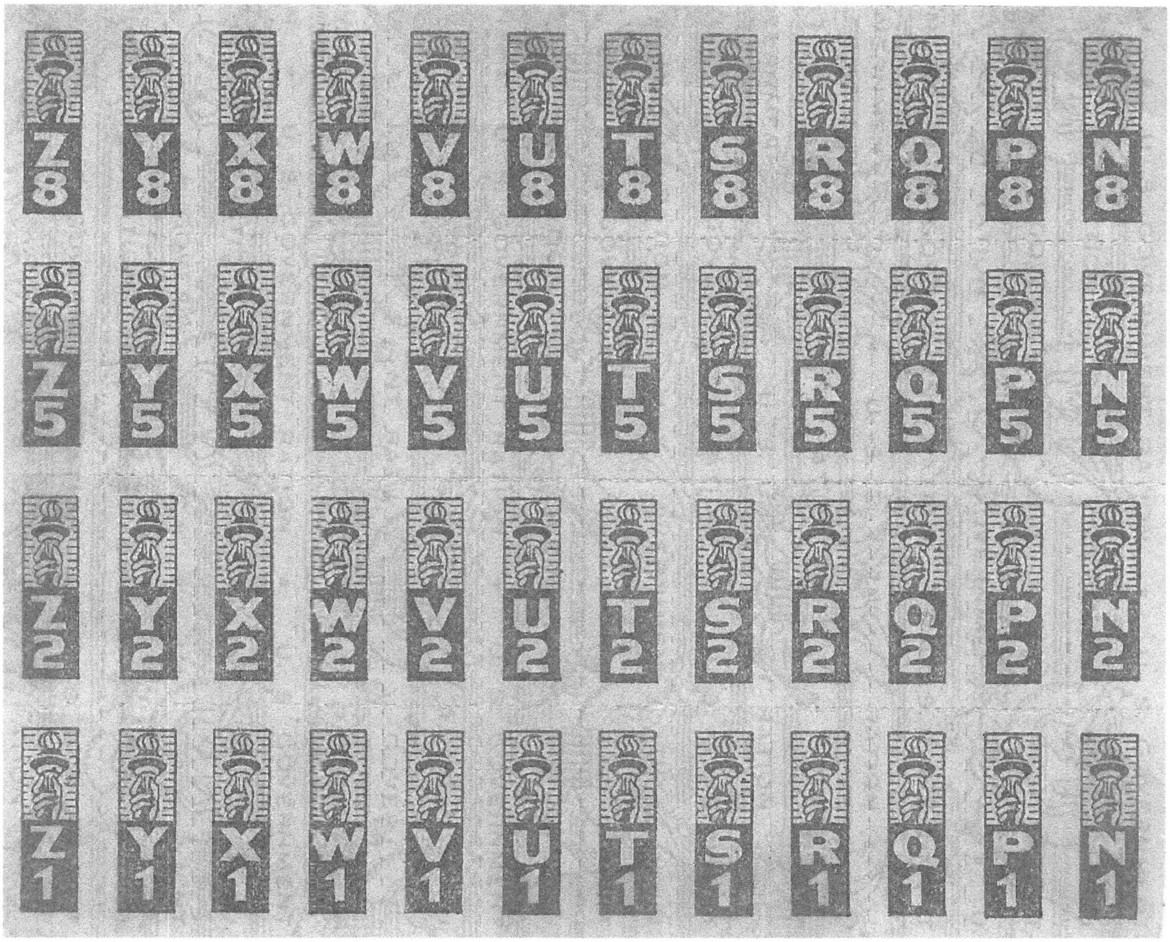

Figure 11 War Rations

There were four different War Ration Books issued by the Federal Government. Each book was for a combination of rationed foods. The store clerk told you how many of which coupon you had to have to purchase that particular food item. It was a violation of Federal Law for a store clerk to sell any ration food item without obtaining the correct amount of ration tickets.

The store clerk gave you a receipt (tax stamps – see Figure 12) in the amount of State Tax you were charged for a taxable item.

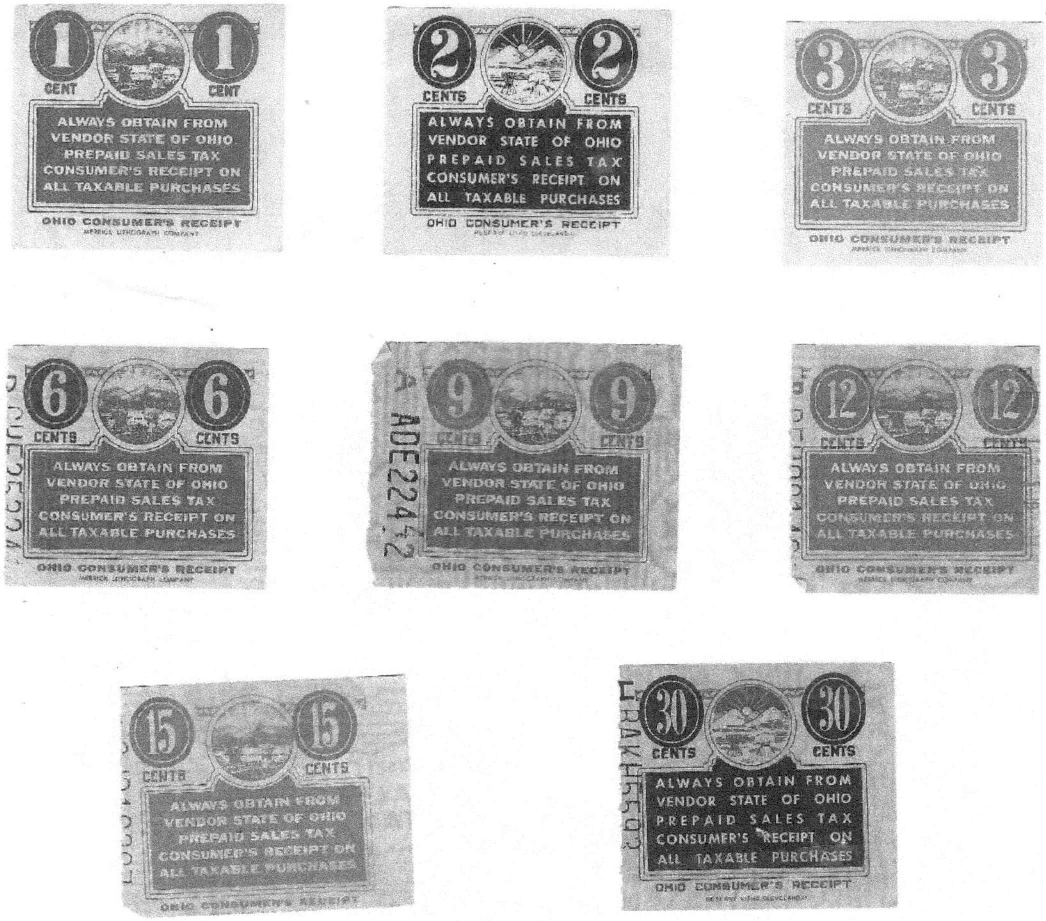

Figure 12 Tax Stamps

In the early 1950's Frank (Chippie) Crothers and Lucille Smith (Deb's mother)managed the ice cream parlor.

Sis Smith has fond memories of work with her mother Lucille in the ice cream parlor. Sis took the order and served the food her mother prepared. This is one of her special memories that lingers in her mind after all these years; during the Vietnam War the government had a "special forces survival training camp" in the wild and desolate woods at Dorr Run. The soldiers were trained to survive in the jungles of Vietnam, to live solely off the land and eat whatever Mother nature provided be it bugs, worms, berries, and nuts, fires for anything were strictly forbidden. The Soldiers were not permitted to have any contact with the outside world. Some of them would disobey this order and slip through the woods in their camouflage disguise, that blended in with the wilderness. Their destination was the ice cream parlor for some real food. They would knock on the back door, so the general public wouldn't see them and place their orders. Sis's mother was afraid of these scary dressed men, it was Sis's responsibility to take their orders, and her mother prepared the real food for these special forces' soldiers. Sis said they always left a large tip supposedly as a bribe "not to tell anyone they had been there."

Figure 13 The Ice Cream Parlor. The gas pumps were removed late 1940. I remember my dad putting a $1.00 worth of gas in our car. $1.00 bought 5-gallons of gasoline.

Figure 14 The Company Store & Office

Chapter 7: Haydenville

S.E.1/4 of Section 13, Green Township
Hocking County, Ohio

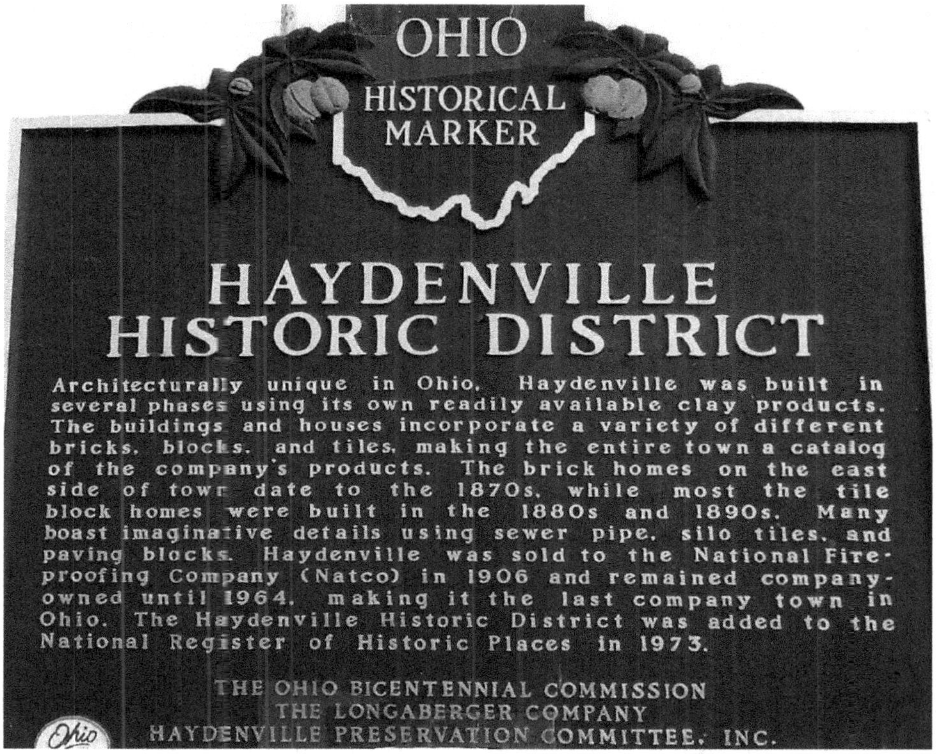
OHIO
HISTORICAL
MARKER
HAYDENVILLE
HISTORIC DISTRICT
Architecturally unique in Ohio, Haydenville was built in several phases using its own readily available clay products. The buildings and houses incorporate a variety of different bricks, blocks, and tiles, making the entire town a catalog of the company's products. The brick homes on the east side of town date to the 1870s, while most the tile block homes were built in the 1880s and 1890s. Many boast imaginative details using sewer pipe, silo tiles, and paving blocks. Haydenville was sold to the National Fire-proofing Company (Natco) in 1906 and remained company-owned until 1964, making it the last company town in Ohio. The Haydenville Historic District was added to the National Register of Historic Places in 1973.
THE OHIO BICENTENNIAL COMMISSION
THE LONGABERGER COMPANY
HAYDENVILLE PRESERVATION COMMITTEE, INC.

In the foothills of Rural Southeastern, Ohio along the banks of Hocking River, Mother Nature shares her picturesque beauty with the little community of Haydenville, the architectural design of the homes and church are truly magnificent, a one of a kind, a town that truly deserves the honor of being listed on the National Registry of Historic Places and holding the distinguished honor of being known as; the last company owned town in Ohio.

In the mid-1800s Peter Hayden constructed two clay tile and brick manufacturing factories. Being a smart, prosperous businessman, he knew that for the factories to prosper, he would need good quality, hardworking labors. To meet those needs he built, with the brick and tile from his factories, the town of Haydenville. These unique, one of a kind, architectural design structures, served two purposes: modern beautiful homes for his employees and eye catching display of the company's manufactured clay products.

Peter Hayden built a company owned town that was a place his employee would be proud to call home, is in Haydenville, Ohio a town with:

- A large, beautiful red brick two-story building, the first floor for company offices, general store, meat shop, and an ice making plant, the second floor was for the doctor's office, hospital and theater. Years later an ice cream parlor and gasoline pumps were added, Chippie Crothers, managed the ice cream parlor, Shorty Seels, managed the gasoline and automotive service.
- A two-story brick boarding house, with four one bedroom units on each floor. The second floor was surrounded by an outside balcony that served as a private entrance to each of the four bedroom units.
- A brick Church, and as a memorial to Peter Hayden, his family donated a large, stained window and the Church bell. Over 100 years have passed since the first service was held. Father Time has not taken his toll, the strength of the Church stands proud and strong yet today.

Building construction and the storm drainage system had to comply with Mr. Hayden's strict guideline. A ditch over 10 feet deep in some place was dug by manual labor to accommodate the 24"X 36"clay storm drain. The storm drain starts at the Church and parallels the highway then in front of the office it went under the highway, across the open fields and emptied into the Hocking River. One section of the original storm drain system is still in use today, it starts at the head Frog Hollow Road, and goes under the highway at intersection on County Rd.25 and (Hunky Row) Wandling Road, on its way to the Hocking River. This explanation, of only a small part, of the storm drain system in Haydenville, is an example of Mr. Hayden strict adherence to detail and strive for perfection. His goals instilled a pride of craftsmanship in his employees that has endured the test of time. His achievements are still standing, more than 100years after being completed.

The Company (Natco), maintained a full-time carpenter /repair, (gang) crew, Red Bert, was the last foreman. The foreman’s job was to maintain all the company buildings and ensure that they remained in excellent condition. Frankie (Weasel) Van Burren was the last foreman in charge of plumbing, trash, and garbage pickup.

The children looked forward to the holiday season, especially Christmas. The Sunday before Christmas, ever pew in the church was packed, and people stood in the aisle to celebrate His birth. The children's Sunday school class put on a Christmas play, in accordance with their age group.

Mr. Hayden, and in later years the Company, always took great pride in helping and being involved in Community activities. Every year the Company would host a Christmas party at the Community Hall; Santa would be there and give each child a bag filled with real chocolate candy, hard candy, some holiday nuts, one large red apple and one large orange. To us kids, this was a special treat, a luxury our parents couldn't afford.

The residents were a self-formed, close-knit family, a philosophy of life they had inherited from their parents; you help thy neighbor. If someone became ill, a neighbor would go to that house without being asked and take over the everyday chores of that family until the person was well.

When death struck someone in the community, a neighbor placed a black wreath on the front door of the deceased. Someone or usually a couple would go door to door through the town collecting money for flowers. Any money not spent was given to the family of the deceased with notes and letters of sympathy. The showing of the deceased was in their home and the funeral was held in the Church, prior to the burial usual in a local or family cemetery. Cremation was an unspoken sin, something that was never discussed regarding a dead person.

All families took great pride in the appearance of their homes both inside and outside. Most of the house had one on two trees in the front yard. This served to help keep the house cool and to enhance its appearance, The summer heat bore down on the houses and sleeping upstairs, all kids sleep upstairs, was sometimes almost unbearable. Few people could afford a window fan and air conditioners were unheard of.

One of Mr. Matheny's unwritten, strictly enforced rule... "He would not tolerate for any reason, unmaintained, trashy looking homes or the blocking of the sidewalk. The Company maintained all sidewalks by driving on them to spread gravel, thus the sidewalks were at least 6 feet wide."

Haydenville was a Company owned town, a world of its own, there was no need to go out of town for anything. The company provided for the everyday needs of the men and their families.

The strength, the bond, and fellowship of the Church was the blood of life for our little town, be it the good times or hard times, the Church was always there to help the people of Haydenville.

Moore Street which is in the middle of town and goes across the railroad tracks to four beautiful brick homes. These are the only brick homes that Peter Hayden did not build. Charlie Moore, an heir to the Wolfe family, and one of the very early residents of Haydenville, build these homes especially for his daughters.

Charlie was one of my 39 *The Logan Daily News* customers. He was a big muscular man and had very large callous hands. He lived by himself, two doors up from Francis Store. His wife, Mrs. Moore lived by herself on the ground floor rear, in one of apartment of the old boarding house. Charlie originally owned the big farm at the top of the hill on Hungery Hallow (holler) road across from Sid Grubb's farm. It later became known as the Ingram (Lew) farm. Lew was a salesman for Natco he and his wife (Audrey) had two sons Phil, and Jack and one Daughter.

In 1903, the post office was moved from the company store to its present location, which at the time of the move, had been the doctor's office. The phone system was also moved into the same building and the postal clerk continued duties as telephone receptionist.

Figure 15 The old boarding house has been abandoned for many years. The original slate roof and interior have not been updated or altered. The building is in remarkable condition with no visible sign of collapsing. This building, like most of those in Haydenville, are an example of the dedication and craftmanship of Peter Hayden's employees over 130 years ago.

Figure 16 H M & M Co. factory provided the red unglazed brick to build its office complex and to the west of that complex is the two-story boarding house, six two-story houses, and the last five one-story houses that included salt glazed drain tile and brick from H.C.M. Co. of Logan,.

Figure 17 One-story red brick house built by H C M Co, Logan, who provided the décor of salt glazed rain tile and glazed brick.

Figure 18 Haydenville chimney tops. This style of chimney top was manufactured by H M & M Co. factory at Haydenville, Ohio They played an integrate role in designing the company houses. Some of the chimney tops were designed to resemblance to chess pieces.

Figure 19 H C M Co. (Hocking Clay Manufacturing Company) Front Street, Logan, Ohio, manufacturers of the Hayden Pavement Brick. US Patent #306.251. Patent October 7, 1884.

Figure 20 This clay drain tile was manufactured at the H C M Co. factory, Logan, Ohio. The forerunner of the present location of the Logan Clay Products Company. It was designed with a taper on each end to accommodate a coupling and the center hole is for a dowel rod to be inserted to keep the tile in alignment. In later years, this drain tile design was modified.

Figure 21 The doctor moved his office to the first house east of his previous office building and this old office building became the US Post Office. My Uncle Harry (Buddy) Mills was born in this doctor's office and probably Dr. R.M. Anderson was the doctor who delivered him.

Chapter 8: Religion

The founders of Haydenville and the surrounding area were pious pioneers who were motivated and sustained by communal worship. There was always a place for song, prayer, and spiritual training for their children.

Religion was an important part of the everyday lives of the men and women in this area, years before the community of Haydenville was founded.

The First recorded document of a church being built close to Haydenville is August14,1850 when George and his wife Mariah by her mark(x) Crawford for the sum of $1.00 deeded.94hds. of an acre to, The Trustee of the Methodist Episcopal Church of the United States of America. The deed set out the stipulation that the said Trustees or successor in trust shall erect or cause to be erected a House or Place of worship for members of the Methodist Episcopal Church of the United States of America.

The property is now known as the Haydenville Cemetery and under strict control and maintenance of the Green Township Trustees.

The Second recorded document is August 1, 1871, when Peter Hayden and his second wife Sarah S. Hayden for the sum of $25.00 deeded 1.34hds.of an acre to, the Trustees of Methodist Episcopal Church.

An 1869 survey by Levi Davis a local (registered surveyor) show the existence of a Church on the property The Church building had been built flat ground, at the bend in the road coming from Hopperville and going through what is now the Haydenville Cemetery. Remnants of the Church's foundation are visible from the abandon road that goes around the hill to the Wolfe Family Private Cemetery.

The Church, in later years, was affectionately call "The Little Church on the hill" it was a 30 feet wide x 40 feet long, frame building, painted white, plain

Figure 22 Early Baptism in Hocking River
Photo from vicinity of bridge on Wandling Road Haydenville , Ohio

glass windows, heated by a coal stove, three rows of straight back seats. There were a several steps leading up to the porch that went across the front of the building to accommodate the two entrance doors. As the custom maintained, in all Church Services, the men entered one door and the women entered the other door.

The seating arrangements for the congregation inside the Church the men sat together on one side, the women, and children sat on the other side.

Several of the older Church Members recall that the Church always had a large attends of adults and children, cold winter days, snow or bad weather, did not keep them from attending Church Services.

In the early days of the Church, there was a man named Ed Lehman. A devout Christian living near the mines, which were about 2 mile from the Church; he felt a need for a way of getting the children to Sunday school. So, he selected one of the clay cars and built a long seat on each side, street car fashion, and then he hitched, "Old Dobber"(pony or mule) to the car and pulled it through the tunnel The children walked about a ¼ mile from the tunnel exit to the Church. The children were always ready and watching for their transportation vehicle and gave it the name *The Gospel Car*.

Early ministers (Preachers) at the little Church on the hill; not in order; Binkley, Finney, Rickets, Sparks, Cooks and Madden. Organists: Mrs. Cora Stiers and Mrs. Kate Stiers. Quartet: Emma Rutter, John Wolf, Alice England, and Martin Olinger.

The community remembers…

- Morris Vollmer and Mrs. Arlie Campbell (Mae Walker) remembers going to school there, and in the fall of 1893, one of the classes was writing on the black board when someone yelled "*fire!*" The teacher Colonel Friesner had the pupils stand in line and march out in an orderly fashion. The building was completely destroyed. Some of the grades were moved to the Old Thompson house, which stood next to the store and office building. Some of the grades were moved to the old Odd Fellows Hall which was located near the Narrow Gauge Trestle. (Concrete foundation beside road up to Cemetery was for the Trestle). Church Services and School classes continued to be held in the Odd Fellows Hall, while the present Church and a school building beside the Church were being built.
- Construction of this Third Church was completed in 1893, Hayden Mining & Manufacturing Co. (H.M. & M.CO) entered into an agreement with the Methodist Episcopal Church to design and construct (the present) Church.

The terms of the agreement were H.M. & M. Co. would be in charge of the entire construction project, provide the building site, the Hayden factories would supply all the building material, and pay 90% of the construction cost The Church and community would be responsible for the remaining 10%.

- The exterior is patented Hayden paving brick, the chip face brick (trade name Mingo) and various hollow tile were all produced at Hayden Clay Manufacturing Co..(H C M Co.) Logan, Ohio the interior Clay terra cotta décor and arch ways are products of H M & M Co. Haydenville, Ohio
- The steeple was removed in the mid 1950 as a safety factor.
- It is safe to assume that Peter Hayden, a devout Christian, was the major supporter of this project. He had a proven passion to improve the quality of life for his employees, their families, and the physical structure of the town. He didn't live to see this major improvement completed. Peter Hayden passed away on the 6th day of April 1888, leaving a legacy that still stands today.
- Mr. Jack Health, of Chicago, Illinois was awarded the building contract. He brought 2 employees with him Harry Zinn and Jack Keegan, both skilled brick mason. During the long and tiring construction process, Harry met and fell in love with Mary Patton the daughter of Eli Patton, one of the original Hocking County families. When the Church building was completed, Harry went back to Chicago to help Mr. Health complete another building, but promptly returned to marry his sweet heart.
- John Smart, Ira Achuaer, and T.A. Wharton hauled the brick and other materials from the factory, by horse and wagon to the Church construction site.
- The Church was completed in May. 1893 the Church cornerstone contains gold coins, a bible, a Sunday School Paper and a daily paper.
- The Churchyard was enclosed with a white picket fence; Mr. Ed. Lehman planted 4 Maple trees on each side of the walk and planted an Ash tree next to the entrance gate, a Walnut tree to the right of the walk The Walnut tree is the only one still standing today.(2020)
- Mr. Ed Lehman was the devote Christian who came up with the idea of building the "gospel car" for the children of the little Church on the Hill, He always sets in the front row of seat, on the left side of the Church. He always stood and faced the congregation when he leads them in prayer.
- Mrs. J. O. Reamy, Peter Hayden's daughter, donated the very large Church bell, which was installed in the bell tower.

- Mrs. Peter Hayden donated the large stained glass windows in memory of her husband.
- The Kings Daughter Sunday School Class October 1939 donated The American flag and the Christian flag.
- The Kings Daughter Sunday School Class June 1945 donated the large pulpit Bible.
- Unknown donator gave three walnut pulpit chairs, which were originally upholstered a bright red plush.
- Mrs. May (Wolfe) McFadden made the first birthday box; a small wooden box covered with black velvet, with "HAPPY BIRTHDAY" embroidered in white letters.
- Mrs. John Wolfe, Mrs. Waldo Chute, and Mrs. John Herald in memory of their parents Mr. and Mrs. Robert Wolfe, donated the large picture the head of Christ, and the beautiful alter and offering plates. Harry Pollack, one of the talented young men of Haydenville, built the beautiful alter for them. *The present alter is not the original.
- Mr. and Mrs. Charles H. Patton date unknown, reupholstered the pulpit furniture in a beautiful dusty rose color material.
- Charles and Dora Anthony May21 , 1893 first bride and groom in the new Church Reverend J. P. Gordon being the first pastor solemnize the rites.
- Mr. and Mrs. Anthony returned in 1943 to celebrate their Golden Anniversary. Mr. Harry Swaim and Mrs. Howard St. Clair furnished special music. Mrs. Charles Patton read a special poem. Mr. and Mrs. Frank Allen and Mr. Robert Swaim were the also guest of the bride and groom 50 years ago.
- Mr. Frank Allen and Mrs. Arthur Kreyssig were care taker of the Church; Walter Gastin rang the bell and fired the coal furnace in the basement . Mr. Allen had been the caretaker for over 20years, when moved from this area in January 1944.
- Mr. Harvey Angle 1948 caretaker
- Mr. Arthur Horn (my father) early 1950's assumed all the maintenance responsible of the Church in addition to his full time job as a labor at the factories. While Dad was working at the factory, many of the responsibilities' rested on my shoulders. The rate of pay to my dad was $20.00 per month.
- September 12, 1948 was the first Homecoming. It was then agreed that the Annual Homecoming would be the Second Sunday of September each year.

MEMORIES OF DAYS GONE BY

- Mr. Jerry Hammon of Logan remembers signing "Marching On" as part of the first Christmas entertainment in the new Church.
- Mrs. Homer Carter was first Cradle Roll Superintend and one of the Church leaders and teachers.
- Mrs. Vern Robinette was very active leader in the Church and work many years with the standard Bearers. She took groups of young people to the Church Camp Grounds in Lancaster, Ohio during the summer months.
- Mrs. Frank Allen was a teacher at the Church Sunday School for over 30 years, and President of the Missionary Society for over12 years.
- Mrs. Harry Swaim (Alice Allen) was in charge of the Primary Department. Will be remembered for her sweet voice, she was always ready to do her part, both for the living on dead.
- Mrs. Wesley Woltz was an active member in the Church and Sunday School she devoted much of her time to the young people of the Church preparing them for plays and special occasion of the Church.
- Mrs. Sarah Tucker was President of the Missionary Society, she brought the missionary program with her from one of the earlier Church.
- Ice Cream Socials and dinners were a regular event of the Church everything was donates in order to make the day a success. Mrs. William Achauer, Mrs. Wesley Woltz, Mrs. Sara Tucker, Mrs. John Matheny and many others, helped to make each event a success.
- One of the many outstanding revivals was in1940 under the pastorate of Evangelists. Rev. W.E. Bancroft. Rev. Watt and Mrs. Walker,
- There was a spirit of harmony in the membership of the Church and "NATCO" stood ready to cooperate in any Church activity. There was always time for kindness and devotion to duty on the part of the Pastors.
- The “NATCO” factories closed in the early 1960 all that remains is a brush field where the factories and kiln once stood. The Church building still stands proud and strong, as in the days it was built. Father time has taken his toll on the membership of the Church congregation. The Church is not dead, but only resting, HIS spirit is in the hearts and souls of those who struggle to breathe the breath of life back into the Church.

HAYDENVILLE CHURCH

Preachers (Ministers)

1893-J.P. Gordon first pastor of the new Church
1897-B.F. Evans Alexander
1901-J.W. Westervelt
1903 -Rev. Oswald
1904-J.W. Orr & W. A. Hunter
1910-J.W. Briscoe
1911-H. S. Yost
1912-G. T. Howard
1914-A. S. Davison
1915-J. C. Plummer
1916-Lot C. Wills
1921-J.W. Steen
1921-W. A. Cooper
1923- Rev. Lockwood
1924-W H. Walker
1926-L.C. Mc Candlish
1929-Edgar B. Dean
1930-G. C. Nutter
-W. E. Bancroft
1936-L O. Lineberg
1944-T. E. Kinnison
1945-C. B. Sees
1947-G. E. Fisher
2015- Dave Sherman

Sunday School Superintendents

J. H. Mc Sherry
Benjamin Harden
T. A. Wharton
John Norris Sr.
J. F. Alexander
Walter Gastin
Nelson Skiver
Homer Carter
Walter Lehman
Roy Crothers

Organists (pianist)
Johnny Williams
Mrs. Cora Stiers
Alta Wharton 8 years
Laurel Pollack
Nellie Allen 18 years

Figure 23 Haydenville Methodist Episcopal Church completed in 1893.

Webb Chapel

A BRIEF HISTORY OF THE CHURCHES FORMING THE WEBB'S CHARGE OF THE UNITED METHODIST CHURCH

1988

Written by: Clarence M. Thompson, pastor

First Settlers

In order to set the stage for this history, I think it would be best to begin at the time the area was first being settled by the early pioneers. The first settlers in Ohio were a few Scotch-Irish families that had made their way across the Alleghenies. It was just after the Revolutionary War, the United States had claimed the Northwest Territory, and the government was offering to pay off many soldiers of the Revolutionary War by offering them western land grants.

In 1787, a land company, the Ohio Company of Associates, a New England group, bought 1,500,000 acres of land northwest of the Ohio River in the Muskingum Valley. The Northwest Ordinance was adopted the same year, and the Ohio country became a part of the Northwest Territory. On April 7, 1788, the Ohio Company established Marietta, the first permanent white settlement in Ohio. These early settlers in Marietta were mostly Puritans and there were no Methodists among them.

In 1798, a Methodist Episcopal minister by the name of John Kobler, crossed the Ohio River from Kentucky. Kneeling there on the river bank he asked God's blessing upon the work he was about to do. On Christmas Day of that year he prepared the communion table and served the sacraments to twenty-five or thirty persons who had gathered for worship. One source claims that this was the first regular preaching and the first Methodist communion in Ohio.

In 1799, Robert Manly formed a circuit in the southeast part of Ohio, extending up the Muskingum River for forty miles. Also in 1799, James Quinn made a missionary tour up the Hocking Valley, preaching to a few families that had settled near the present site of Lancaster. In 1804, Asa Shinn organized the Hocking Circuit out of this territory. The following year, James Quinn and John Meck were sent to this circuit.

Webb's Chapel Orgainized

In 1810, the Ohio Conference was organized at Portsmouth. By this time classes and societies were being formed in most of the settlements within the area. Between 1811 and 1830, a number of circuits were formed. Among them was the Fairfield Circuit. By 1817, a Methodist Episcopal Church was built in Logan and their records show that they were a part of the Fairfield Circuit with Michael Ellis and J. McMahon as the circuit riders. The little community where Webb's Chapel is now located, as well as other communities in the area, was probably visited by these itinerant preachers.

In 1818, Benjamin Webb organized the class that was to become the Webb's Chapel Methodist Episcopal Church. The newly formed group built a log structure in section 29 of Falls Gore Township in Hocking County. The log structure was used for nearly a quarter of a century. In 1851 the membership roll had grown to sixty members and the congregation built a new frame structure. In a history written around 1880, it tells of the present pastor, Rev. A. B. Shaw, holding worship services and class meetings on alternate Sundays and prayer meetings every Thrusday night. Sunday School was conducted for six months during the year.

Maxville Church Organized

A class of Methodists was organized in Maxville in 1845. Membership increased and a building was erected and used by the new society for a few years. The structure was later to be used as the school when a new frame structure was built in 1852. This structure is still in use today and is in excellent condition. The Maxville Methodist Episcopal

Chruch, being situated about three miles from Webb's Chapel Methodist Episcipal Church, made it possible for the two churches to be placed on a charge together. During the period from 1855 to 1872, it is believed that these two churches were on the same charge.

South Harvey Organized

The church that is now South Harvey United Methodist Church, was the former Harvey Chapel Methodist Episcopal Church. It, too, is quite old and was probably organized at about the same time as the Maxville society. When it was first organized, and a log structure was built, it was called "Black's Meeting House." The church structure was also used for a school and was sometimes referred to as "Black's Schoolhouse." But its organization was much like the others. The pattern was much the same for all denominations. First there would be meetings in the homes, then maybe in a barn, then a log structure would be built. After a few years, a larger structure would be erected.-- sometimes a frame building or sometimes brick would be used. Almost always a steeple would be added and a church bell to call its members to worship and to Sunday school. Many of those structures are still in use today.

Methodism Flourishes

The Methodist Episcopal Church flourished in and around this area if Ohio. By the middle and latter part of the 1800s, Methodist societies and classes were found in practically every community. In 1883 it was reported that the Methodist Episcopal Church had more members than any other denomination in the area. The societies of Webb's Chapel, Maxville, and Harvey Chapel would be placed on different charges over the years. Sometimes a charge would consist of only two and sometimes as many as seven churches were placed together to be referred to as a "charge," or "cluster," or "parish."

All three of the churches enjoyed quite a number of activities within their memberships. There were womens' societies. The men were organized in the Webb's Chapel Church for a while. The youth were organized and active in many ways. The MYF in Webb's Chapel, for example, became very active in 1944 and in the years to follow. They put up a tent at the county fair and sold food to earn money for their organization. With the money they bought folding chairs for the church. They decided to take on the project later of building a basement under the church and completed it. The youth decided to continue to have food for the county fair and built a booth, and the project prospered. The youth involved themselves in outreach programs as well.

They would visit the sick and nursing homes, taking gifts at Thanksgiving and Christmas time.

The food booth at the fair is still an active project for the Webb's Chapel United Methodist Chruch each year. The only difference is that the whole church gets involved now. Those who were members of the youth fellowship are now adult members and still work very hard to make it a success. The money that is earned helps to fund the many missionary and outreach programs the church supports.

1968 Union of EUB and Methodist Churches

In the early part of the twentieth century, before the reunification of the Methodist branches, and before the uniting of the United Brethren and Evangelical Association, the small congregations throughout the area would attend one another's revival meetings and special functions on a regular basis. The Methodist Episcopal Churches and the United Brethren Churches by far out numbered other denominations in this part of the country and these small churches were the center of social activity in every community. But it was very common for people throughout the area to gather for any special function, in any of the churches, and denominational lines would virtually disappear. However, whether because of the rise of New

Reformation Theology, the effects of the fundamentalism movement, or for some other reason, denominational lines seemed to be more finely drawn toward the middle of the twentieth century.

In 1968, the union of the Methodist Church and the Evangelical United Brethren Church took place to form what is now the United Methodist Church. In 1970, after this union of the two denominations, a meeting was called by the district superentendant, Joe Graham, to deal with restructuring the charges in the immediate area; because now there were several small churches, all in the same general area, some very close together. Some of the older members remember it to be a very emotional meeting. One church member attending the meeting made the suggestion that the smaller churches be closed. This only added to the fear, mistrust and suspision that already existed. After some discussion, a seven church charge was organized that included Webb's Chapel, Maxville, South Harvey, (former Methodist Chruches) and four churches that were former Evangelical United Brethren Churches. The new charge was pastored by a husband and wife team, Fred and Betty Wintermute. Later, Harold and Golda Kochersperger, another husband/wife team, were assigned to the seven-point charge. The husband, who was a licensed local paster, would alternate worship services in the churches, holding services one Sunday while his wife, who was a licensed lay speaker, would follow the next Sunday. This arrangement of the seven-point charge functioned for some time, but after a few years some of the congregations became dissatisfied with the arrangement.

A Time of Crisis

In 1977, at a meeting with the district superentendant, the former EUB churches stated that they would like to be placed on a charge by themselves. The emotions were somewhat high during that meeting, as some of those in attendance recall. One of the members from Webb's Chapel, a PPR committee member, suggested that it would be agreeable with their congregation to be placed on a charge with the two smaller, former Methodist Churches. The district superentendant, Wesley Clark, was very pleased with that offer and the seven church chagre was made into two separate charges. It has remained this way to the present time.

Other Times of Crisis

During the past few years, the population has decreased in the area. Many of the little communities have suffered the loss of local businesses, small industries, and service organizations. Schools have consolidated and moved to larger, more centrally located communities. And, of course, the churches have suffered with the loss of members. Along with that is the fact that the church is no longer the center of social activity in most places. It has been replaced by a multitude of other interests; everything from television to football, from golf to camping, from jogging to movie going, and the list could go on and on. This could be seen as a critical point in the life of each church in this area.

Hope for the Future

Even though the churches on this charge are struggling, they have not given up hope. These little churches are searching and looking to the future with the expectation of being able to continue offering the gospel to others and serving others in the immediate area and throughout the world.

Chapter 9: Church Classroom & Community Building

In the spirt of helping the community the elders of the Church decided to clean out the old school building and make it into a Church classroom. The building sat empty for several years after students had transferred to the new school on State Route 595.

In 1976 Charlotte Crothers was the Youth Fellowship leader. Youth Fellowship class painted (free hand) large full-color murals on each wall as a memorial to Alice Swaim. Alice passed away July 10,1976. She will always be remembered for the positive influence she had on the community of Haydenville.

Photographs were taken of all the murals Charlotte's Youth Fellowship class had painted on the old school band room walls. Each photograph was laminated and mounted in a beautiful 8 x 10 frame for permanent display. I took a photo of two of the murals to share here:

Figure 24 Youth Fellowship Class Mural

Figure 25 Youth Fellowship Class Mural

Every child comes with
the message that God
is not yet discouraged of man.

Part of the Haydenville School
Old Band Room
Wood Working Class Room

Paintings:

The Youth Fellowship Class of 1976 under the leadership of Charlotte Crothers had her class write memorial tributes on the walls of Alice Swain who passed away July 10, 1976. Alice Swain will always be remembered for the positive influence she had on the community.

Charlotte Crothers 1976

History:

Built as part of the school	1924-1952
Church Classroom	1952-
Mr. Matheny (Superintendent)	
The NATCO Co. gift to Church	1962

Uses:

Community Events
Church Functions

These paintings on the walls were 33 years old.
In 2009 pictures were taken to preserve their history.

Dedicated to passed and future generations of Haydenville
By Larry Horn and Patty Hampshire Horn

Figure 26 Old Band Room Dedication

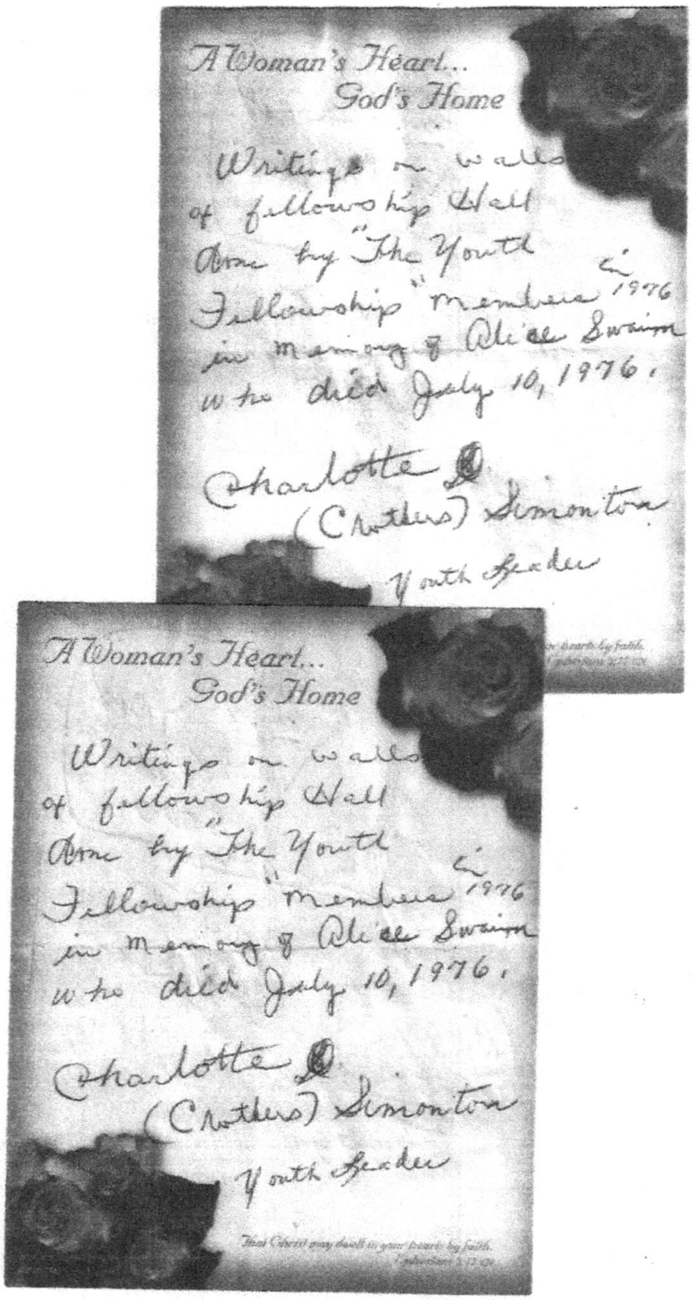

Figure 27 Charlotte Crothers Youth Leader

I witnessed Charlotte (Crothers) Simonton write this memo. She wanted to be sure that her 1976 Youth Group received credit for the painting on the interior wall of the old school band room building. She said, "The paintings were from the hearts and minds of the youth painting them." She wrote a separate memo with the name of each youth in the group. She thanked me for photographing and framing each painting.

Chapter 10: Education

Early settlers realized education was needed to break the stigma of poverty and isolation their children were enduring. Though the humble one room school houses only offered classes from the first grade to the eight. It provided a limited education and social life that would help prepare the children of Rural America meet the challenges of the outside world.

School attendance became mandatory state wide in 1877. In 1889 a new statute on school attendance was added to the mandatory statute, it set the requirements; that children between the ages of eight and fourteen must attend school, student between the age of fourteen and sixteen that had a full time job could be excused from school. The new statute also set out that a Truant officer would be used to ensure that all students went to school.

Fannie McFadden Horn's book about growing up in Haydenville, talks about her experience of walking from her house in Hopperville to the Coakley one room school on Hunger Hollow Road (now Purdum road). "I remember my first days; it was a mile or more over the hills from our home at the mines to the Coakley School. My teacher was Minnie Crow then I had J.B. Mathias. We had some bad snowy weather in those days, Nora (my sister) and I wore rubber boots with one buckle, over our high top shoes, but the snow was so deep it would get inside out rubber boots. Our mother made us wear long black stocking to help keep our feet warn, but when we got close to the school house we would take the off and hide them in an old tree stump. Then after school we would struggle to put those frozen stocking on before we went home. I remember the teacher let us get two buckets of drinking water, which we pass up one aisle and down the other until everyone had a drink, we all drank out of the same tin cup."

Mrs. Kapple life stories of the one room school East of Haydenville, the now forgotten town of The Diamond and Glenn Gary, Diamond Brick plant.

In1914-1915, a 24foot wide x 35 foot long, 14 foot high ceilings, building, with a slate roof, and one foot thick brick walls would become the Diamond's one room school. Ralph (Hammy or Ham-bone) was paid five dollars a month to provide all the custodian services.

The Pattonville one room school house stood at the junction of Route 33 and 595, on what was part of the Wright farm and close to the Wright canal locks. In later years it was converted to a saloon by the Sharb family. Haydenville was a dry town (no alcohol sales permitted) local residents referred to the saloon as the 5 mile inn. A thriving alcohol business, but always very clean an orderly.

Mrs. Alice (Evans) Saunders recalls, The Greenland one room school, remnants of the building stands on the Evans farm at the junction of Route 595 and Green Township Rd. 348-A and close to the Ebenezer Church. She recalls that all eight grades of students were seated in the one room school house, boys on one side and girls on the other. Each grade level of student would rotate from front to back of the room, while the teacher taught the next grade level. Some of those students she remembers, who attended Greenland school:

Becky R., George Evans, Harold Carpenter, Hubert Lambert, Donald Lambert, Clarence Lambert, Guy Champ, Donald Conner, Ester Lehman, Frances Walker, Ruth Chute, Ruth Barnhart, Ruth Lehman, Clare Belle Lambert, Betty (?), (?) Schultz, Grace Chute, Irene Lehman, Gerald Lehman, and Merlen Hemsworth.

At the Western edge of Nelsonville is a creek identified as Dorr Run, up in the haller (slang) where the creek starts was the Dorr one room school house. The Dorr family married into the Wolf family in the late 1800's.

The Haydenville's one room school classes were held in the Methodist Episcopal Chapel that sat in the bend of the road about one hundred feet below the present Haydenville Cemetery.

In Louise Ohlinger notes of Haydenville; recalls that during the week days the building was used as a school, and on weekend and after school it was used for Church purposes. The wooden frame building was completely destroyed by fire about 1898, but no one was injured. The teachers held classes in; company donated houses and the odd fellows' hall, while a new school was being built beside the new Church in Haydenville.

Paul Leroy Reider (Born Sept 4, 1916) letter to me says "I started to school at Haydenville in 1922. This is the year the school burned to the ground. Then I went to school in 2nd house in Hunky Row (Walhanding Rd.) Then in 1923 the new school building was built I went there until the school closed in Sept 1933. (Note the school did not close, but all high school students were transferred to Logan City School).

Figure 28 An 1898-99 photograph shows: the new two-story school building, on the lot adjoining the Church property. The school building sat against the hill, six wide steps were part of the building's foundations retaining wall.

Figure 29 Haydenville School built in 1923 on the site of the first school. A separate building was built beside the school for shop classes and band practice. Local residents and students referred to the building as the "band room". The school closed halfway through the school year in 1952. The building sat empty for several years before it was torn down. In 2008 the land was purchased for $40,000. The first ever Community Park was built on the property.

The new "1923" Haydenville School building was constructed on the site, were the other 2 story school building sat, before it was destroyed by fire the year before. The new build was a two-story “school” building the first floor accommodated grades one through eight and the second floor was for the high school students. High school students had separate stairway entrances in the rear of the building.

Small brick buildings were built at the rear left and right side, of the school building. I (Larry Horn) remember these small buildings were outside toilet, one for the girls and one for the boys, "inside plumbing was unheard of".

Jack Sharb (B. 1926) comments to Larry Horn "I was 6-1/2 years old which would have been 1932, when I started to school at Haydenville and went there for eight years. The school did not close in 1933, but that was the year all of the High School students had to transfer to Logan. The school then had a classroom for each of the eight grades and the adjacent building, which is still being used(2020), a vocational and band room building.

In 1952 Haydenville and the outlying schools combined to make the Green School District. Halfway through the 1952 school year, Haydenville and outlying students transferred to the new school building at the junction of U.S. Route 33and 595.

Shortly after the Haydenville school closed in the late 1950’s L. M. Hutchison and his sons John and Bill started an electric motor repair business in the lower half of the building. Several years later they went out of business, the building sat idle and decayed until it reach the point of no return. The County Highway Department demolished the "old school" and used the brick to repair the landslide on Greasy Ridge Road.

Haydenville Green Marching Band
The band practice their music in the build adjacent to the school building,
And everyone referred to this building as the "band room."
It was a spectacular sight for the resident to watch the band
Practice their marching formations while marching though town.
Haydenville Green became Green School District
With the advent of moving into the new school
At the junction of Rt. 33 & 595

Figure 30 Marching Band.

Haydenville Grade School Students around1910

Information and picture provide to Logan Daily
News by Mabel Rardain of Limebank Rd. Logan

Teacher: Georgia Hickman.

Student: ? Davis, Carl Pollock, Roland Schrater, Midge Matheny, Buss Matheny, Rosie Ademskie, Martha Ervin, Fred Norris, Paul Howard, Charles Horn. Flossie Myers, Gladis Mount, Charles Wolfe,? Moore, Stanley Hall, Rose Mount, Flossie Price, Helen Stimmel, Frank Rouggie, Stanley Mc Daniel, Willie Forbes, John Besermenskie, Roy Rieder, Harold Davis, Roy Lenegar, Paschel Tigner, Clarence Rouggie, Edith Helber, Dorothy Hall, Debee Hall, Francis Lehman, Harry Kerns, Chester Ademskie

1914-Haydenville Eight-Grade Graduating

Information and picture provided to Logan Daily
News by Mrs. Lottie Moorehead and Mrs.
Blanche Tucker

Teacher:

Fred Duffy taught grade7-8, Effie Wolf Poston taught grade ?, Agatha Fox Brown taught grade ?

Students: Lester Achauer, Lottie 'Tignor' Moorehead, Pauline 'Davis' Louden, William Irvin, Louise Ohlinger , Goldie 'Wharton' Dupler, Terrance Wharton, Blanche 'Pollack' Tucker, and Lillian 'Bond' Brown.

HAYDENVILLE
Special School District
...AND...
Green Township
BOXWELL COMMENCEMENT

WEDNESDAY, JULY 2, 1913.

PROGRAM

Music—Piano Duette

Sketch, "Tom's Arrival" . . } Mary Bond, Leta Davis assisted by Fannie Walker

Music—Quartet

Class History . . . . Mary Bond

Music—Piano and Mandolin

Reading . . . . Leta Davis

Music—Vocal Solo

Reading . . . . Sam'l Drake

Music—Quartet

Address . . . . Mr. T. D. Brown

Song—by audience
"The Star Spangled Banner"

Benediction . . . . Rev. G. T. Howard

Graduates
Mary Bond   Leta Davis   Sam'l Drake

Haydenville
Special School District
And
Green Township
Boxwell Commencement
Class of 1913

Figure 31 Boxwell Commencement Class of 1913

1917 "First" Graduating Class of Haydenville High School

Louise Ohlinger, Mildred Moore, William Irvin

1932 "Last" Graduating Class of Haydenville High School

Margie Matheny, Jane Nutter, Phyllis Swaim, Eileen Pollock, Garnet Gleason, Kenneth Woltz, Dale Primmer, Dale Arnold, Nellie Campbell, Leland Walters, Roy Nutter, Mary Kovach, Ruth Sinnott

HOCKING COUNTY

HIGH SCHOOL LYCEUM

1930-1931

HAYDENVILLE HIGH SCHOOL

Presents

"RUTH IN A RUSH"

A Three Act Comedy

Miss Mabel Cary, Director

CAST OF CHARACTERS

Mrs. Brownell, Ruth's aunt.......Phyllis Swaim
Juliet Raymond, Ruth's secretary.......Eileen Pollock
Ruth Moore, always in a rush.......Margie Matheny
Susie, a maid.......Garnet Gleason
Leonard Bruce, poor but aristrocrat.......Hallie Campbell
Wayne Ashley, rich but uncultured.......Roy Nutter
Dwight Lambert, an eloper.......Kenneth Woltz
Peggy Patton, another eloper.......Jane Nutter
Gilbert Lansing, a writer.......Leland Walters
Philip Grant, a millionaire.......Dale Primmer
Sadie Sodastorm, a ticket agent.......Mary Kovach
Jean Foster, Ruth's sister.......Ruth Sinnott

Time—The Present.

Place—An Eastern City.

Act I. Room in Ruth Moore's residence.
Act II. Waiting Room at Sunshine Junction.
Act III. The same as Act II a few hours later.

SYNOPSIS

Act I. Ruth in a Rush—to obtain a secretary's position. She shocks an aunt, dismisses two persistent suitors and advises a prospective bride and groom.

Act II. Ruth in a Rush—for a train. She and Juliet share the waiting room with two travelers with a confusion of identities, elopers and lunatics.

Act III. Ruth in a Rush—for the border line.

High School Lyceum
Haydenville High School
Class of 1930-1931
*Lyceum, Institution of Higher Education

Figure 32 Haydenville High School Class of 1930-31 Playbill

The Boxwell Law

Alexander Boxwell, a school teacher who also served five consecutive terms in the Ohio House of Representatives, pursued a way in which to incorporate a fair practice of allowing the county school students to be admitted to high school without added expenses. A council of teachers appeared before the Committee of Schools and presented arguments for a "ninth grade proficiency test" as proposed in the bill by Mr. Boxwell which stated, "the boys or girls in the county schools shall have the equal opportunity for a high school education, as the pupils in the town or city schools."

The Boxwell Law would give aspiring young adults, whose roots were in the rural areas and not in the city, the opportunity to proceed with his or her education. The Boxwell Law which was passed in.1892, stated in certain terms "that township boards of education are obligated to pay the successful student's tuition at the city high school of their choice, but the students must provide for their own transportation or living accommodations." Under the new law, an examination would be given, that tested the scholastics skills of all rural students, prior to acceptance into high school.

Two examinations were to be given a year. Passage of these tests made the student eligible for admission to any high school in the County in which the pupil lives, or a neighboring county.

The law also read that a county commencement for all graduates under this act would be held. Successful students were required to present an oration or read an essay at that commencement. The Boxwell Law had clearly done more for the county schools of Ohio than any other law previous passed.

The "one room schoolhouse" was struggling in its composition of too little education and no future for the students to advance. The Boxwell Law made it possible for young students to excel and make a place for them self in society.

The Boxwell Test consists of the following subjects: Arithmetic, English Grammar and Composition, Orthography, Geography, United States History including the Civil War and Physiology.

ARITHMETIC

Find the amount of the following bill, retaining all fractions.

1-300 pounds sugar at 4-34 cents a pound

2- 1 dozen and ten eggs at 3 2 cents a dozen

3- 1 dozen knives and forks at $2.50 a dozen

4- 12-1/2 yards of toweling 12-Y: 1 cents a yard

5- Take the two numbers 445.3 and .073, find (a) their sum (b) their difference (c) their product, (d) the quotient of the first divided by the second (2 1/2 credits for each part).

6- A field is half a mile long and a quarter of a mile wide. If 2-1/2. acres are plowed each day. How many days will be required to plow it?

7- Having the radius of a circle, how can you find the area of the circle? Having the dimensions of a joist, how do you find the number of board feet it contains?

8- A house and lot are worth $3,500. The house is worth six times as much as the lot. Find the value of each.

9- Find the simple interest on $2347.50 for 3 yr. 6 mo. 15days at 4 1/2 % per annum.

10-There are 40 pupils in a class, and each needs a ruler and a drawing compasses. The price of the rulers is $035 per doz. Net, and of the compasses $ 1.65 per doz. less 10 per cent and 5 per cent. What will the supplies cost the school?

11- The floor of a room is a square and contains 144 sq. ft. The room contains 1268 cu. ft. Find the three dimensions of the room.

12- (a) A boy was present 304 half days during the school years which contains 320 half days. What was his percent of attendance? (b) In the same school a girl attended 313 half days. What was her percent of attendance?

13- The center pole of a circus tent is 3 5 ft. high and a guy rope is stretched from the top of the pole to a stake 56 ft. from the bottom. How long is the rope supposing the ground level and rope straight allowing 4 inches for tying?

GRAMMAR

1- Define language, word, grammar, and sentence, appositive.

2- Give examples of how sentences are classified (a) in regard to meaning (b) in regard to form.

3- Use a word in a sentence as an adjective. Expand the phrase into an equivalent clause.

4- Use in sentences and name each of the following: (a) a collective noun (b) a relative pronoun (c) a descriptive adjective (d) an adverb of degree (e) a present participle.

5- Give the synopsis, first person singular of the verb see in all the tenses of the indicative mode, active voice.

6- Write the possessive singular and plural of each of these words: child, deer, wolf, fly, turkey. (b) Compare the following: fine, worthy, thin, splendid, much.

7- Name the part of speech of each word in the following: We believe that the truth has never changed from the beginning of creation.

8- Write the proper reference to capitals and punctuation: the teacher quietly turned to the class and remarked, "You see children I have placed on the board a stanza for you to learn……

in learning proudly said the birch
I once played quite a part.
whenever little boys were dull why.
I would make them smart."

ORTHOGRAPHY

1- For what do you use a dictionary? Name a good one.

2- Copy the following sentences, using the correct word selected from the words in parentheses: (a) A (vale, veil) of mist enveloped the mountain.(b) Members of the cat-tribe (clime, climb) by means of their (claws, clause). (c) His (style, stile) in (right, rite, write, writing) was excellent.

3- Indicate by the use of the proper diacritical marks the sound of the vowels in the following words: arc, fur, more, food, lost.

GEOGRAPHY

1- Define the following terms: orbit, meridian, continent, isthmus, delta.

2- What conditions determine (a) the climate of a country (b) the occupations of men.3.

Mention three kinds of government and tell which kind is found in each of the following: United States, Japan, France, Russia, England.

3- Write a paragraph on the Panama Canal.

4- Name and locate ten of the world's leading seaports.

5.- Mention five countries, two rivers and three cities of South America.

6- Take an imaginary trip across the United States. Name in their order the states through which you would pass and the important cities you would see.

7- Name five products the people of the United States send to other countries and name the country to which is sent.

8- Of what interest to the American government are the following: Cuba, Puerto Rico, Hawaii, Panama?

9- Draw a map of Ohio. Locate thereon your county seat, five important cities and three important rivers.

UNITED STATES HISTORY INCLUDING CIVIL GOVERNMENT

1- Who were the Cabots ? From what country did they sail'? Tell what they discovered.

2- Tell the story of Ponce de Leon, of De Soto.

3- What is each of the following: retina, esophagus, cerebrum, pericardium, diaphragm?

4.Apply these adjectives to the correct nouns: flexor, vitreous, hepatic, pulmonary, mitral.

5-Name the digestive fluids and state the office of each.

6- What two companies were formed in England in the early part of the seventeenth century for the purpose of colonizing America? Tell briefly what was done by each.

7- Tell something about each of the following: King Philip, Father Marquette, General Oglethorpe.

8- Why did the colonists claim that Parliament had no right to tax them? What was the Stamp Act?

9- Name five important men connected with the American Revolution, and tell for what each is noted

10- When were the railroads first built in America? Tell the story of the invention of the telegraph or of laying of telegraph cable under the ocean.

11- Why did the people of South wish to leave the Union in 1861? How many states seceded? What name did the seceding states take?

13- Mention three great surrenders that were made to General Grant during the Civil War and give an important result of each surrender.

14- What does the Constitution say in regard to the election of members of the House of Representatives?

PHYSIOLOGY

1- Name five organs of the body and state a function of each.

2- State the difference between arteries and veins.

3- Describe the ribs as to shape, arrangement, number, attachment.

4- Describe the structure of the teeth. In the care of the teeth what should be observed? What should be avoided?

5- What are the effects of impure air upon the system?

6- Illustrate by diagram the circulation of blood, showing the two systems of circulation.

7- What is the use of respiration? Explain.

Chapter 11: Haydenville Grade School Bell

After the school building was abandon, the bell was referred to as

The Old School Bell

The Haydenville Grade School Bell sat on a two foot high 'unenclosed' pedestal and was mounted permanently to the roof of the last school in Haydenville. A rope was connected to the bell and came through the ceiling of the foyer at the top of the stairway on the second floor. One of the teachers or an appointed student who had won the honor pulled the rope to ring the bell at the designated times. A 90 degree angle, ladder went from the foyer through a trap door in the ceiling, thus giving access to the roof. This opening and ladder were used daily to connect the American Flag to the flag pole permanently mounted on the school building roof.

The Bell was rung manually (electrical technology was not available yet) at 8:30 (first bell) and 9:00 (second bell) if you came to school after the second ringing of the bell, you had to go directly to the principal's office and be disciplined. The bell was also rung at lunch time and start of school after lunch. The school playground was across the "Road" (then U S Route 33) and the bell was rung as the notice, recess was over, report back to class. One student was given the special honor by the teachers, to be the safety patrolman, who would stop all vehicle traffic prior to any student attempting to go across the "Road". The safety patrolman was the "Law" of the school and heaven help you if you questioned his authority.

Haydenville and other rural schools in the immediate area combined to form the Green School District. A modern one floor plan school building was constructed at the junction of US 33 and 595. Half ways through the 1952 school year, all the students from these rural schools were transferred to the recently constructed Green Elementary School Building (Green School), and their formal schools were abandon. The new school was a modern marvel, a breath taking

"AWE" to most of the students, a classroom for each of the eight grades, a cafeteria to server lunch, a gymnasium, and modern indoor plumbing.

The Haydenville school building sat empty for several years until: L. M. Hutchison and sons John and Bill started a commercial electric motor repair business on the first floor. They ran the business for several years but they could not compete with modern technology and mass production. The demand for their expertise slowly diminished and they we force to go out of business. During this time period the factories were still working and the only change in the community was the abandoning of the old grade school building.

Mr. Matheny the General Manager of the factories (NATCO) and in this capacity had complete control and authority of all the building in this Company Owned Town of Haydenville. He donated the school desk and scrap iron to the Haydenville Boy Scout Troop number (?). The money raised from the sale of the scrap iron went toward the purchase of uniforms for the scout troop.

Boy Scout leaders at that time were Chuck Moore, Neil Geirheart, Roy Crothers and Jim Moore.

The Scout Leaders realizing the historical value of the school bell and did not permit the "Bell" to be sold as a piece of scrap iron.

Jim Moore's house is adjacent to Green School and he remembers that between1964and 1966 he stood on his front porch and filmed a Parade lead by the Haydenville Boy Scout Troup and the Haydenville Band. They had marched from the old Haydenville School Building, to celebrate the mounting for display the Old Haydenville School Bell at the then new Green Elementary School (Logan Daily News also covered this parade, (an article is in their archives).

Lester Crothers, the custodian at the new Green Elementary School, made arrangements to have the "Bell" and a time capsule displayed, on a brick monument at the edge of the school's circle driveway.

The following Haydenville residents, and brick layers by trade, built the brick monument and installed the time capsule; Chuck Moore, Neil Geirheart, Jud Skiver, Creighton Lehman, and Roy Crothers. The time capsule was opened and recorded on film Octerber14, 2008 by Green Elementary School teacher, Rob Lamage.

A precedence was set in the early1950's by the Crothers family to preserve the Old Grade School Bell and keep it directly associated with Haydenville, the Crothers Family are/were, Roy Crothers, Lester Crothers, Martin (Buddy) Crothers, (all deceased) and Bret Crothers of Haydenville, Ohio

About 2008 a new Green Elementary School building was built, beside the Logan Middle School on Maysville Road Logan. The Green Elementary School at Route 595 and 33 was sold and is being used as a school for Handicap and

Disable Children (MRDD). The new owners ask that arrangements be made to remove the brick bell monument.

The old Haydenville School Bell is now prominently on display on the lawn of the museum in Logan, Ohio. Although the physical appearance of the "bell" is not in Haydenville, its memory is now etched in time.

Chapter 12: Haydenville Postmasters

Haydenville's Postmasters or Officers-In-Charge

Name	*Title*	*Date Appointed*
Oliver C. Pierce	Postmaster	01-10-1870
John W. Jones	Postmaster	04-18-1883
Herman W. Giesecke	Postmaster	05-16-1893
Kirby Wolfe	Postmaster	06-15-1897
Fannie McFadden[1]	Postmaster	09-29-1903
Robert J. Thompson	Officer-In-Charge	07-21-1904
Frank S. Shepard	Postmaster	02-05-1907
Fred P. Linscott	Postmaster	11-14-1910
Ethel W. Snoke	Postmaster	06-21-1911
Dais D. Waugh	Actin Postmaster	01-01-1921
Dais D. Waugh	Postmaster	03-25-1921
Thomas D. Brown	Actin Postmaster	01-01-1922
Thomas D. Brown	Postmaster	04-21-1922
Ethel W. Snoke	Actin Postmaster	09-01-1931
Olive Ruble	Postmaster	12-16-1931
Anna L. Moore	Actin Postmaster	11-30-1961
Anna L. Moore	Postmaster	10-16-1963
Karen Bullington	Officer-In-Charge	10-09-1980
Jud G. Hampshire	Postmaster	05-02-1981
Robert J. Cassady	Officer-In-Charge	02-28-1985

[1] Fannie McFadden Horn

John C. Bankes	Officer-In-Charge	05-02-1986
Robert J. Cassady	Officer-In-Charge	08-28-1986
Alicia Wells	Officer-In-Charge	11-12-1986
Carol J. Williams	Officer-In-Char	03-18-1987
Peggy J. Howard	Officer-In-Charge	04-29-1987
Peggy J. Howard	Postmaster	06-03-1989
Elizabeth Riley	Officer-In-Charge	11-05-1999
Jeffery M. Bullock	Officer-In-Charge	06-23-2000
Alicia Ann Walls	Postmaster	01-27-2001
Lisa Carter	Officer-In-Charge	07-31-2009
Deborah M. McGhee	Officer-In-Charge	07-30-1912
Tonya Smith	Postmaster Relief	01-12-2013
Kathy Lauderback	Postmaster Relief	04-29-2013

Fannie McFadden Horn held the position of postal clerk to postmaster Kirby Wolf. The original post office was in the company store; in addition to being postal clerk, Fannie was also responsible to answer all telephone calls, and take the outgoing mail over to the railroad depot.

George Finney was the railroad telegraph operator and was responsible for the mail being loaded onto the train mail. There were five trains a day passing through Haydenville; the 7:15 a.m., the 10 a.m., and the noon trains went North. The 5:28 p.m. went South, and the 6 p.m. went North.

In 1903, the post office was moved from the company store to its present location, which at the time of the move, had been the doctor's office. The phone system was also moved into the same building and the postal clerk continued duties as telephone receptionist.

Our little post office life span of over 100 years, in the same location, may be coming to an end soon, another milestone for Haydenville, and another end of an era. A postal clerk is only on duty two hours a day, local residents have access to their free locked boxes in the lobby 24/7.

Chapter 13: Telephone

Peter Hayden purchased a telephone system at the 1876 Centennial in Philadelphia and installed it in his Company office in Haydenville. This was the first telephone system in the Hocking Valley, and the first long distance call was to Hayden office stating that one of his employee wife had a baby girl and they had nick name her "Telly."

Joan (Lehman) Rose tells this story of her Grandmother Myrta (Kasler) Lehman using the telephone during an unexpected thunder storm:

My Grandfather Jacob (Bert) Lehman had a coal mine just off Cohagan Road, in Green Township. Grandfather and his sons, plus several other men he hired worked the coal mine. My Grandfather and his sons also hauled coal to individual houses and to the NATCO factory at Haydenville Their first means of hauling coal to customers was with a horse drawn wagon, a few years later they purchased a dump truck to replace the horse and wagon.

Grandfather needed a telephone to operate his business, but the telephone company would not run a telephone service line the 9/10 of a mile from Route 595 (which was a county road at that time) to his house. So grandfather and his boys strung the telephone wire on the fence post along Cohagan Road to his house.

Grandfather purchased a battery operated, telephone and mounted it on the wall, he kept the telephone batteries charged from electricity generated from a windmill. You had to ring the operator and tell her who you wanted to call and she then made the proper connection.

One day my pregnant Grandmother Myrta (Kasler) was on the telephone talking to one of my grandfather's coal customers. A storm came up unexpectedly and lighting struck the telephone my grandmother was using, she went around in a circle three times before falling to the floor. The ambulance at the Cherrington Hospital in Logan was called and she was taken to the hospital in a horse drawn ambulance wagon. Her baby was still-born. She named him Henry Gerald Lehman and he was laid to rest at the Ebenezer Methodist Church Cemetery on Route 595. Grandmother was in the hospital for a month. Her Doctors, Murrit Halstead Cherrington and his brother, were in touch with doctors in London, England for advice.

To make a phone call in 1915 required for you to crank the handle on the side of the large telephone box mounted on the wall, speak into a cone shaped micro-phone while holding the receiver to your ear. After you turned the handle a couple of times, a live operator would answer, you would tell the operator to ring the party you wanted and she would connect you to that person's phone. Each house had its own phone sequence, two longs, one short or other various combinations.

I remember the episode in the early 1950's when my dad went to the phone company in Logan and told them he wanted a phone installed in our house. The receptionist started to fill out the paperwork and about halfway through the application she ask dad if he was in debt to anyone, that was a big mistake on her part. He gave her a lecture on the fact that when he wanted something he saved his money and paid for it. She explained why she had to ask about his credit. A few days later the phone company ran a line from their main line to our house.

There were five or six other houses connected to each line. It was referred to by the phone company as a *party line*. Anyone on your line could hear your conversation (eavesdrop) and when you wanted to make a call you had to pick up the receiver to be sure the line was not in use before you dialed.

The phone was the standard desk type rotary dial phone, you put your finger in the hole that had the number showing you wanted and turned the dial until it stopped. Then you took your finger out of the hole and let the dial face return to start. You had to dial the complete seven-digit phone number to make a connection. Any number out of your area code was a long distance call and the operator had to dial it for you.

Our first phone number was EV5.... I don't remember the other four numbers, an alphabet letter preceded all phone numbers. The telephone service area out of the Haydenville was very limited, it went to Logan and only a few of the small surrounding towns. The phoneline from Nelsonville came up to Johnnie Norris' Shell gasoline station (demolished years ago) across the road from the entrance to Company Road. It was common practice to dial "0" for the operator and tell her you wanted to make a long distance telephone call, all long distance calls were an additional charge to your monthly service bill.

1915

HAYDENVILLE, OHIO DIRECTORY

A

Achauer, Charles C., clerk
Achauer, Raymond F., emp. N. F. P. Co.
Achauer, William L. (Jennie), miner
Adams Express Co., Gomer Lewis, Agt.
Adamski, Tony (Helen), emp. N. F. P. Co.
Alexander, Porter (Debbie), barber
Allen, Willis (Mary), foreman N. F. P. Co.
Alton, John, emp. N. F. P. Co.
Ander, Russel S. (Clara), grocer
Arnold, William D. (Ardis)

B

Best, Harold S., ceramist
Black, Frank B. (Mary), emp. N. F. C. Co.
Bolden, George W. (Goldie), emp. N. F. C. Co
Bond, Pearl (Nellie), emp. N. F. C. Co.
Bond, Simon O. (Ida), miner
Brady, Charles, janitor
Brown, Donald, stu.
Brown, George F., farm mgr. N. F. P. Co.
Brown, Jean, music teacher
Brown, Mary, stu.
Brown, Thomas D. (Anna), mgr. N. F. P. Co.
Buren, Frank, emp. Ohio F. P. Co.
Burns, Andrew (Bridget), ceramist N. F. P. Co.
Burns, Robert (Goldie), emp. N. F. P. Co.
Burns, William (Delphia), emp. N. F. P. Co.

C

Caian, Geo., emp. N. F. P. Co.
Caian, Mike, emp. N. F. P. Co.
Cello, John, emp. N. F. P. Co.
Carpenter, George E., emp. N. F. P. Co.
Carpenter, John W. (Rosa), emp. N. F. P. Co.
Chilcote, Alva, emp. N. F. P. Co.
Chilcote, David R. (Lena), emp. N. F. P. Co.
Chilcote Samuel E. (Bertha), emp. N. F. P. Co.
Cigaro, John, emp. N. F. P. Co.
Cochran Edward B. (Naoma), emp. N. F. P. Co.
Coll, William, emp. N. F. P. Co.
Coko, John, emp. N. F. P. Co.
Coko, Mike (Annie), emp. N. F. P. Co.

Cooley, Edward C. (Mary), mgr. N. F. P. Co. store
Cooley, Harriet
Cooley, J. Mac, stu.
Costierre, Mike, emp. N. F. P. Co.
Covacis, Mike, emp. N. F. P. Co.
Crane, Albert (Cora), emp. N. F. P. Co.
Crane, J. Wilson (Amy), emp. N. F. P. Co.
Crassa, Joe, emp. N. F. P. Co.

D

Davis, Eli (Dora), supt. N. F. P. Co.
Davis, Leta, stu.
David, Mildred, stu.
Davidson, Arthur S. (Ada), pastor Meth. Episc. Church
Dawroff, Tudor, Mary), emp N. F. P. Co.
Deidreichs, Ernest, emp. N. F. P. Co.
Dobias, Frank, emp. N. F. P. Co.
Dosticic, Mike, emp. N. F. P. Co.
Dosticic, Tom (Lulu), emp. N. F. P. Co.
Dougherty, James W., farmer
Duffey, Fred H., school teacher

E

Eaton, Charles A. (Irene), emp. N. F. P. Co.
Eaton, Edward J., emp. N. F. P. Co.
Eaton, Fred W., emp. N. F. P. Co.
England, William R. (Idella), machinist
Ervin, Edward (Ella), emp. N. F. P. Co.
Ervin, Elizabeth
Ervin, Grant, stu.
Ervin, Jane (wid. Edward)
Ervin, Leroy, emp N. F. P. Co.

F

Fercas, Pete, emp. N. F. P. Co.
Francis, Clyda M., stu.
Francis, Jesse (Isabelle), grocer
Francis, Mary O., school teacher

G

Ginther, Daniel A., emp. N. F. P. Co.
Ginther, Jacob (Loretta), emp. N. F. P. Co.
Goodfellow, James (Elizabeth), miner

H

Haydenville Public Schools, Fred H. Duffy, supt.
Heading, Albert J.
Heislein, L. McKinley, school teacher

Chapter 14: Nicknames

Being called by a nickname was the common and the excepted means of communication. The following is a list of nicknames of Haydenville residents and laborers. Some people did not have quirky nicknames, but, they are listed just the same with their position and workplace. The words are typed just the way they were pronounced back in the day (and present day), some with Appalachian dialect.

Special thanks to Martin (Buddy) Crothers, Bill and Norma Lehman, Delbert (Deb) and Casey Smith. Without their help, this bit of unique Haydenville history would be lost forever. They contributed the nicknames below from memory for the sole purpose of preserving a part of Haydenville history. Accuracy is not guaranteed.

The nicknames and positions are typed the way they were pronounced, mostly in slang. #1 and #2 refer to the plants/factories. The *set gang* manually stacked conduit in the storage yard. The *draw gang* manually removed glazed conduit from the kiln (kils) and stacked it in the storage yards. *Kil farman* (kiln fire man) were the manual laborers who shoveled the coal into the fire boxes of the kiln. A *trussel* (trestle) is a bridge over the highway (State Route 33), that carried the narrow gauge railroad cars from the mines to the factory. A *reamer* manually beveled the interior ends of the conduit tile before they dried.

Name	*Nickname*	*Position or Workplace*
Clarence (C.S.) Matheny	Hoot	General Manager of Natco and Haydenville Plant,
Alguren Beougher	Red	Foreman Kill-far (Kiln Fire) man
Allen McMillin	Mac	Foreman #1 yard
Carl Bond	Carl	Foreman #2 yard
Charles Horn	Callie	Foreman #2 plant
Charles Lehman	Hump	Main Office
Clarence McMillen	Pete	Superintendent #2 plant
Irvin Keels	Fuzzy	Foreman #1 plant
James Karshner	Jim	Foreman
Lewis Ingram	Lew	Company Salesman

Raymond Mills	Ray	Foreman
Sanford Boals	Boalie	Mine Superintendent
Walter Swaim	Walt	Superintendent #1 plant
Lincoln Swaim	Abie	Foreman #2
? Keels	Fuzzy	Foreman
?	Hotnips	#1 Shop (from Jamaica)
Arthur Ethelbert Horn	Art	Yard crew clean up
Albert Bailey	Honey Dipper	Clean outside toilet by dipping waste out by bucket and putting into barrels
Albert Sparks	Red	#1 yard gat builder (wood partition to secure material when loaded in railroad cars), box car loader
Allen Miller	Allen	Set Gang
? Angle	Shorty	
Jim Barron	Shovel	
Bill Harper	Harp-po	
Bobbie Ruble	Bobbie	Postmaster Haydenville Post Office
? Brown	Cap	Skid building (wood pallet maker)
Ralph Campbell	Hump	
Carl Warren		
Charles Campbell	Sonny	#2
Charles Gastin	Chuch	#2 Shop
Charles Mettler	Pee Wee	
Charles Vollmer	Chuck	Set Gang
Charles Waugh	Charlie	#1 Shop
Chester Spellman Sr.	Wimpy	#1 yard box car loader
Clarence Angle	Short-tee	
Clarence Nihiser	Nank	#2
Clarence Wingman	Red	Shop
Cleveland Thompson	Cleve	Night watchman
Coby Pounds	Kobe	
Conrad Clouston	Con	#1 yard draw gang
Creighton Lehman	Fade-e	Brick layer
Dale Wittekind	Dale	Mechanic
Delbert Smith	Deb	#2 tow motor operator (trussel)
Delmar Martin	Shine	Brick layer
Donald Keels	Don	#1 Shop
Donald Hopstetter	Rink	
Donald Turner	Stub	#1 yard set gang

Earl Wittekind	Ham	Mechanic
Eddie Pedigo	Pedigo	Boiler room operator
Edger Bert	Red	Carpenter for company houses
Elmer Van Curren	Elmer	
Ernie McCune	Wooly-bogger	#2 draw gang
Ethelbert Horn	Art	Yard maintenance
Everett Stover	Everett	
Floyd Matheny	Buss	
Floyd Webb	High Pockets	#1 yard Kill-far (Kiln Fire) man
Francis Lehman	Jake	#1 Shop
Frank Stewark	Chick	#1 Shop
Frank Brown	Frank	Kill-far man
Frank Crothers	Chippie	Ice cream par-lar (parlor)
Frank Van Buren	Weasel	Carpenter, company houses, pipe fitter
Frank Keels	Frank	#1 Shop
Fred Mormon		Farmer and worked in clay mine
Fred Mount		
Fred Norris	Fred	
Fred Vollmer	Monkey	#1 yard shop
Fred Waugh	Fred	
George Bond	George	
George Walker Jr.	Junior	
Gerald Jeffery	Tip	Shop, fitting maker for clay tile
Gerald Karins	Karnsey	
Gerald Knapp	Nappy	#2 truck driver
Gerald Vollmer	Moussie	Clay mine
Glenn Danielson	Slim	#1 shop
Glenn Farley	Glenn	Clay mine
Gus Wachenschwanz	Gus	
Harold Gastin		
Harold Vollmer	Peanut	#2 yard
Harry Pa-lick (Pollack)	Bake	Plant carpenter
Harry Crane	Hap	#1 Kill-far (Kiln Fire) man
Harry Swaim	Harry	
Henry Oliver	Hickory	#1 yard
Henry Skiver	Skillet	Dry pan
Hickory Oliver	Hickory	#1 yard box car loader
Homer Carter	Democrat	Company store meat cutter
Hubert Lehman		Loader

Jack Barney	Jack	
Jacob Lehman, Pastor	Jake	Shop
James Barron	Fat	
James Hood	Jimmy	Set gang
James Moore	Jim	Machine shop
John Bailey	Johnny	
John Clouston	Johnnie	Company store meat cutter
John Hooper	John	Boiler room
John Oliver	John	#1 Shop
Jr. Miller	Flowerbed	Tow motor operate, donkey on trestle
Kenneth Chaffin Sr.	Doke	
Kermit Swaim	Tumble	Clay mine
Larry Horn	Larry	Company store clerk
Lawrence Jones	Jonesy	
Lee McQuaid	Lee	
Leonard Lehman	Len	
Leroy Mace	Shrimp	#2 yard
Lester George Turner	Boots	
Lester Crothers	Les	
Lewis Feeback	Feeback	
Libby Phillips	Libby	Company store clerk
Louie Coleman	Hunkie Louie	Kill door builder
Lucille Smith		1950-53 Ice cream parlor manager
Luther Skivers	Jud	#1 yard drove tractor for set gang
Martin Crothers	Buddy	Pulled clay mine cars on trestle over Rt33
Mary Fisher	Mary	Company store clerk
Morgan Bailey	Guy	#1 shop reamer
Morse Clouston	Morman	Cleaned rings in pipes
Morse Vollmer	Murl	Kil far box cleaner
Nelson Skiver	Nelson	
Newton Spencer	Newt	Gas Station Corner of Purdum Road, Hungry Hollow Road/Haydenville Road
Okey Smith	Okey	Yard set gang
Opera Sharb	Gip	#2 yard brick layer shop
Page Martin	Page	#1 set gang
Paul Barroues	Paul	
Paul W. Fielder	Hope	#1 yard door builder

Pearl McGathey	Perk	#1 set gang
Pete Jurgenmire	Pete	Made brick samples
Phillip Devol	Nance	#1 yard
Phillip Moore		
Porter Moore	Port	Yard maintenance
Ralph Martin	Grassy	#2 brick inspector
Raymond Vollmer		
Raymond F. Achauer		
Raymond (Ray) Turner	Cracker	#1 shop
Raymond Brown	Ray	Kill-far (Kiln Fire) man
Raymond Mills		
Raymond Stover	Ray	#2 shop
Reeves Jack	Whiskers	Mix room
Richard Crane	Dick	
Robert Auflick	Bob	
Robert Gastin	Bob	
Robert Hopstetter	Bob	
Robert (Bob) Lehman	Dad	Reamer
Robert Morgan	Bob	
Robert Swaim	Bobbie	
Robert Weaver	Bob	
Roger Campbell	Happy	Gae builder for box cars
Roger Moore	Popeye	#1 shop reamer
Roy Crothers	Byde	Bricklayer
Roy Glenn Jr.	Roy	Electrician
Roy Glenn St	Roy	Electrical Foreman
Roy Reider	Dusty	Pulled clay mine cars from mine to factory
Same Chilcote		
Sam Hiles	Popcorn	Hauled town trash and maintenance
Bill Seels		#2 yard loading gang
Sheldon Hartgrove	Shell	Green township trustee
Sherman Dicken	Sherm	Yard and tractor driver
Sidney Grubb	Sid	Produce and commercial flower farmer – Purdum Road/Hunger Hollow Road
Stanley Norris	Stan	Company mechanic
Vern Robinette	Slim	Company store meat cutter
Virgil Slay	Virg	
Virgil Smith	Virg	#1 Set gang

Waldo Lehman	Hump	
Walter Gastin Jr		
Walter Gastin Sr		
Ward Phillips	Ward	Company store manager
Wilbur Lightfoot		
Willard Seels	Shorty	Meat cutter ran ice cream parlor/town deli. Seels Sohio, St. Rt. 595 and 33
William Reeves		
William Evans	Willie	Yard maintenance
William Lehman	Bill	Geiger, #1 Shop and kiln fire man
Wilmer Crothers	Jerry	#1 yard, set gang

Chapter 15: Struggles & Hard Times

Roy Rieder lived in the end house in block row. Block row is a short distance from Red Row. All 5 house in block row were 2 story single family hollow salt glazed tile made in Haydenville by National Fire Proofing Company. All houses are occupied as of 9/2020. Roy told me "He started working at Haydenville in 1940 for 40 per hour."

Harry "Jim" Brown was born in 1879. His wife was Rachel J. Brown. They were our neighbors when I was just a little boy. Mr. Brown told me of the experiences of the kill farman (kiln fire man). They worked a 12-hour shift for $2.52. Bonus pay for weekend and holidays was unheard of, they were just another day. Once the fire was started in the Kill (kiln) fire box it was a continuous 24-hour work cycle, regardless of the weather. He recalled ice skating on the old canal almost every winter and getting a shave and hair cut for 25 cents at the local barber shop. The barber shop sat across the road from the school and straddled the canal. No man had long hair as that would be a Cardinal sin. He told me his big fish story, and I remember seeing the monster fish (carp) Jim and his son Cap had caught it on a trot-line in the Hocking River. It had to weigh over 25 pounds and was over 5 feet long. I saw Jim bringing this fish home, he had his hand on his shoulder holding the fish by its gill and its tail was dragging the ground.

The fish was a blessing for Jim's family and friends. A welcome change to have fresh fish to eat and the women didn't have to worry about what they were going to fix for their families to eat.

Jim's son Raymond worked at Haydenville factory for 37 cents an hour, sawing fire brick into loaf size brick for stove liners. In later years several men were dying from a lung disease locals referred to it as the Haydenville cough. It was determined that the men sawing the fire brick were breathing the fine dust and over the years their lung became infected from the dust. The medical term for this disease is "silicious".

When Raymond passed away he willed his house to the Haydenville Methodist Church who then promptly sold it.

Pete C. recalled catching the school bus a few houses up the holler (hollow) from his house. There was a neighbor family that had to send their kids to school in the winter barefoot. He remembered watching the kids run from their house barefooted in the snow to get on the school bus.

It was necessary for all students to carry their lunch to school. Those barefoot children would bring "grease sandwiches" (grease from the frying pan spread between two slices of bread). Pete would go up to their house to play and in the wintertime the kids had to brush the snow off the floor to play. The floorboards didn't fit close together and the snow would blow up through the cracks. Some of the siding was missing, it had been pulled off to make firewood to heat the house. Pete's Mother cooked the family meals on a kerosene stove, the height of the flame was controlled by turning up the wick (similar to the Coleman lantern of today).

The Keels family were life-long residents of Haydenville. Don and his family lived on Mine Hollow (haller) Road in the section of town called Red Row.

The two-story houses in Red Row were rough cut, wood planks directly from the local saw mills, as was the custom in the late 1800's. Several years after they were built the Company painted the houses red.

In the late 1800's Red Row was considered a part of Hopperville and the road in front of the houses went direct to the mines, which was referred to as Mine Hollow (haller) Road.

Don was a good friend of mine and he asked me to put these copies of his pay stubs in my book "so people could see just how hard it was to raise a family on factory wages."

*Note item # 7 on his pay stub $7.00 per month, but "the town had no utilities" coal oil lamps were the only light, wood and coal-fired cook stoves and potbelly stoves for heat, drinking water was out of a bucket of water carried in from the outside well and the bathroom was a path to the outside toilet behind the house.

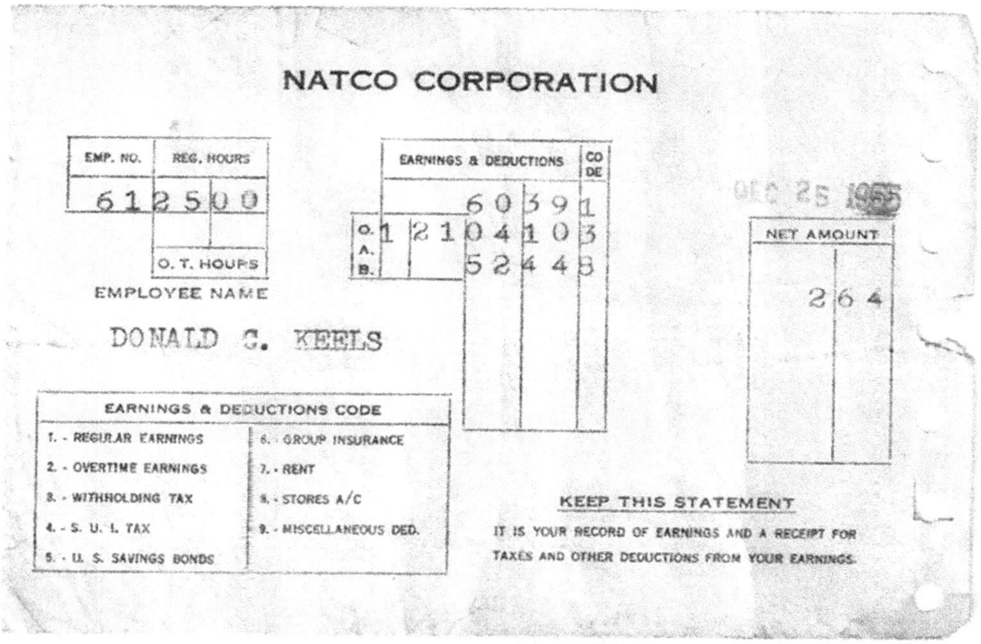

NATCO CORPORATION

EMP. NO.	REG. HOURS
61	2500
	O. T. HOURS

EMPLOYEE NAME

DONALD C. KEELS

EARNINGS & DEDUCTIONS	CODE
60391	1
O. A. B. 1 21041 0	3
5244	8

DEC 25 1955

NET AMOUNT

264

EARNINGS & DEDUCTIONS CODE

1. - REGULAR EARNINGS	6. - GROUP INSURANCE
2. - OVERTIME EARNINGS	7. - RENT
3. - WITHHOLDING TAX	8. - STORES A/C
4. - S. U. I. TAX	9. - MISCELLANEOUS DED.
5. - U. S. SAVINGS BONDS	

KEEP THIS STATEMENT

IT IS YOUR RECORD OF EARNINGS AND A RECEIPT FOR TAXES AND OTHER DEDUCTIONS FROM YOUR EARNINGS.

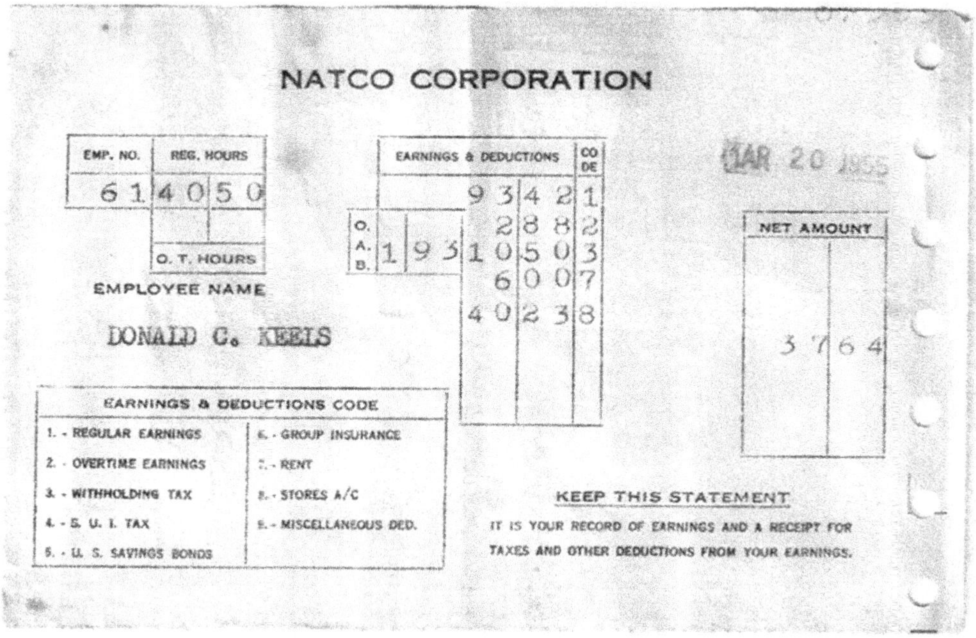

NATCO CORPORATION

EMP. NO.	REG. HOURS
61	4050
	O. T. HOURS

EMPLOYEE NAME

DONALD C. KEELS

EARNINGS & DEDUCTIONS	CODE
9342	1
288	2
O. A. B. 1931 050	3
600	7
4023	8

MAR 20 1955

NET AMOUNT

3764

EARNINGS & DEDUCTIONS CODE

1. - REGULAR EARNINGS	6. - GROUP INSURANCE
2. - OVERTIME EARNINGS	7. - RENT
3. - WITHHOLDING TAX	8. - STORES A/C
4. - S. U. I. TAX	9. - MISCELLANEOUS DED.
5. - U. S. SAVINGS BONDS	

KEEP THIS STATEMENT

IT IS YOUR RECORD OF EARNINGS AND A RECEIPT FOR TAXES AND OTHER DEDUCTIONS FROM YOUR EARNINGS.

Figure 4 Don Keels "Natco" Paystubs

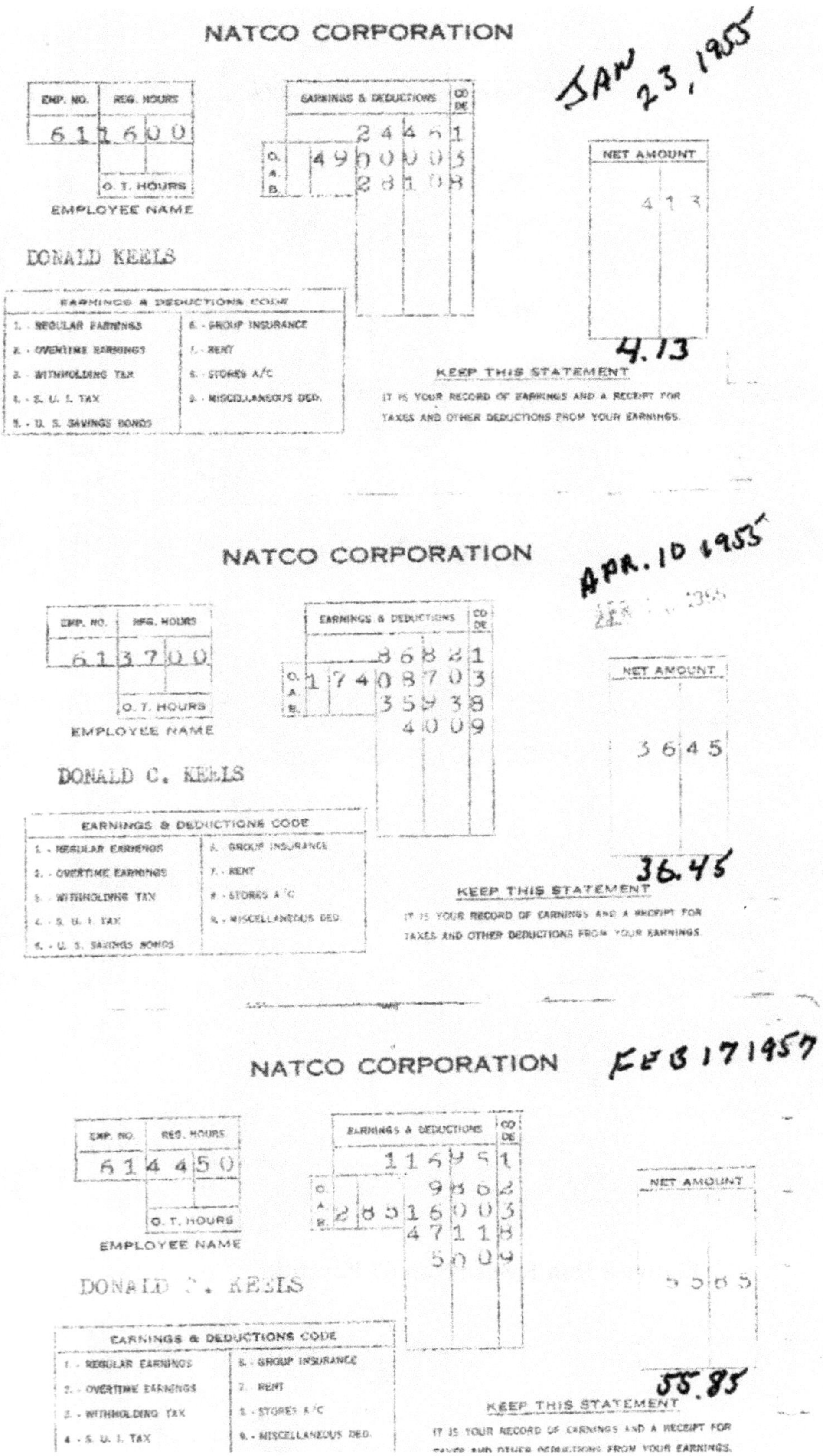

NATCO CORPORATION

JAN 23, 1955

EMP. NO.	REG. HOURS
61	1600
	O. T. HOURS

EMPLOYEE NAME

DONALD KEELS

O. A. B.	EARNINGS & DEDUCTIONS	CODE
	2446	1
49	0000	3
	2810	8

NET AMOUNT
413

4.13

EARNINGS & DEDUCTIONS CODE	
1. - REGULAR EARNINGS	6. - GROUP INSURANCE
2. - OVERTIME EARNINGS	7. - RENT
3. - WITHHOLDING TAX	8. - STORES A/C
4. - S. U. I. TAX	9. - MISCELLANEOUS DED.
5. - U. S. SAVINGS BONDS	

KEEP THIS STATEMENT

IT IS YOUR RECORD OF EARNINGS AND A RECEIPT FOR TAXES AND OTHER DEDUCTIONS FROM YOUR EARNINGS.

NATCO CORPORATION

APR. 10 1955

EMP. NO.	REG. HOURS
61	3700
	O. T. HOURS

EMPLOYEE NAME

DONALD C. KEELS

O. A. B.	EARNINGS & DEDUCTIONS	CODE
	3682	1
174	0870	3
	3593	8
	400	9

NET AMOUNT
3645

36.45

EARNINGS & DEDUCTIONS CODE	
1. - REGULAR EARNINGS	6. - GROUP INSURANCE
2. - OVERTIME EARNINGS	7. - RENT
3. - WITHHOLDING TAX	8. - STORES A/C
4. - S. U. I. TAX	9. - MISCELLANEOUS DED.
5. - U. S. SAVINGS BONDS	

KEEP THIS STATEMENT

IT IS YOUR RECORD OF EARNINGS AND A RECEIPT FOR TAXES AND OTHER DEDUCTIONS FROM YOUR EARNINGS.

NATCO CORPORATION FEB 17 1957

EMP. NO.	REG. HOURS
61	4450
	O. T. HOURS

EMPLOYEE NAME

DONALD C. KEELS

O. A. B.	EARNINGS & DEDUCTIONS	CODE
	11695	1
	986	2
2851	6003	3
	4711	8
	500	9

NET AMOUNT
5585

55.85

EARNINGS & DEDUCTIONS CODE	
1. - REGULAR EARNINGS	6. - GROUP INSURANCE
2. - OVERTIME EARNINGS	7. - RENT
3. - WITHHOLDING TAX	8. - STORES A/C
4. - S. U. I. TAX	9. - MISCELLANEOUS DED.

KEEP THIS STATEMENT

IT IS YOUR RECORD OF EARNINGS AND A RECEIPT FOR TAXES AND OTHER DEDUCTIONS FROM YOUR EARNINGS.

Figure 5 Don Keels "Natco" Paystubs

Chapter 16: Tragedies, Grief and Sorrow

As told by those who were a witness or have knowledge of the event: Martin (Buddy) Crothers, Casey and Delbert (Deb) Smith, Kellie Rutter, Larry Horn, and Don Keels

The most feared sound was when the Company's main whistle started blowing unexpectedly to alert the town that a tragedy had happened. The factories immediately switched to emergency shutdown mode and remained in the emergency mode until Mr. Matheny gave the orders to resume work. Regardless of what you were doing, everyone rushed to the to the company office building, hoping and praying silently that the tragedy didn't involve one of your family members.

Mr. Matheny would be standing in the office building balcony, everyone stood silent when he explained why the whistle had blown. When the tragedy involved one of the workers, the town "keeping with tradition" became one family. Volunteers automatically took over the everyday chore of the grieving family and the Church extended spiritual strength, with no questions ask.

- James (Jimmy) Sharb, Jimmy was spectator setting in the bleachers watching the cars races, on the dirt race track at Walker Speed Way (Davis Chapel Road). During one of the races a wheel came off a race cars and hit Jimmy in the head. Resulting in permanent physical impairment.
- R. Pauline (Weede) Martin, shot and killed in the family bedroom she was the wife of Paige Martin.
- Jody Ann Martin, shot and killed in her bedroom, she was the daughter of Paige and Pauline Martin.
- Paige E. Martin, husband of Pauline, father of Jody Ann drowned in the family pond suspected suicide, all 3 lived same house on Hungry Hollow Road (Purdum Road).

- Johnny Russell drowned in the Hocking River. Lee McQuaid was part of the search party and the one who recovered Johnny's body from the water. Johnny was a relative of Stub Turner.
- Luther Burch died from a poisonous snake bite.
- Mary Lou Martin, at the age of 14-15 when the family coal heating stove exploded, setting her clothes on fire, she suffered burns over 50% of her body. Bret Crothers and Eva Amos assisted her, until the Logan fire department arrived. the fire department had to use the water in the Mr. /Mrs. Amos swimming pool to put out the fire. Mary Lou survived.
- Monte Amos, son of Ed and Evelyn (Eva) Amos, was struck by a car while riding his bicycle on the highway in town, then State Route 33. The car was driven by Paul North, Monte survived, but has permanent physical impairment.
- Mr. and Mrs. Walter Gastin killed in a head on collision on Route 33 East of Laurel Run Road (Blood Alley). Mrs. Gastin died at the scene of the accident; Mr. Gastin died a few days later.
- Kenny Gastin died unexpectedly from an aneurysm. Kenny was born July 23, 1960, died October 3, 2005.
- Henry Ohlinger (husband of Nora, father of Louise) died unexpectedly while hunting rabbits with Jim Farley. His body was discovered by one of the local youths.
- Pat Sherritt slipped on wet conduit tile, fell into the canal, jammed a broken glass bottle into his back. Pat survived the accident.
- Paul Matheny committed suicide in C.S. Matheny's home.
- Reed Warren shot himself with a shotgun but survived.
- Richard Sparks, son of Albert Sparks, fell down a flight of stairs and choked to death on a hall tree. Richard was a young man, just starting high school.
- Mrs. Kovach, wife of Sam Kovach, short herself with a .22 rifle on the other side of the Hocking River, at the town trash dump.
- Fannie (Mount) Sparks, wife of Albert Sparks, was hit and killed by a car in Nelsonville, Ohio. Fannie was born April 10, 1910, died October 25, 1941.
- Jimmy Van Bibber was hit by a train behind Johnny Norris' Pure Oil Gas Station at Laurel Run Road and State Route 33. Jimmy lived on Laurel Run Road.
- Richard Van Bibber, resided on Laurel Run Road, choked to death in the back seat of his car. Alcohol (tequila) was suspected cause of death.

- Edna (Wade) Van Bibber, born in 1922, wife of Charles Van Bibber, shot and killed herself in June of 1962.
- William Evans, Jr., residing on Hungry Hollow Road, was found dead in the gravel pit close to Route 328 and Route 33 on October 23, 1977. Authorities never determined if William's death was suicide or murder.
- Curtis (Curt) Keels shot and killed himself at home.
- Francis E. Swaim, born January 28, 1920, son of Robert and Maud Swaim, was hit and killed by a car while walking with friends in Haydenville on October 12, 1933.
- Raymond Stover, Jr., born October 4, 1944, lived in the first house on the left in Hunkie Row. Raymond was killed on Poston Curve while assisting another driver whose car had gone into the old canal. Jimmy Sharb's car hit Raymond's car, knocking it into the canal, landing on top of and killing Raymond.
- James Robert Sharb was killed in a car accident outside of Nelsonville in 1970.
- Raymond F. Archuer, born October 30, 1898, was killed by an industrial accident at the Haydenville Plant machine shop. Raymond had clasped his gloved hands around the high-speed main 4" power shaft, a burr on the shaft snagged his glove and spun him to death.
- Arthur (Art) E. Horn, born September 18, 1912, Larry Horn's father, was hit by a car driven by Carl Bond while walking to work on a foggy morning. Art suffered physical damage to the side of his face but survived. The accident occurred at the intersection of Route 33 and Hunkie Row Road in the late 1940s.
- Bill Mace, born Mary 6, 1922, unexpectedly died while sitting alone on his front porch in his wheelchair on September 12, 1990.
- Bobbie Williams, son of Bob Williams, was riding his bicycle on Hunkie Row Road and was hit by "Honey Dipper's" septic-cleaning truck. Bobbie survived.
- Casey Smith jumped out of a tree while playing at his uncle's house. Casey impaled himself on an iron fencepost. He survived.
- Christina Williams lived in one of the round houses across the Hocking River beside the bridge. The heating stove blew-up when she threw kerosene on hot coals. She suffered severe burns and had permanent physical impairments.
- Fred (Monkey) Vollmer, lived on Main Street (Rt 33) close to the Ruble St. intersection, walked out into his back yard and killed himself with his .22 rifle.

- June Sharb, born 1926, died 1972 wife of Jack Sharb, Sr. was riding in the car with her son Jimmy when their car went off the road at Poston Curve and into the old canal bed, killing June (Jimmy's mother).
- Jane (Matheny) Karshner was killed in a private airplane crash, on Greasy Ridge hillside close Route 328.

I remember that on a hot summer evening one of the kiln-fire men sat down on the bench outside of the kiln-fire man's office/shack and died. He never said a word, just fell over dead. The death was suspected as a result of the extreme work environment.

The factory imposed hidden dangers to employees and the town. In later years it was determined that employees exposed to fine dust created by the griding and glazing of tile could become victims of Silicosis (otherwise known as the Haydenville Cough), a respiratory disease, similar to Black Lung in coal miners.

Sudden, unexpected death was not uncommon and an accepted hazard.

Chapter 17: Civil War Veterans

We remember and honor those who served during the Civil War and are buried in Haydenville Cemetery.

Name	*Branch of Service*
Allen, Cornelius Battelle 9/3/1845 – 5/27/1926	Army Pvt. Co. C 182nd Regt OV 1
Lent, Stephen 5/1/1821-11/13/1883	Army Pvt. Co. E 90th Regt Ohio Infantry
Levering Jacob 5/25/1815-2/15/1899	Army Pvt. Co. F 186th Regt. Ohio Infantry.
Loomis, Russell J.	Army Pvt Co. B 31st Regt. Ohio Infantry
Mitchell, Adams 12/3/1844-5/11/1931	Army Pvt, Co. 1 & B 75th OV 1 Andersonville survivor
Wycuff, Joseph 7/8/1826-1/24/1906	Army Pvt. Co. H 114th Regt. C V 1

Chapter 18: WWI and WWII Veterans

World War I and World War II Haydenville military veterans. The names listed below were engraved in an Honor Roll Monument, located in the (former) empty lot between the ice cream parlor and the boarding house. Early history notes put the Thompson house on this lot before it burned to the ground, prior to that it was the location of the Iron Ore Smelting Furnace.

Name	*Branch of Service*	
Achauer, William	Army	WWII
Allberry, Jack	Navy	WWII
Bailey, John	Navy	WWII
Barney, Cliff	Army	WWII
Barney, Donald	Army	WWII
Barron, James L.	Navy	WWII
Bond, Clifford	Army	WWII
Bond, Murl	Army	WWII
Bond, Wilbur	Army	WWII
Brooks Sr., Kenneth	Navy	WWII
Brown, Eldon	Army	WWII
Brown, Raymond	Army	WWII
Burns, Clarence Edison	Army	WWII
Bums, Harold Wayne	Army	WWII
Campbell, Paul	Army Air Core	WWII

Carter, Homer	Army	
Carter, Raymond	Navy	WWII
Conrad, Terry	Navy	WWII
Crothers, Hod	Army	WWII
Crothers, Lester Dale	Army	WWII
Crothers, Roy	Navy	WWII
Devol, Phillip (Nance)	Army	WWII
Farley, Donald	Army Air Core	WWII
Gastin, Charles	Navy	WWII
Gastin, Walter	Navy	WWII
Glenn Jr., Roy	Army	WWII
Gray, Marion	Army	WWII
Grubb, Donald	Navy	WWII
Grubb, Leslie	Army	WWII
Hood, James	Army	WWII
Hopstetter, Donald (Rink)	Army	WWII
Horn, Charles (Callie)	Army	WWII
Hurl, Judson	Army	WWII
Hutchinson, Bill	Navy	WWII
Jones, Lawrence	Army	WWII
Keels, Curt	Army	WWII
Keels, Wendell Sylvester	Army	WWII
Kovach, Samuel	Army	WWII
Lehman, Charles Dewey	Army	WWII
Lehman, Creighton V.	Army	WWII
Lehman, Jacob M.	Navy	WWII
Lightfoot, Allen	Army	WWII
Lightfoot, Benton	Navy	WWII
Lightfoot, Donald D.	Navy	WWII

Lightfoot Jr., Wilbur	Navy	WWII
Lightfoot Sr., Wilbur	Navy	WWI & WWII
Lowell, May	Army	WWII
Martin, Ralph	Army	WWII
Matheny, Paul	Army	WWII
May, Donald	Army	WWII
May, Lowell	Army	WWII
Maze, David	Army	WWII
McCandish, Eugene	Army Air Core	WWII
McIntosh, Albert	Army	WWII
McQuaid, Lee	Army	WWII
McQuaid, Gene	Army	WWII
Mettler, Robert	Navy	WWII
Miller Jr., Gerald	Army	WWII
Miller, John	Army	WWII
Moore, Dorothy	Navy Waves	WWII
Moore, Charles	Army	WWII
Moore, Lewis L.	Army Air Core	WWII
Moore, Paul	Army	WWII
Moore, Rover V. "Popeye"	Army Air Core	WWII
Moore, Victor	Army Air Core	WWII
Moore, William F.	Navy	WWII
Mount, Orval E.	Army	WWII
Nihiser, Clarence (Nank)	Army	WWII
North, James	Army	WWII
Oliver, Donald	Navy	WWII
Oliver, Henry (Hickory)	Navy	WWII
Oliver, James	Navy	WWII
Oliver Sr., James	Navy	WWII

Pollock, George	Army	WWII
Saunders, Danny	Army	WWII
Sharb Sr., George	Navy	WWII
Sharb, Jack	Navy	WWII
Sharb, Victor	Navy	WWII
Skiver, Donald Robert	Army	WWII
Skiver, Merle	Army	WWII
Sparks, Lester	Army	WWII
Spencer, Forrest Dee	Army	WWII
Stover, Harry Everett	Army	WWII
Stover, Raymond M.	Army	WWII
Swaim, Kermit H.	Navy	WWII
Swaim, Wendall	Navy	WWII
Thompson,Clarence (Grinner)	Army	WWI
Thompson, Earl	Army	WWII
Thompson, Raymond	Army	WWII
Tucker, Clarence	Army	WWII
Tucker, Raymond	Army	WWII
Turner, Ray (Cracker)	Navy	WWII
Van Bibber, Charles Frederick	Army	WWII
Van Curen, Leory	Army	WWII
Van Curen, Sam	Army	WWII
Vollmer, Roy D.	Navy	WWII
Walker, Clarence	Army	WWII
Weaver, Bob	Army	WWII
Wyskiver,	Nany	WWII

Chapter 19: Haydenville Military

Honor Roll

All gave some, some gave all.

These brave men are now preserved for generations to come. Thanks to James Moore, Casey Smith, Delbert (Deb) Smith, Kellie Rutter, Bill & Norma Lehman

These brave men's names are now preserved for future generations:

ALL gave some, and some gave ALL

Name, Date of Birth--Deceased	Branch of Service
Allen, Cornelius Battelle 09/03/1845-05/27/1926	Civil War PVT Co. C 182nd Regt OV 1 Buried in the Haydenville Cemetery
Amos, Edward E. 03/25/1925-08/21/1997	Navy WWII
Barron, James L. 12/28/1916-01/12/2009	Navy WWII
Boals, Terry	
Boals, Steven	
Bond, Murl 06/18/1916-07/08/1980	WWII Army PFC Buried in the Haydenville Cemetery
Bond, Wilbur 05/02/1918-04/30/1971	WWII Army PVT Co. L 168th Infantry Buried in the Haydenville Cemetery
Brooks, Kenneth E Jr. (Sonny) 11/11/1947-03/26/1996	Army Vietnam
Brooks, Kenneth Sr.	Navy WWII

02/15/1925-08/10/1984	
Burch, Luther	
Burch, Tony	
Burchfield, Roger	
Burns, Clearance Edison 10/19/1914-08/22/1959	WWII Army PVT Buried in the Haydenville Cemetery
Burns, Harold Wayne 04/02/1921-11/03/1950	WWII Navy GM1 Buried in the Haydenville Cemetery
Campbell, Charles (Sonny)	
Campbell, Robert	

Carpenter, George	WWII Army PVT Co G. 7th OH Infantry Buried in the Haydenville Cemetery
Carter, Bernard	
Clouston, John Lloyd (Jack) 06/13/1940-06/23/2020	Navy (1958-1961)
Crane, Gene	
Crothers, Lester Dale 05/24/1909-03/10/1983	WWII Army
Crothers, Wilmer (Jerry) 11/29/1931-07/09/2019	Army Korean
Crothers, Roy	Army
Crow, George	Army
Devol, Phillip (Nance)	WWII Army
Evans, William Jr.	
Feeback, Louis	
Gastin, Kenneth D. 07/23/1960-10/03/2005	Army National Guard
Gastin, Mark	
Glenn, Roy Jr.	WWII Army
Gump, Scott	
Harkless, James C. 08/31/1907-03/09/2010	Army Korean

Harkless, Rocky	
Hinerman, Keith A. 10/19/1933-07/22/2006	Army National Guard
Hopstetter, Donald (Rink)	WWII Army
Hopstetter, Robert	
Horn, Charles (Callie)	Army
Horn, Danny K. 03/4/1945-	Army Vietnam
Horn, Larry A. Sr. 07/19/1939-	Army Germany
Howard, Margie	WWII Buried in the Haydenville Cemetery
Hutchinson, James Sr.	
Hutchinson, Charles E. 04/23/1923-05/1979	Army
Jeffery, Gerald (Tip) 10/03/1910-03/09/1998	
Jeffery, Ralph L.	WWII Buried in the Haydenville Cemetery
Johnson, George 10/03/1914-02/10/1995	WWII Army
Keels, Curt	
Keels, Frank	
Keels, Timothy	
Keels, Wendall Sylvester 06/16/1924-11/16/1994	Army
Keeney, Donald Sr.	Army
Kern, Earl	WWII Buried in the Haydenville Cemetery
Kline, Merlin E. 01/31/1923-5/24/2000	WWII Army
Klinebriel, Gary	
Klinebriel, Joseph	
Klinebriel, Larry	
Klinebriel, Lawrence Sr	
Klinebriel, Richard 07/22/1945-01/21/2019	Army Vietnam

Knight, Allen P. 02/15/1916-5/28/1993	WWII Army (Purple Heart)
Lehman, Charles (Dewey) 04/21/1913-02/02/1965	WWII Army
Lehman, Jacob M. 09/12/1917-06/12/2003	WWII Army
Lehman, Clarence 04/14/1929-01/27/2010	Army
Lehman, Ray	
Lehman, Robert (Bob)	
Lehman, William Maxwell 01/18/1933-03/29/2021	Army Korean
Lent, Stephen 05/01/1821-11/13/1883	Civil War Army PVT Co. E 90th Ohio Infantry Buried in the Haydenville Cemetery
Levering, Jacob 05/25/1815-02/15/1899	Civil War Army PVT Co. F 186th Ohio Infantry Buried in the Haydenville Cemetery
Lightfoot, Allen	WWII Army
Lightfoot, Benton	WWII Navy
Lightfoot, Daniel 11/17/1928-02/28/2014	Navy Korean
Lightfoot, Donald D. 10/28/1925-03/18/2014	WWII Navy
Lightfoot, Wilbur Jr.	WW11 Navy
Lightfoot, Wilbur Sr. 10/16/1894-09/23/1969	WWI and WWII Navy
Long, Robert W. 01/29/1950-06/06/1996	Vietnam (KIA)
Loomis, Russell J. 1844-1914	Civil War Army PVT Co. B 31st Ohio Infantry Buried in the Haydenville Cemetery
Mac Intosh, Eugene	
Mace, Leroy Jr. (Butch)	
Martin, Paige 08/22/1931-09/ /1990	Army Korean

May, Jack	Army
May, Larry	Army
May, Lowell	WWII Army
Mc Gathey, Bill	
Mc Gathey, Richard	
Mc Gathey, Robert	
Mc Gathey, Wayne	
Mc Quaid, Lee	
Miller, Allen	
Miller, Timothy	
Miller, Pool	Army Air Core (KIA)
Mitchell, Adam 12/03/1844-05/11/1931	Civil War PVT Co 1 & 75th OV 1 Andersonville Prisoner of War Survivor Buried in the Haydenville Cemetery
Moore, Roger V. (Popeye) 01/16/1928-06/03/2024	WWII Army Air Core
Moore, James 10/31/1929-10/21/2019	Army Korean
Moore, Jimmy Joe	
Mount, Orval E. 12/08/1918-05/15/1993	WWII Army PVT Buried in the Haydenville Cemetery
Mouser, Ronald	
Myers, Melvin 02/09/1949-06/13/2015	Army Vietnam
Nihiser, Clarence (Nank)	
Oliver, Charles B. 08/14/1947-10/ /1976	Army Vietnam
Oliver, Donald	WWII Navy
Oliver, Hickory	
Oliver, Jonathan 08/31/1918-08/03/1979	WWII Navy
Oliver, John Jr.	
Oliver, John Sr.	

Pool-Reeves, Richard	
Seels, William	Army Korea
Sharb, George Sr. 11/28/1921-03/12/2005	
Sharb, Gideon	
Sherritt, Elmer Sr.	
Shiver, Donald Robert 10/17/1921-05/14/1994	WWII Army
Skiver, Jack	Navy
Skiver, Merle	WWII Army
Skiver, Luther (Jud)	
Skivers, Richard (Dick)	
Smith, Lawrence	Korea (MIA)
Souders, Ed	
Sparks, Robert (Bob)	
Sparks, Wilbourn T. (Wib) 06/10/1939-09/20/2015	Army
Stover, Charles F. (Charlie) 11/09/1939-05/05/2007	Army
Stover, Harry Everett 07/01/1914-10/04/1967	WWII
Stover, Raymond M. 01/29/1922-10/27/1981	WWII Army
Swaim, Graham	Navy
Swaim, Kermit H. 12/21/1915-01/27/1986	WWII Navy
Swaim, Raymond E 04/20/1938-01/19/2000	Navy
Swaim, Ronald E. Sr. (Ronnie) 04/20/1938-02/05/2003	Army Korea
Swaim, Robert (Bobbie)	WWII Navy
Swaim, Kyle	
Thomas, Donald	
Thomas, Jerry	
Troops, Jerry	Vietnam (KIA)

Tucker, Clarence	
Tucker, Raymond	WWII Navy
Turner, Donald (Stub)	
Van Bibber, Charles Frederick 06/19/1912-02/05	WWII Army
Van Bibber, Lawrence Edward 04/01/1939-08/28/2012	Army
Van Bibber, Randy Charles 02/11/1949-10/31-2020	Marine Corp Vietnam
Van Curen, Leroy	WWII Army
Van Curen, Martin	
Vaught, Jerry	
Vollmer, Bill	Air Force
Vollmer, Chuck	
Vollmer, Donald 04/22/1927-07/21/2011	
Vollmer, Roger	Army
Vollmer, Roy D	WWII Navy
Warthman, Eddie	
Weaver, Bob	
Webb, Bob	WWII Army
Wilkes, Denny K 09/12/1914-09/09/1979	Navy
Wolford, John (Jack) 12/30/1928-03/03/2009	Army Korea
Wycuff, Joseph 07/08/1826-01/24/1906	Civil War Army PVT Co H 114th Reg CV1 Buried in the Haydenville Cemetery

Special thanks to James Moore, Delbert (Deb) Smith, Casey Smith, Kellie Rutter, Bill and Norma Lehman

Chapter 20: Haydenville Cemetery

And

Site of the First Church

Established August 14, 1850

Figure 33 Haydenville Cemetery. This picture was taken looking down the hill while standing l while standing in one of the ruts made the wagons bringing raw materials from the mines to what is now Haydenville. The first church was possibly erected in right corner of the distance tree line.

As a seasoned resident of Haydenville, with ancestors buried in the Haydenville Cemetery, it has always been a place of reverence and peace. Established August 14, 1850, the Haydenville Cemetery was also the site of the first Haydenville church. Old photographs confirm that this first church was built at the same location as the current Haydenville Cemetery. The original iron gate to the church was to the right of grave #145.

Hocking County Records Deed Book "L" page 184, shows George Crawford and his wife Mariah (X) her "mark" for $1.00 deeded .94 acres to Trustee of the Methodist Episcopal Church in the United States of America… "The said trustee or successor in trust shall erect and build or cause to be erected a House or Place of Worship for members of the Methodist Episcopal Church in the United States of America" signed by John Gibbon, Henry Myers, George Crawford, Benjamin Hanby, Thomas Mitchell, Thomas A. Gibbon, John Webb (Trustees).

My relatives, including Skivers, Mills, Mundy, Wycuff, and Green, buried in the Haydenville Cemetery, I often visit just to revisit the past. On one occasion, I had a rare – strange – true life experience. In October 2011 I was at the cemetery conducting research and compiling information for this memoir. It was a warm, sunny afternoon. I was standing in the vicinity of Grave #117-118-119 when a movement at the edge of the woods by Grave#160 got my attention. To my amazement there stood three children (two boys and one girl) who were about 10 or 12 years old. They were watching me. The boys were wearing long sleeve shirts and long pants (not levies), the girl was wearing a full ankle length dress, with long sleeves, her hair was brown, and extended well below her waist. When they saw me looking in their direction, both boys drifted back into the woods out of my sight. The girl hid behind some small trees and continued to watch me. I waved to her and shouted "Hello," she then turned and also drifted into the woods out of my sight. I immediately walked up to where they had been standing, in hopes that I could see these three children again, but without any success. These three children were standing on the hill at the N.W. corner of the cemetery which is the boundary line of the Wayne National Forest. This area is all woods; there are no houses in the general vicinity. Still determined to find an answer, I immediately left the cemetery and drove into town, then up and down Frog Hollow Road, then up and down Wandling Road, then I drove through town looking for these three children, but none were seen. The school bus had not returned any children home from school yet, so that rules out the possibility these three were local children.

I have been back to the Cemetery many times since to finish compiling the historical information in the Haydenville Cemetery and out of curiosity, but regretfully never saw the three children again.

The question will always linger in my mind, who were these children, why were they there? Or is it proof that *angels* are amongst us and we are not alone?

Follow me through historic Haydenville Cemetery. To ensure that the memory of those buried here are not forgotten, the names and legible inscriptions from the headstones are noted when possible. Other marked include tile, brick, a rock, a concrete slab, and numerous other items, indentations in the ground are noted as possible unmarked graves.

Each row was carefully walked, several times, one foot at a time, by me to ensure that as many indentations in the ground were recognized as probable Unmarked Graves or possible burial sites; 113 unmarked graves and possible burial sites were located. All others are now know but to God! The last person buried in the cemetery was Cottie Alexander on September 9, 1995.

In the cemetery rests many veterans; six Civil War, two WWI, seven WWII, and at least one unknown veteran.

Figure 34 Salt Glazed Headstone. Probably made at Haydenville by one of the family members and glazed in a kiln with clay conduit pipe.

Hocking County Records Deed Book "L" page 184, shows George Crawford and his wife Mariah (X) her "mark" for $1.00 deeded .94 acres to Trustee of the Methodist Episcopal Church in the United States of America... "The said trustee or successor in trust shall erect and build or cause to be erected a House or Place of Worship for members of the Methodist Episcopal Church in the United States of America" signed by John Gibbon, Henry Myers, George Crawford, Benjamin Hanby, Thomas Mitchell, Thomas A. Gibbon, John Webb (Trustees).

An old photograph confirmed that a Church/ House or Place of Worship was built at the location currently known as The Haydenville Cemetery. Martin (Buddy) Crothers told me "The original iron gate to the Church was to the right of grave#157 in Row#21 and the initial G C on the cement headstone is a Crothers member."

To ensure that the memory of those buried here are not forgotten, the names and legible inscriptions from the headstones are noted when possible. Other markers include tile, brick, a rock, a concrete slab, and numerous other items.

I have identified 199 names and grave's locations, and 104 names only of unmarked graves.

The last person buried in the cemetery was Cottie Alexander on September 9, 1995.

My ancestors Skivers, Mills, Mundy, Wycuff, and Green, are buried in the Haydenville Cemetery.

A path close to the tunnel entrance goes up to the cemetery (one sandstone step and remnants of hand-dug water well remain). This walking path was a short cut from town to the cemetery and comes out close to grave # 47

This cemetery is the final resting place for; six Civil War, two WWI, seven WWII, and ? unknown Veterans.

In October 2011, I was at the cemetery conducting research and compiling information for this memoir. It was a warm, sunny afternoon. I was standing in Row #16 at Graves #119-120-121 when a movement at the edge of the woods by Grave#163 got my attention. To my amazement there stood three children (two boys and one girl) who were about 10 or 12 years old. They were watching me. The boys were wearing long sleeve shirts and long pants (not levies), the girl was wearing a full ankle length dress, with long sleeves, her hair was brown, and extended well below her waist. When they saw me looking in their direction, both boys drifted back into the woods out of my sight. The girl hid behind some small trees and continued to watch me. I waved to her and shouted "Hello," she then turned and also drifted into the woods out of my sight. I immediately walked up to where they had been standing, in hopes that I could see these three children again, but without any success. These three children were standing on the hill at the N.E. corner of the cemetery which is the boundary line of the Wayne National Forest. This area is all woods; there are no houses in the general vicinity. Still determined to find an answer, I immediately left the cemetery and drove into town, then up and down Frog Hollow Road, then up and down Wandling Road, then I drove through town looking for these three children, but none were seen. The school bus had not returned any children home from school yet, so that rules out the possibility these three were local children.

I have been back to the Cemetery many times since to finish compiling the historical information in the Haydenville Cemetery and out of curiosity, but regretfully never saw the three children again.
The question will always linger in my mind, who were these children, why were they there? Or is it proof that angels are amongst us and we are not alone?

Row #1

1. Arthur Bond: 03/03/1897- 07/27/1940. Former wife: Ethel (Smart) Bond, Son of Levi and Rebecca (Asbell) Bond
2. Margie Howard: 01/13/1926 - 09/27/1968, WWII Vet
3. Cheryl R. Howard: 06/16/1955 - 06/19/1973. Beyond the Sunset
4. Agatha Six: 1878 – 1918
5. Orval Raymond Denny: 1902- 11/10/1918, 6y. 2m. 13d.
6. Unknown: Haydenville tile marker and blank original marker

Row #2

7. Unknown: Haydenville tile marker
8. Unknown: Nelsonville paving brick marker
9. Fredrick Paul Eaton: 03/09/1917- 12/04/1918, 1y. 8m., Son of Fred and Mable (Meek) Eaton

Row #3

10. Unknown: 4 lot markers "P" and Haydenville tile
11. Harold Ellsworth Cochran: 08/28/1916 - 11/11/1920, Son of Bert and Naomi (Bond) Cochran
12. Bert E. Cochran: 1883 – 12/12/1926
13. Juanita Bond: 05/20/1914-1914- 1/05/1918, Daughter of Simon and Ida (Lehman) Bond, Original marker "B"

Row #4

14. Roy M. Lenegar: 06/17/1903 - 09/08/1928
15. Evelyn A. Lenegar: 02/28/1928- 02/28/1928
16. Eugene E. Lenegar: 02/22/1927 - 03/26/1927
17. Unknown: Brick outline of plot
18. Unknown: Haydenville tile marker
19. Charles C. Smith: 02/19/1891- 11/21/1918, Son of Joshua & Maude (Patton) Smith
20. Mary Jane Smith: 1918 – 1919

Row #5

21. Lata Alice Lehman: 03/04/1915 - 11/06/1921, Daughter of Charles and Leona (Ingram) Lehman
22. Leona Blanch Lehman: 1888-07/25/1940, Wife of Charles B. Lehman, Mother of Lata Lehman
23. Unknown: Sandstone rock marker
24. Catherine Zora Patton: 05/25/1884 - 10/24/1949, Wife of Frank Patton
25. Frank Patton: 05/25/1884-10/24/1949. Husband of Catherine (West) Patton
26. Concrete slab marker
27. Unknown: Veteran, Haydenville tile marker, 4 lots

Row #6

28. Charolette A. Skiver: 1937 – 1937, metal marker
29. Barbara E. Skiver: 1934 - 04/27/1934, Daughter of Ernest & Elsie Mae (Skivers) Mills, Metal marker
30.Jack Wesley Mills: 1932-1932, Son of Harry C. & Eliza Mae (Skiver) Mills
31.Unknown: Sandstone rock marker
32.Dora E. Lehman: 1884 1911, Wife of Eugene Lehman
33.Eugene Lehman: 1884- 19??, Husband of Dora E. Lehman
34.Charles E. Ruble:1887 – 1915, original marker "R"
35.Unknown:

Row #7

36.Richard Rieder: 1873 - 1967
37.Grace Rieder: 1880 - 1960
38.Melvin Rieder: 1818-1911, metal marker
39.Unknown: stone marker
40.Unknown: stone marker
41.Charles O. Tignor: 1894-1912, Our Boy, son of William & Ida Tignor
42.Nellie V. (Skivers) Mundy: 02/29/1892 - 09/15/1967, Mother
43.Mariah E. (Wycuff) Skiver: 03/18/1865 - 05/05/1929, Wife of William Wesley Skiver, Daughter of Joseph Wycuff Our Mother

Figure 35 The Haydenville Cemetery, row #7, grave #40

My Grandfather Harry C, Mills, General Manager of the Greendale Brick Co., made this headstone for his mother- in- law Mariah E. Skiver. The arm represents under the arm of God.

44.William Wesley Skiver: 05/10/1868-08/08/1959, Husband of Mariah E. Wycuff Skiver, Larry Horns' Great Grandparents
45. Gay Arlene Powell: 04/17/1916 - 01/26/1917, Our Darling
46. Rollo Wayne Walker: 04/18/1909-08/22/1919

Row #8
47. Dickie Bernard W. Turner: 1933-1939, 4 lots
48. Unknown: stone, brick marker, two graves

49. Leta Ladonna Keplar: 02/04/1931-10/08/1932, Daughter of Clarence & Mabel (Skivers) Keplar
50. Hazel Campbell: 10/31/1899 - 08/31/1904, Daughter of C.E. and B. Campbell
51. Alvil L. Matheny: 07/24/1894 - 05/24/1904
52. Unknown: stone marker
53. Unknown: paving brick marker
54. Unknow: concrete marker
55. Russell J. Loomis: 1844-1914, Husband of Mary Loomis, Civil War Vet, Co. B31 Ohio Infantry
56. Mary Loomis: 1855-05/12/1929, Wife of Russell Loomis
57. Clinton Loomis: 1880-1904, Son of Russell & Mary Loomis
58. Unknown: brick marker
59. Unknown: 2 sandstone rock markers

Row #9
60. Cottie A. Alexander: 09/06/1936 - 09/09/1995
61. Lester L. Alexander: 06/16/1908 - 05/05/1983
62. Fred William Tucker: 09/27/1914 - 11/??/1974, Husband of Mary (Six) Tucker, Son of Joseph & Mary (Appleton) Tucker
63. Marilyn Irene Tucker: 06/07/1940 - 09/03/1940, Daughter of Fred & Mary (Six) Tucker
64. Francis M. Tucker: 04/21/1842 - 03/10/1903, Husband of Doris (Clark) Ailes
65. Doris (Clark) Ailes: 1894-05/09/1918, Wife of Francis Tucker
66. Unknown: brick marker
67. Elizabeth Clark: 1885 – 1927, Wife of Owen Clark
68. Owen S. Clark: 1879 – 1942, Husband of Elizabeth Clark

Row 10
69. Unknown: Haydenville building tile marker, 4 lots
70. Ce? Smith: 1801 – 1804, first name is not legible
71. Alice Keller: 1870 - 1893
72. Elizabeth Clark: 1885-1927, concrete marker

Row #11
73. Minnie O. Mount: 1885 – 1971, Wife of Samuel H. Mount
74. Samuel H. Mount: 1885 – 1952, Husband of Minnie O. Mount
75. Unknown: stone marker
76. Unknown: brick marker

77. James F. Allen: 07/10/1879- 03/02/1888, 8y. 7m. 21d., Son of J. & M. Allen
78.The Mundy Children of George & Nellie (Skivers) Mundy
79. Infant Daughter Mundy: 07/22/1915-07/22/1915
80. Melvin Orville Mundy: 08/17/1919-03/18/1932
81. Wavel Mundy: 06/29/1920-06/29/1920, Twin brother of Wayne Mundy
82. Wayne Mundy: 06/29/1920-06/29/1920, Twin brother of Wavel Mundy
83. Hazel Virginia Mundy:11/13/1923-07/14/1925
85. Venice Arvilla Mundy: 01/31/1925-06/17/1926
86. Wilma Mundy: 02/11/1928- 02/11/1928
87. Norman Jean Mundy: 01/12/1932-03/18/1932

Row #12
88. Frank Pickett: 03/12/1856 – 12/10/1936, Husband of Julia (Carr/Crow) Pickett
89. Hubert O. Pickett: 09/08/1886 - 02/11/1877
90. Charity Liman: 1831-1921, Daughter of Richard & Mary (Young) Matheny
91. Unknown: Haydenville building tile marker 4 Lots
92. Unknown: small concrete slab marker
93. James B. Hiles: 04/17/1852, 25y. 23d. Son of C. and M.A. Hiles,
94. James R. Cook: 01/13/1875, 20y. 4m. 3d.

Row #13
95. John Rieder: 08/29/1850 – 1929, Husband of Rebecca Rieder
96. Rebecca E. Rieder: 1856 – 1934, Wife of John Rieder,
97. Francis C. Rieder: 07/10/1886, 5y. 3m. 7d., Daughter of J.A. and R.E. Rieder,
98. Harry P. Rieder: 1887 – 1888
99 Unknown: concrete marker, base only
100.Unknown: above ground concrete slab marker, 4 lots
101.Ira W. Achauer: 03/16/1877 - 8/15/1927, Husband of Sara J. Achauer
102.Sara J. Achauer: 09/??/1869 – 1911, Wife of Ira W. Achauer
103.Donald Achauer: 09/27/1905 - 02/05/1905, Gone home
104.Freda J. Giesecke: 1897 - 1898
105.Nellie C. Humphrey: 03/10/1901, ly.8m.2d., Daughter of A.M. & M. Humphrey
106.Helen L. Loomis: 1907-1909
107.Unknown: flat upright stone marker, no inscription
108.Minta Myers: 1878-1948, Wife of George Myers
109.George Myers: 1868-1941, Husband of Minta Myers

Row #14
110.Unknown: Haydenville tile marker
111.Matilda Ross: 12/27/1833 – 06/08/1890
112.Elizabeth Wyskiver: 06/29/1831-10/25/1909, Mother and Daughter, original lot marker inscribed letter "Y"
113.Christena Campbell: 11/11/1864-02/07/1910, Daughter
114.Nellie Loomis: 11/09/1896, 11y. 4m.14d. Daughter of J. & M. Loomis
115.Frederick Myers: 1907 - 1907
116.Ethel Myers: 1902 - 1908
117.Mary Myers: 1899 - 1901
118.Florence Myers: 1897 – 1899

Row #15
119.Walter D. Lehman: 06/11/1888, ?m. 11d., Son of S. & L. Lehman
120.Unknown: Haydenville brick marker
121.Unknown: Haydenville brick marker
Children of M. & S. Arnold Cuardner: 12/19/1878, 13y.6m.8d., original marker M.A.A.
122.Children of M. & S. Arnold Cuardner: Mary A. 10/10/1895, 13y. original marker M.A.A.
123.Unknown: monument base only with no inscription
124.Christina Campbell: 05/20/1811-11/03/1897
125.Wesley Campbell: 11/17/1807- 01/29/1894
126.Francis A. Bennett: 07/10/1829, 34y. 6m. 6d., Wife of D. Bennett
127.Unknown: Lamb marker name not legible

Row #16
128.Jessie O. Mitchell: 04/24/1886, 2y. 3d., Daughter of J. & A. Mitchell
129.Francis T. Smirclift: 05/02/1873, 12y. 1m. 19d.
130.James R. Smirclift: 07/17/1871, 8y. 9m. Id.
131.Unknown: monument with no name.
132.Unknown: original marker inscribed L.H.C.
133.Unknown: stone marker
134.Barney Vollmer: 1850 – 1902, Husband of Mary Vollmer
135.Mary Vollmer: 1858 – 1928, Wife of Barney Vollmer
136.George Heine: 1889 - 1891
137.Mary Heine: 1889 - 1891
138.John Heine:1886 - 1891
139.Unknown: Haydenville tile marker

Row #17
140.Mattie M. Quillen: 10/3/189?, 36y. 16d., Wife of John Quillen, original marker M.Q.
141.Unknown: above ground concrete slab, 4 lots, original marker letters C.L.
142.William Fisher: 1862 - 1910
143Anna Fisher: 12/26/1903, Daughter of Wm. & Katie Fisher, original marker letters A.F.

Row #18
144.Fannie Ruble: 06/16/1895, 4y.
Row #19
145.Unknown: Haydenville brick marker
146.Unknown: Haydenville brick marker

Row #20
147.Annie M. Parsons 10/03/189? 1y. 10m.?d., Daughter of M. & C. Parsons, Only A Sleep
Gina put the photo of the Scholl head stone here see hard copies.
148.John S. Scholl: 12/27/188
150.Unknown: Haydenville tile marker
151.Unknown: Haydenville brick outline of lot
152.Judy: Only writing legible on child monument

Row #21
153.Unknown: Haydenville brick outlines original marker S.L.
154.Anna R. Lent: 03/07/1839- 01/28/1914, Daughter of Gilbert Vankenberg:, Mother of Perry, Lovina, Stephen, Charles, Mimmie, John
155.Stephen Lent: 05/01/1821- 1/13/1883, 62y.7m.12d., Civil War Vet
156.Unknown: sandstone rock marker
157.G.C. - This concrete marker is for a Crothers family member, as per family member Martin (Buddy) Crothers who, also states original entrance to the first Church was to the right through an iron gate, this marker was to the right of that iron gate.".

Row #22
158.Cornelius Batelle Allen: 09/03/1845, Husband of Mahala Allen, Civil War Vet
159. Mahala Allen: 04/28/1848 - 08/09/1902, Wife of Cornelius B. Allen
160.Joshua Tanner: 1848-1896, Husband of Jane Tanner

161.Jane Tanner: 1846-1899, Wife of Joshua Tanner
162.Allen Primmer: 02/14/1888 - 03/15/1888, Son of J.A. & L.E. Primmer
163.Lora Sparks: 1899-1931, Wife of Fernando Sparks
164.Fernando Sparks: 1879-1940, Husband of Lora Sparks

Row #23
165. James Kenner: 02/26/1806 - 12/18/1807, 1y.10m. ?d., original marker J.K.J.
166.Idella Tucker: 01/08/1885 - 03/19/1961, Son Arlie: 1908
167.Joseph Tucker: 06/03/1883 - 02/23/1960, Charlie: 1918
168.John Price: 1850 - 1918
169.Unknown: 2 Haydenville brick markers
170.Clarence Edison Burns:10/19/1914 - 08/22/1959, WWII Army Vet
172.Harold Wayne Burns: 04/02/1921 - 11/03/1950, WWII Army Vet

Row #24 located at the Northeast corner of the cemetery.
163.Joubert Jeffery: 1900-1979
164.Alfred Jeffery: 1872- 1963, Husband of Grayce Jeffery
165.Grayce Jeffery: 1883-1970, Wife of Alfred Jeffery
166.Ralph L. Jeffery: 1927-1947, Son of Emmit Jeffery, WWII Vet
167.Emmit H. Jeffery: 1893-1940, Father of Ralph Jeffery
168.Jacob Henry Loomis: 06/20/1867-08/14/1917, Husband of Nellie Loomis, Father
169.Jeannette Nettie Loomis: 04/19/1866-19?? (07?) Wife of Jacob H. Loomis, Mother
170.Russell S. Loomis: 1894 - 1910
171.Albert R. Davis: 01/20/1888 - 03/16/1903, 6 lots
172.Unknown Davis: Monument Base Only
173.William Burns:1877 – 1937

Row #25
175.Unknown: stone marker
176.Murl W. Bond: 06/18/1916 - 07/08/1980, WWII Army Vet
177.Wilbur L. Bond: 05/02/1918 - 04/30/1971, WWII Army Vet
178.Gertie M. Bond 1887 – 1959, Wife of William Bond: Son Gerald D. Bond
179.William H. Bond: 1885 – 1941, Husband of Gertie Bond
180.Unknown: cement block marker
181.Unknown: cement block marker
182.John Bond: handmade metal marker & monument base
183.Unknown:

184.Smith: possibly by big hickory tree, info by Delbert Smith family
185.Unknown: concrete marker
186.Delphia Burns: 08/16/1893-02/06/1931, Wife of William Burns,
187.Garnet Irene Burns: 05/05/1912-05/10/1922, Daughter of William and Delphia Burns
Row
188.Unknown:
189.Mary Blair: 1908 – 1964, Wife of William Blair,
Parents of: Bob, Don, Margie, Gerald, Wave, Roger
190.William Blair: 1906 – 1964, Husband Mary A. Blair
191.Orvale E. Mount: 12/08/1918 – 05/15/1993, WWII Army Vet
192.Elizabeth H. Mount: 1892-1986, Wife of Kella Mount
193.Kella O. Mount, 1883-1963, Husband of Elizabeth Mount:
Children: Florence, Harold, James, Merlyn
194.Arvil A. Wallet: 10/19/1901-01/07/1909, name cast in concrete not legible:
195.James L. Mount: 08/01/1931-09/19/1932, Son of Kella & Elizabeth Mount
196.Chloe R. Mount: 08/15/1925 - 09/30/1925
197.Adam Mitchell: 12/31/1844-05/11/1931, Husband of Alice A. (Roby)
198.Michell, Children: Joseph, Mary, Civil War Vet, Co Ohio Infantry199.
199.Edward S. Six: 1889 - 1944

The southeast corner of cemetery by a Big Oak tree.
The final resting place of these 104 adults/children in the Haydenville cemetery is unknown.

1.Geneva L. Black: 03/14/1917-03/31/1918, Daughter of Frank & Mary (Lehman) Black
2.Lawrence Black: 11/30/1919-09/24/1921, Son of Frank & Mary (Lehman) Black
3.Melvin Eugene Black: 02/17/1914-05/18/1914, Son of Frank & Mary (Lehman) Black
4.Charles Blair: 04/18/1866-03/13/1937, Husband of Ida M (Taylor) Blair
5.Charles Blair Jr: 07/25/1909-09/24/1917, Son of Charles & Ida (Taylor) Blair
6.Erma Blair: 04/18/1903-08/18/1918, Daughter of Frank & Mary (Lehman) Blair
7.Luther Blair: 09/01/1899-02/27/1916, Son of Frank & Mary (Lehman) Blair
8.Charles Bond: 03/19/1895-11/17/1918, Husband of Cora (Poling) Bond
9.Ellen Rebecca Bond: 02/21/1864-08/27/1940, Wife of Levi Bond

10.Gerald Delmar Bond: 04/28/1917-04/29/1917, Son of William H & Gertie M Bond
11.Joe Bob Bond: Unknown-12/01/1931, Son of Simon & Ida Bond
12.John Wesley Bond: 06/? /1882-06/14/1944, Son of Levi & Ellen Bond
13.Levi Bond: 01/21/1859-09/04/1941, Husband of Ellen Bond,
Son of Leonard & Viancia (Disbennett) Bond
14.Ronald Eugene Bowersock: 04/20/1931-04/20/1931, Son of Jacob & Ellen (Patton) Bond
15.Paulene Gale Brown: 06/03/1921-08/11/1921, Daughter of Elisha Brown
16.Cryus Buttermore: 06/24/1856-08/27-1938, Husband of Susan (Lyons) Buttermore
17.Susan Buttermore: 4/05/1856-04/01/1936,Wife of Cyrus Buttermore
18.Bettie Campbell: 02/16/1922-01/18/1922, Wife of Floss Campbell
19.George Carpenter: 01/4/1938, WWI Army Vet, U.S. Army PVT. G7 Ohio Inf
20.Margaret Francis Coakley: 03/11/1909-08/30/1909, Daughter of Darl & Elsie (Casto) Coakley
21.Eva Mae Conley: 01/02/1931-05/03/1921, Daughter of John & Dora (Blair) Conley
22.J.F. Conley: 1870-12/26/1924
23.Mary Jane Crothers: 05/04/1921-05/04/1921, Daughter of Frank & Mabel (Martin) Crothers
24.Esther Denney: Unknown- 10/31/1923
25.Chester Dunes: Unknown- 03/06/1917
26.Edward Ervin Jr: 10/?/1871-04/13/1918, Son of Edward & Elizabeth
27.Elizabeth Jane Paxton: 01/15/1838-03/10/1917, Wife of Edward Ervin Sr.
28.Jeannine Ervin: 09/21/1911-11/13/1911, Daughter of Edward
29.Naomi Ervin: 03/07/1909-02/23/1911,
30.Mary Marguerite Evans: 03/01/1931-04/04/1931, Daughter of Otto & Mary (Forest) Evans
31.Mary Catherine Fullem: 11/04/1916-11/04/1916, Daughter of John & Mary (Eakin) Fullem
32.Phillip France Fuselli: 03/03/1922-09/06/1923
33.Anna Grant: 1867-04/03/1910, Daughter of Fountain & Jane (Busby) Grant
34.Fountain Grant: 1847-02/13/1929, Husband of Katherine (Dickerson) Grant

35.Henry Eugene Helber: 01/16/1909-01/22/1909, Son of Jonathon & Berta (Swick) Helber
36.Christopher Hill 1856-07/14/1903, Husband of Margaret (Downing) Hill
37.Florence Hill 03/06/1919-12/05/1925, Daughter of Howard & Sylvia (Keplar) Hill
38.Ida Jane Finefrock Hill 04/10/1888-06/09/1913
39.Margaret Ann Browning Hill: 09/04/1860-02/13/1937, Wife of Christopher Hill
40.Sylvia (Keplar) Hill: 07/12/1896-01/04/1929, Wife of Howard Hill
41.Infant Female Jaqnes: 03/17/1923-03/19/1923, Daughter of John & Katha (Knuckles)
42.Gerald Jeffrey: Unknown- 02/06/1913, Twin of Gerald Jeffrey
43.Harold Jeffrey: Unknown- 02/08/1913, Twin of Harold Jeffrey
44.James Alfred Jeffrey: 07/21/1923-07/21/1923, Son of Janbert & Gladys (Rolland) Jeffrey
45.Mamie Mae Blair Keplar: 08/06/1888-02/24/1931, Wife of Pearl W. Keplar
46.Alfred Leroy Kern: 04/17/1918-12/06/1918, Son of Earl & Effie (Buttermore) Kern
47.Earl Kerns: 1876, Grandson of Isaac & Eliza Kerns, WWI Vet
48.Earl Kern Jr: 06/24/1927-09/09/1929, Son of Earl & Effie (Buttermore) Kern
49.John Calvin Kern: 02/13/1927-02/13/1927, Son of Earl & Effie (Buttermore) Kern
50.Pearl Kern: 07/24/1929-09/22/1929, Daughter of Earl & Effie (Buttermore) Kern
51.Nellie Hester Knapp: 05/13/1909-05/13/1909, Daughter of Samuel & Henrietta (Stant)Knapp
52.Edward Deford Lehman: 01/16/1852-07/30/1903, Husband of Mary E (Sudlow) Lehman
53.Francis Marion Lehman: 04/02/1853-06/10/1917, Husband of Mary Catherine Lehman
54.Mary Catherine Lehman: 04/06/1856-12/12/1912,Wife of Frances Marion Lehman
55.Mary Ellen Sudlow Lehman: 06/29/1857-02/03/1940, Wife of Edward D. Lehman
56.Meredith Eugene Lehman: 08/18/1883-11/08/1945, Husband of Jennie (Six) Lehman
57.Charles Lent: 02/24/1871-05/30/1939, Son of Rachael

58.John Lent: 04/23/1876-01/07/1929, Husband of Ann (Nye) Lent
59.William Nelson Lent: 11/17/1912-03/10/1913, Son of John & Anna (Nye) Lent
60.Ida Mae Patten Lesley Patton: 07/03/1882-05/05/1911, Daughter of Ohio & Margaret (Skivers)
61.Jacob Levering: 05/23/1815-02/24/1899, Civil War Pvt. Co. "F"
62.John Marcovitch: Unknown- 09/12/1942
63.Betty June McDaniel: 07/21/1921-07/26/1921, Daughter of Virgil & Florence (Wolf) McDaniel
64.Ella Beatrice Mettler: 09/24/1917-10/11/1917, Daughter of William & Mary (Nutter) Mettler
65.Goldie Faith Mettler: 01/06/1919-07/12/1919, Daughter of William & Mary (Nutter) Mettler
66.Nellie May Mettler: 05/26/1922-11/02/1922, Daughter of William & Mary (Nutter) Mettler
67.Roy Stanford Mettler: 03/08/1910-09/29/1910, Son of William & Mary (Nutter) Mettler
68.William Mettler: 10/02/1879-11/25/1941, Husband of Emma May Nutter
Son of Charles &? (Dupler) Mettler
69.Alice A. Toby Mitchell: 04/26/1852-05/02/1926, Wife of Adam Mitchell
70.Annabel Mount: 07/08/1923-07/16/1923, Daughter of Samuel & Minnie (Lehman)
71.Charles Ambrose Mount: 01/20/1921-08/19/1921, Samuel Minnie (Lehman) Mount
72.Willard Mount: 1922-08/25/1922, Son of Samuel & Minnie (Lehman) Mount
73.Catherine Ilene Pettit: 03/21/1918-08/04/1918, Daughter of Can & Ethel (Westenbarger) Pettit
74.Infant Male Pickett: 08/19/1920-08/19/1920, Son of Arthur & Mayme (Wilmink) Pickett
75.Wilford Pickett: Unknown 11/20/1927, Son of Frank Pickett
76.David Pierce: 09/10/1869-04/29/1938, Husband of Mary Pierce
Son of 77.William Pierce
78.Goldie Barbara Pierce: Unknown-02/03/1933, Daughter of Leroy and Goldie Pierce
79.Emma Krontey Polakovitz: 1876-08/12/1915, Daughter of Charley Krontey
80.Herbert Rheinshceld: 03/14/1894-03/26/1920, Son of Valentine & Ida (Koble) Rheinshceld

81.Minnie Hoyle Robinson: 1897- 10/28/1924, Wife of Emmett E. Robinson Daughter of James & Linda (Wolfe) Robinson
82.Jimmy Roegge: 11/05/1918-11/06/1918, Son of William & Etta (Newlin) Robinson
83.Johnathon "Johnie" Roegge: 12/10/1911-12/10/1911, Son of William & Etta (Newlin) Robinson
84.Walter Roegge: 08/28/1910-08/31/1910, Son of William & Etta (Newlin) Robinson
85.Carolyine Slatzer Rose: 04/02/1862-04/17/1940, Wife of William Rose Daughter of Christopher & Mary (Engle) Rose
86.William Rose: 03/08/1856-09/06/1945, Husband of Caroline (Slatzer) Rose Son of David Rose
87.Wiley Rutter: 07/25/1897-06/10/1916, Son of Peter & Rosa (Baker) Rutter
88.William Eden Rutter: 08/02/1910-11/11/1917, Son of Peter & Rosa (Baker) Rutter
89.Infant Male Six: 07/15/1936-07/14/1936, Son of Edward & Irma (Rieder) Six
90.John Edward Six: 02/04/1915-09/14/1916, Son of Edward & Irma (Rieder) Six
91.Vernal Slevester Six: 04/24/1926-05/14/1926, Son of Edward & Irma (Reider) Six
92.Delmero Skivers: 06/07/1905-04/20/1921, Son of William & Marion (Wycuff) Skivers
93.George Gilbert Skivers: 04/16/1915-09/11/1915, Son of Gilbert & Marion (Smith) Skivers
94.Infant Male Smith: 12/20/1911-12/22/1911, William Lucy (Leach) Smith
95.Infant Male Smith: 06/10/1910-06/10/1910, William Lucy (Leach) Smith
96.Olive Watkins Smith: 03/04/1895-12/18/1932, Wife of Okey Smith Daughter of James Watkins
97.Bonnie Lou Sparks: 03/23/1940-04/22/1940, Daughter of Lester & Erma
98.Fannie Pearl Mount Sparks: 04/07/1910-10/25/1941, Wife of Albert Sparks, Daughter of Samuel & Monnie (Lehman) Mount
99.Alvin Tanner: 08/28/1857-08/01/1928, Husband of Elveretta (Johnson) Tanner, Son of Kinsey Tanner
100.Arlie Tucker: 1908-1908,Son of Joseph & Mary
101William Paul Vanbibber: 07/24/1924-03/03/1925, Son of William & Flora

102.Malinda Ellen Vanbibber: 01/09/1925-05/12/1926, Son of William & Flora
103.Perry Woolery: 09/24/1859 – 05/02/1941
104.Joseph Wycuff: 06/08/1826-01/24/1906, Civil War 1862-1865
Husband of Lucy (Green) Wycuff, Children Mariah E. (Wycuff) Skiver

Figure 36 Larry Horn, Sr. at the Haydenville Cemetery, row #7, grave #40

My Grandfather Harry C, Mills, General Manager of the Greendale Brick Co., made this headstone for his mother- in- law Mariah E. Skiver.

~~declared that she did voluntarily sign seal and acknowledge the same and does now acknowledge the same and that she is still satisfied therewith Witness my signature this 12th day of March AD1857 Rec'd for record July 22nd 1857 George Payne J.P. (seal) and Recorded July 22 1857 Jas Gregen Recorder H. Ohio~~

George Crawford & wife To The Trustees of M E Church DEED

This Indenture, made this fourteenth day of August in the year of our Lord one thousand Eight hundred and fifty between George Crawford of the County of Hocking in the State of Ohio and Mariah his wife of the one part and John C Gibbons Henry Myers George Crawford Benjamin Hardy Thomas Mitchell Francis A Gibbons & John Webb trustees, in trust for the uses and purposes hereinafter mentioned all of the County of Hocking in the state of Ohio aforesaid, of the Other part (in trust for the uses) Witnesseth that the said George Crawford and Maria his wife for and in consideration of the sum of One dollar specie, to us in hand paid at and upon the sealing and delivery of these presents the receipt whereof is hereby acknowledged have given granted bargained sold released confirmed and conveyed and by these presents do give grant bargain sell release confirm and convey unto them the said Trustees, all the estate right title interest property claim and demand whatsoever either in Law or in Equity which he the said George Crawford and Maria his wife have in to or upon the all and singular a certain Lot or parcel of Land situate lying and being in the county and State aforesaid bounded and butted as follows towit, beginning at a Stone in the County Road & running North west thirteen & a half rods thence North East Eleven rods, thence South East Twelve & a half rods thence south west twelve rods and two thirds to the place of beginning. Containing and laid out for ninety four hundredths of an acre of Land together with all and singular the houses, woods, waters ways privileges and appurtenances thereunto belonging or in anywise appertaining. To have and to hold all and singular the abovementioned and described lot or piece of Land situate lying and being as aforesaid together with all and singular the houses woods and ways water courses and privileges thereto belonging or in anywise appertaining unto them the said trustees and to their successors in Office forever in trust that they shall erect and build or cause to be erected and built a house or place of worship for the use of the members of the Methodist Episcopal Church in the United States of America according to the rules and discipline which from time to time may be agreed upon and adopted by the Ministers of the said Church at their General Conferences in the United States of America and in further trust and confidence, that they shall at all times forever hereafter, permit such ministers and preachers of the said Methodist Episcopal Church, belonging to said Church as shall from time to time be duly authorized by the said General Conference [of the said Methodist Episcopal Church or by the annual conferences of said Church authorized by the s'd General Conference] to preach and expound God's Holy Word therein And the said George Crawford doth by these presents warrant and forever defend all and singular the abovementioned and described Lot or piece of Land with the appurtenances thereunto belonging unto them the said trustees and their successors, chosen and appointed as aforesaid. —

Figure 37 Deed to the Cemetery - Book L Page 184

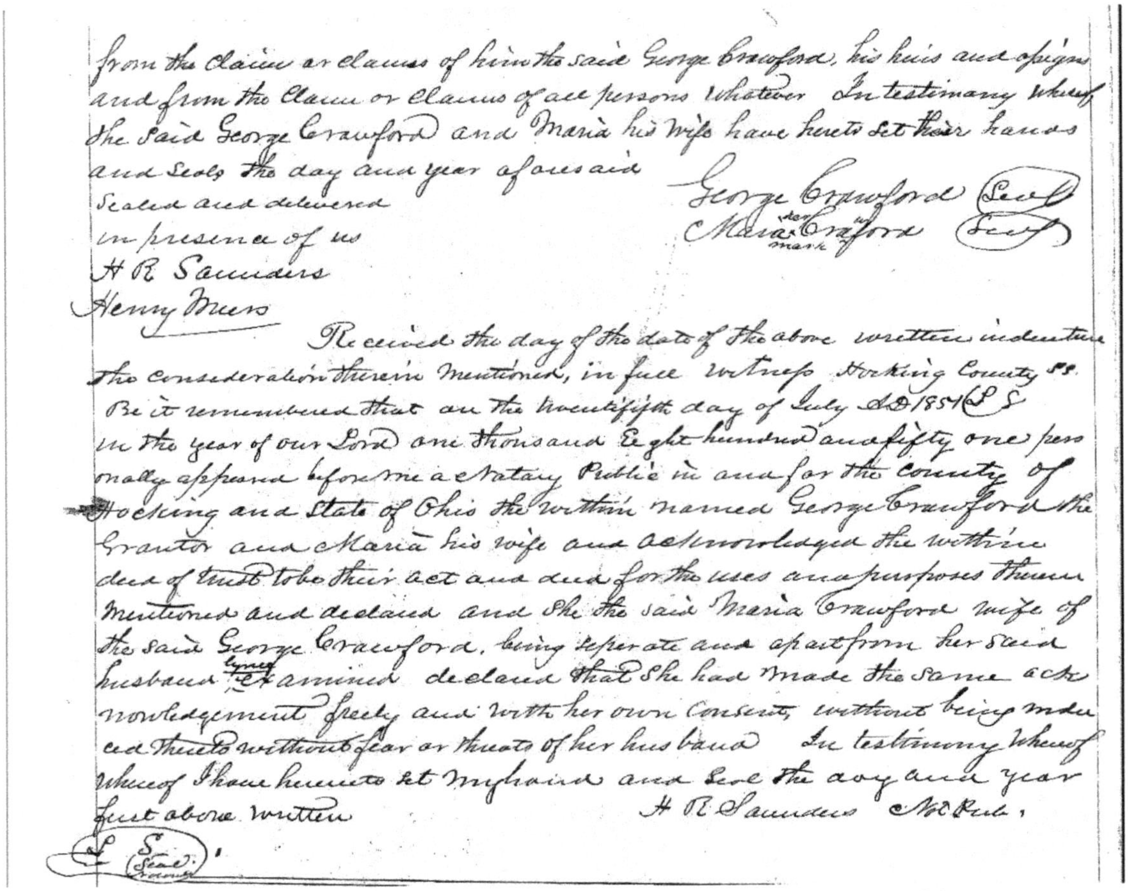
from the claim or claims of him the said George Crawford, his heirs and assigns
and from the claim or claims of all persons whatever In testimony whereof
the said George Crawford and Maria his wife have hereto set their hands
and seals the day and year aforesaid George Crawford (Seal)
Sealed and delivered
in presence of us Maria her mark Crawford (Seal)
H R Saunders
Henry Miers

Received the day of the date of the above written indenture
the consideration therein mentioned, in full witness Hocking County ss.
Be it remembered that on the twentyfifth day of July AD 1851 (L S)
in the year of our Lord one thousand Eight hundred and fifty one personally appeared before me a Notary Public in and for the County of Hocking and State of Ohio the within named George Crawford the Grantor and Maria his wife and acknowledged the within deed of trust to be their act and deed for the uses and purposes therein mentioned and declared and she the said Maria Crawford wife of the said George Crawford, being seperate and apart from her said husband by me examined declared that she had made the same acknowledgement freely and with her own consent, without being induced thereto without fear or threats of her husband In testimony whereof whereof I have hereunto set my hand and seal the day and year first above written H R Saunders No Pub.
(L S Seal)

Figure 38 Deed to the Cemetery - Book L Page 185

Chapter 21: National Fireproofing Company

National Fireproofing Company acquired Haydenville Mining & Manufacturing Co. (H M & M Co.) in 1906 from the Peter Hayden heirs. The factories were in full production, producing various quantiles of fireproof clay products The new company made changes to the production equipment and the kill (kiln) operation, and began production of hollow square tile. These tile required high heat to vaporize the salt the kill far man would add to the kill fire boxes after the internal temperature of the kill reach 2000 degrees. This process was referred by the fire man as "high fire" the vaporized salt produced a clear hard glazed coating that penetrated the conduit and made them almost inducible.

A few years later the company upgraded the production machinery for the mass production of clay conduit tile. These simple modification were to existing machinery that were in operation and most had been installed when Peter Hayden built the factories.

National fireproofing Company changed its name to National Automotive Tool Company "NATCO" and continued to produce top quality clay conduit tile to meet the needs of underground utilities.

Natco was able to survive the great depression of the 30's and two world wars and still hold the completive edge over competition. It owned existing coal and clay mines and the rail transportation system that delivered the needed raw material to its factories. After several years of continues mining the coal and clay reserves were depleted. The mines were closed and seal as per State regulations. Natco had lost its competitive edge, it was forced to purchase all needed raw material from independent mining companies.

- A brick two-story school house adjacent to the Church

- A "new" brick railroad depot, Ed Amos was the last station master. Hocking Valley Scenic Railroad is in the process of restoring the depot back to its original condition.

- A brick one room U S Post office building and a postmaster has provided mail service to the community every business day since it was opened.

- Seven glazed title two-story single family "Silo" houses, nicked named round house, Casey Smith resides in the last remaining round house.

- 47 brick two-story single family houses, 40 remain in use today.

- Nine brick one-story single family houses, seven remain in use today.

- Seven brick one-story double family houses nicked named "doubles" - two remains in use today.

- 10 brick two-story double family houses nicked named "doubles" - two remain in use today.

- Several one and two-story wood frame houses were built after Mr. Hayden passed away, most remain in use today.

- A large wood frame building for community activities nicked named community hall.

Labor was becoming a serious expense, the men would go on strike for higher wage and more company paid benefits. The margin of profit was becoming smaller and expenses were increasing.

Natco began improving its Indiana and South Carolina factories with modern production equipment that required less labor to operate.

Haydenville Natco failed to see the writing on the wall when its mines closed, they could have installed modern equipment to off-set the third party expenses.

When the factories closed in the late 1950's they were still operated by most of the same equipment Peter Hayden installed when he built the factories.

Natco Labor Strike Settlement

The strike lasted from March1, 1957 until May 17, 1957, a total of 78 days. The factory started back to full production on May 20, 1957. This copy of the contract was obtained from Jim Moore a life resident of Haydenville and personal friend who was a big support in compiling this book.

Author personal memories of the strike:

March 1, 1957, the United Brick Workers Union as representative for the factory employees, called for a general strike and shut down at the Haydenville factories.

My personal knowledge, it was a long drawn out nonviolent strike. The union did open a small store beside the barber shop that supplied the workers with the bare necessities to survive and feed their families. The very few varieties of food that were available came from contribution of other Natco factories not on strike.

Assistance as we know it today did not exist, this strike was one of the many hard time the families of Haydenville endured , but they always came together and lived by the community tradition "help thy neighbor".

A few of many incidences during the strike I will never forget:

- My mother was frying some meat in a cast iron skillet, the next door neighbor came over and ask my mother if she could have some of the grease from the meat to flavor her gravy.

- Pancakes were simply flower and water, the syrup was boiled down sugar water.

- Mayonnaise and catsup sandwiches were standard food items.

- Cookies were gram crackers, the filling was powered sugar with a dab of water stirred in to make it like a paste.

- Gravy was often referred to as "slop gravy" flour browned in the skillet, then water, salt and pepper were added. Most of the time there was no meat for flavoring, and many time the only food on the table was slop gravy and homemade bread.

May 17th, 1957, the Union and Natco came to a labor agreement and the men went back to work under the following terms:

1. $2,000 life insurance.
2. $2,000 principal sum accident and death benefit.
3. Sick and accident benefit $20 per week for maximum of 26 weeks.
4. Blue Cross and Blue Shield hospitalization and surgical benefits for employee and semi-private room.
5. The three existing paid holidays to be counted as day's worked in computing weekly overtime pay.
6. 5-cents per hour raise across the board.

Second year of the new contract and effective March 1st, 1958

1. Three additional paid holidays making a total of six to be computed as days worked in computing weekly overtime.
2. Increase in sick and accident benefits to $25 per week for a maximum of 26 weeks.
3. 5-cents per hour raise across the board.

The long duration of the strike resulted in the Haydenville factories to losing many of its longtime customers.

The factories struggled on until the late 1950's, by that time it had become financially impractical to sustain the day to day operations.
The Company call an "unannounced shut down" of the factories, and a few month later sold them to a scrap dealer.

The following is a copy of correspondence and agreement of the 1957 labor strike by the union at Haydenville. Jim Moore gave me these and told me "This may be something to put in your book about Haydenville." Jim passed away before this book was published. In 2019, a rare flash flood devasted his home. The original contracts were lost in the flood.

NATCO CONTRACT

These are some letters the company sent to us, trying to get us to vote.

The contract was ratified Friday, the 17th of May, 1957. I was supposed to work Saturday May 18th to get the Number 1 shop ready to run production on Monday the 20th. My oldest daughter was born the morning of the 18th so I missed the first day. I think we were on strike 99 days.

James B. Moore

Page 1

Figure 39 NATCO Contract

NATCO CORPORATION

PITTSBURGH

J D Moore

March 30, 1957

TO OUR EMPLOYEES:

You have now been on strike for 30 days. A large number of NATCO employees have been asking company representatives, storekeepers, bankers and others why they are on strike and why the strike is not being settled. We of Natco management are asking the same question. WHY?

Prior to the strike your Union represenatives were offered a settlement of 7 cents per hour across the board. This offer was in line with or better than settlements your Union had made with competitive companies in the localities where our plants are located, and also settlements your Union has made since our offer was made.

Your Union has settled with the Canton, Port Washington, and Uhrichsville plants of the Belden Brick Company. It has also settled with the Stone Creek Brick Company and Ava Brick Company, Fairfield Brick Company, with the Canton and Minerva plants of Metropolitan Brick, Inc., the Claycraft Company, the Evans Brick Company, and others. The employees at these plants have continued to work.

All of the above settlements have been made with your Union and it is common knowledge in the areas surrounding these plants that none of these settlements have been better than the offer Natco made to your Union representatives prior to our strike.

We have had several meetings with your Union representatives since the strike started. Your Union representatives expressed a desire to enter into a 2-year agreement, and also stated that the issues of certain benefits, such as insurance and paid holidays, were very important to our employees. As a result of these discussions, we revised our original offer so as to include these benefits. The cost of these benefits -- and they are substantial -- included in this revised offer is such that the offer now outstanding is substantially above the settlements your union has made with our competitors.

The revised offer is as follows:

Effective March 1, 1957 --

1. $1500 Life Insurance
2. $1500 Accidental Death and Dismemberment Insurance
3. Sick and Accident Benefits - $20 per week for a maximum period of 26 weeks.
4. Blue Cross and Blue Shield Hospitalization and Surgical Benefits for the employee on a ward basis.
5. The above Insurance to be paid for entirely by the Company.
6. The three existing paid holidays to be counted as days worked in computing weekly overtime pay.
7. 5 cents per hour across the board.

Figure 40 NATCO Contract

\- 2 -

For the second year of the proposed contract, and effective March 1, 1958:

1. 3 additional paid holidays, to be counted as days worked in computing weekly overtime pay.
2. 5 cents per hour across the board.

In view of the fact that the company offered before the strike a settlement equal to or greater than settlements made with our competitors, and has further increased the offer since the strike started, we are at a loss to understand why this strike must continue.

The company has lost business that it can never regain because of this strike, and each employee is losing earnings that can never be regained. The company must have profits from sales to put back into the business, new improvements and new machinery, in order to make your job more secure. Without these sales you can not hope to have a secure job. As for the terrible losses incurred, you have been out of work for the entire month of March, and the loss in wages per man, depending upon his particular job, have ranged from $350 to over $500. This money can never be regained and it is all so unnecessary.

Your company, in order to secure business, must be in position to offer to sell its products at prices that are competitive with those plants of our competitors. The policy of your Union in keeping our plants on strike and shut down, while making settlements with competitive plants at less than the offer we have made, can only lead to one result -- your continued unemployment and loss of pay.

We are writing this letter to you to explain the company's offer and position. If you believe as we do that Natco has been fair with you, we urge you to so express yourself to your union representatives.

Yours very truly,

NATCO CORPORATION

Vice President - Operations

LAB:G

Figure 41 NATCO Contract

NATCO CORPORATION

PITTSBURGH

May 2, 1957.

To Our Employees:

You have begun your third month of the strike. While we have made every effort to settle with you, and will keep on trying to settle, we do not believe that Eugene Johnson, Representative of the United Brick and Clay Workers of America, wants a fair settlement, and that you will continue to lose your wages week after week. It makes no difference to him how long he keeps you out of work, because he gets his pay right along.

We ask you to read the questions and answers below, which should tell you why we feel as we do about the matter.

1. What is Natco's final offer?

In addition to agreeing to numerous contract changes, and a number of special job rate adjustments, the offer is as follows:

Effective March 1, 1957 -

1. $2,000 life insurance.
2. $2,000 principal sum accidental death and dismemberment insurance.
3. Sick and accident benefits $20 per week for a maximum period of 26 weeks.
4. Blue Cross and Blue Shield hospitalization and surgical benefits for the employee on a semi-private room basis.
5. The three existing paid holidays to be counted as days worked in computing weekly overtime pay.
6. 5 cents per hour across the board.

For the second year of the proposed contract and effective March 1, 1958:

1. 3 additional paid holidays, making a total of 6, all to be counted as days worked in computing weekly overtime pay.
2. Increase in sick and accident benefits to $25 per week for a maximum period of 26 weeks.
3. 5 cents per hour across the board.

2. How does this offer compare with other settlements?

In our letter to you dated March 30 we pointed out that your Union had settled with many of our competitors for amounts less than our offer to you, which

Figure 42 NATCO Contract

JB Moore

- 3 -

to many changes in the contract. We have agreed to make special adjustments for certain jobs. Yet, no matter what we offer, Eugene Johnson always brings up new things which make a settlement impossible.

Is it his objective to drive us out of business in Ohio and destroy your jobs completely?

6. __How much has the strike cost you?__

Depending on your particular job, from $700 to over $1,000. In our opinion, this can never be made up during your working life, no matter what the final settlement is.

7. __Are you entitled to vote on the company's last offer?__

We have always been led to believe that you are. If you have not been given this right, we suggest that you take this up with your committee members - that is unless you want Eugene Johnson to keep on making your decisions.

8. __Where do we go from here?__

Natco will never refuse to bargain with Eugene Johnson or any other representative that you may choose. However, it is perfectly clear to us that Eugene Johnson does not want a fair settlement and does not want to end this strike for reasons of his own, at which we can only guess.

We suggest that you give serious consideration to whether you consider it is in your best interests to be held out on strike, going into the third month, with no end in sight, while all of the competitive plants have settled for less than you have been offered, with no loss of work.

Very truly yours,

NATCO CORPORATION

R.A. Bretz

LAB:G

Vice President - Operations.

Figure 43 NATCO Contract

Figure 44 National Fireproofing Company
Predecessor of H M & M Co.

Hollow 'salt glazed' tile

This particular series of hollow tile was used to build several houses in the Haydenville in the early 1900's. Shortly after the Company began producing clay conduit tile for underground utility companies, this series of tile was discontinued.

Figure 45 At the east end of Haydenville stands the only remaining silo round house.

*KILL-FARMAN

The final process in the manufacturing of the clay products.

The clay products were put in large air tight bee hive *kills, the *farman would start a fire in the kill fire boxes. They would continue stoking the fire 24/7 until the inside temperature of the kill exceeded 2000 degrees F. Then they would shovel salt into the fire boxes, this was referred to as "high fire", the salt vaporized in the kill and form a hard glade on the clay products inside the kill. After a specific time the kill farman covered the fire in the fire boxes with coal ashes, and let the fire die out. Several days would pass before the kill was opened and the glazed products were cool enough to be manually removed.

(*Local slang) Kiln (kill) Farman (Manuel laborer who shoveled coal into the kiln fire boxes)

Figure 46 Nine-way conduit tile

The conduit in this picture was referred to as a 'nine-way' which is the number of separate channels in the tile, the small holes were for dowel pens to be inserted to keep the tile in proper alinement. This style of conduit was also available with two, four, six, and twelve separate channel and dowel pen holes.

The salt glaze made the ends very rough and sharp. It was almost impossible to pick one up bare-handed.

To overcome this problem the men would cut from old innertubes pieces of rubber in the shape of a baseball catcher's mitt. Then on one end, cut a slit just large enough to slide their hand through and still be tight around their wrist. They wore this for a glove and would have to replace it at least four or five times in an eight hour shift.

Fire proof building tile
By
National Fireproofing Co.
Haydenville, Ohio

Figure 47 Haydenville salt glazed homes

National Fireproof Company predecessor of H M & M Co. built several two-story silo (round) houses (see page 158).

Figure 48 Steam compressor

The steam from the boilers was used to run this mammoth machine, which in turn produced constant powers to turn a four-inch solid steel shaft the full length of both factories. Flat surface belt pullies were mounted to the shaft at locations that needed power to run a machine. A flat belt pully was attached to the machine and vice-versa to the four-inch power shaft, then both pullies were connected via a flat belt. The speed the machine was to run was controlled by the size of the pully arrangement.

I remember when a control valve malfunctioned and the huge fly wheel keep turning faster and faster and everyone run for cover. The centrifugal force was so great the huge flywheel disengaged. Large chunks of steel 'weighing over two ton' tore out a brick wall and landed over a quarter mile from the base of the machine. The production from both factories came to an abrupt halt for several weeks while repairs were being made.

Lucky no one was injured. From the time the valve malfunctioned until the flywheel disengaged was about twenty minutes.

Figure 49 Haydenville Plant #1 & #2 about 1950. Ledger Ref page 166.

Ledger of Haydenville Factories
See Figure 36 Haydenville Plant #1 & #2 about 1950

The factories and storage yards covered an area of over 12 acres.

1-Upper right corner is the Hocking River and was subject to flooding, flood water never got high enough to reach the factories or the town

2-Local ball diamond

3-New Railroad depot

4- Narrow gauge railroad (trussell) trestle over route #33 for loaded clay cars from the mines to the factories, the electric power unit,(motor) to move these car was via of overhead electric cable , similar to the electric trolly busses in the big cities

5(Ressie) reservoir water was pumped from the river to ensure amply supply of clean water to operate both factories.

6-The original Wolfe Homestead (family residents 2020)

7-Repair shop and holding area for clay car waiting to unload at the factories

8-Boiler room had 4 huge coal fired boilers in operation 24/7

9-(Plant)#1 factory

10- (Plant)#2 factory

11-Original railroad depot

12-(The barn) repair shop for trucks, tow motors and their overnight storage

13-(Kills) kiln

Chapter 22: The Last Employee

Mr. C.S. (Clarence Sylvester) Matheny, General Manager, Haydenville (Natco) Factories

Figure 50 Mr. (C.S.) Clarence S. Matheny - the Last Employee

I remember Mr. Matheny from my early childhood. He was not office bound but made frequent trips through the factories, always spoke with his employees and was ready and willing to listen to their concerns or problems. The families of Haydenville treated him with respected and understanding. They felt comfortable and secure knowing someone of authority was willing to listen to them.

Figure 51 The original H M & M Co. office and company store Haydenville, Ohio.

Mr. C.S. Clarence Sylvester Matheny, then General Manager, Haydenville (Natco) Factories, was the last employee. Mr. Matheny was a small town boy and made a proud name for himself and his family. Here is a list of Mr. Matheny's genealogy, his family line from U.S. Census reports and local gravestones:

Clarence Sylvester Matheny, born Hocking County, Ohio April 10, 1890; died November 29, 1977. Final resting place, Oak Grove Cemetery, Logan, Ohio.

Mr. C.S. Matheny was the son of John E. and Mary Drollinger Matheny…

Family Member	Age	Notes
From the 1900 U.S. Census:		Living in Starr Township, Hocking County, Ohio
John E. Matheny	31	
Mary Drollinger Matheny	32	
Clarence Sylvester Matheny	10	
Alva L. Matheny	7	Not listed in any future Census reports
Irvin Y. Matheny	5	
Nellie Matheny	2	
From the 1910 U.S. Census:		Living in Green Township, Hocking County, Ohio
John E. Matheny	41	
Mary Drollinger Matheny	41	
Clarence Sylvester Matheny	20	General Store Salesman (Haydenville)
Irvin Y. Matheny	16	
Nellie Matheny	12	
Robert Matheny	7	
Floyd Matheny	4	
Lloyd Matheny	4	
Hester Matheny	4	
From the 1920 U.S. Census:		Living on Greendale Haydenville Pike, Haydenville
Clarence Sylvester Matheny	29	Shop Foreman Title Factory (Haydenville- Natco)
Freda A. Achauer Matheny	25	Married to C.S. Matheny November 12, 1912, born February 18, 1894, died September 1, 1976, final resting place, Oak Grove Cemetery, Logan, Ohio
Margaret Matheny	5	
Paul F. Matheny	3	
From the 1930 U.S. Census:		Living in a rented house #88, Haydenville, Ohio
Clarence Sylvester Matheny	49	General Superintendent (Natco)
Freda A. Matheny	46	

Paul F. Matheny	23	WWII Veteran, died August 22, 1977, final resting place Oak Grove Cemetery, Logan, Ohio
Jane Matheny	19	Jane married Jim Karshner and was killed in a private airplane accident in the late 1950s
From the family archives		
Margaret Matheny Hess		Married Ralph Hess, died January 4, 1970, final resting place Jackson, Ohio. Margaret was in the last graduating class from Haydenville High School 1932

Chapter 23: Louis Dudos Coleman

June 6, 1882-October 30, 1976

Louis Dudos Coleman was also known as Hunky Louie by his coworkers, friends, and neighbors. It seems that everyone who lived in Haydenville, Ohio back in the day when the factories were booming knew Hunky Louie or at least they knew of him. He was among the immigrants who came from Europe and settled into one of the homes on Hunky Row Road, (Now Wanderling Road). Hunky Row is a road that turned off from the main Haydenville Road and went towards the Hocking River. Hunky Louie lived on the left side of the road in the second house from the end. (The term Hunky is an ethnic slur that the Americans used to use for people immigrating from Hungary).

Louis Dudos Coleman was born June 6, 1892. He arrived in America in 1902. It is most likely he came to New York as an immigrant and passed through Ellis Island. He migrated from Hungary to America when he was twenty-one-years-old, (in 1902 it was the Austro-Hungarian Empire). It is unknown if he came with his family or if he traveled alone. His natural spoken language was Hungarian Magyar. People who knew him reported he had a difficult time speaking English and often they did not understand him. The name Coleman was probably spelled Claman or Kalman which was a Yiddish or Hebrew name and was changed after arriving in America.

The exact year that Hunky Louie came to Haydenville is unknown, however, he was listed as living here in the 1930s and 1940s.

He worked as a labor for the National Fireproofing Company, in Haydenville, Ohio, which went out of business in the late 1950s. He was a hard worker, never missed a day work, and was known to save all his money. The locals who knew him said he lived alone, he was single man without a family or any known relatives.

The following is a sweet and caring story which came from his next-door neighbor… Mary Jo Leffler:

Hunky Louie lived right beside us for about eight years! He became friends with my mom and us kids! He would always open his window (where he would sit daily) and he would always talk to all of us as we came out our backdoor which faced his back window. He was a very caring man to our family, even though us kids were not allowed to go inside his home…his rule.

Our Mom and sister visited him and would take him occasional meals. Also, they swept and cleaned his home. I do not think he used the upstairs!

Once a week he would yell for me, (I was the youngest) to come to his window and he would lean out and give me an apple filled with pennies, nickels, dimes, and quarters. And I do mean filled!

He called us all, including our mom and the other kids... "Kid".

He would yell to the other kids: "Hey kid, come here to the window!" He would hand apples filled with coins and then say, "Buy you some candy kid". The he would close the window almost shut and sit down and wave.

We respected him and he was so good to our whole family. A great neighbor.

Many stories have been told about how much he loved children. He would buy candy for them and loved to just have them around. One person reported he would let them play with money when they came to visit. Money would be thrown all over the floor. There were never any reports of a bad nature or anything wrong as one might think considering the world we live in today. The children brought him a little joy since he did not have a family.

Louie Coleman's obituary reads: October 30, 1976, formally of Haydenville, died on Thursday in a nursing home in West Lafayette, Ohio. Burial was in the Oak Grove Cemetery, Logan, Ohio.

My research was done and this story was written on October 30, 2020, exactly forty-four years after his burial. The story of his life remains a mystery to us. Between 1880 and 1920 more than 20 million immigrants arrived in America. Hunky Louie was one of them. Nevertheless, he came to America as a young man with hopes and dreams of a better life. Thanks to Mary Jo Leffler for this wonderful story.

Many years ago, Mr. Matheny's granddaughter Paula, told the author this story. This is one of the many acts of compassion and respect that the author witnessed of Mr. Matheny.

When I was a child, I never knew Louie's last name and it did not matter, I did not like him. He was a faceless intruder at our family's Thanksgiving celebration.

Louie was a skilled craftsman who began working for my grandfather during the 1930s and had immigrated to his promise land. He had no family, and his broken English keep him from making any friends. His house was sparsely decorated, for Louie was not a collector of thing. His work was his pride.

One day, as the Great Depression wore on, Louie went to see my grandfather in his office. In one of the drawers of my grandfathers' large oak desk, was a pistol. A plant manager in the coal and clay county of Southern Ohio could not be too careful during those troubled times. When Louie entered my grandfather's office, shuffling his feet nervously and looking down at his hands, grandfather knew the gun would remain out of site.

With no friends, Louie had sought the one man be believed would not laugh at his request for help. Louie wanted to open a savings account, but he did not know how. Later that day, management and labor entered the local savings and loan together. Minutes later, Louie walked out with a savings passbook clutched in his hands. To him the book symbolized his new American citizenship and the scared oath of loyalty.

For years thereafter Louie deposited his meager savings of a few dimes and dollars into his account. His deposits never amounted to much, but faithfully followed each payday.

Then the deposits stopped, Louie was forced to retire. But his rainy-day saving account was never touched. In retirement, Louie lost the most important thing in his life - his work. But he retained the admiration of my grandfather.

I do not remember when I first became aware of Louie's Thanksgiving intrusions, but in my eyes they were totally unwarranted. The whole family would be gathered in the dining room as the turkey was being carved and the dressing and vegetables were put on the table. The aromas of freshly baked pumpkin and pecan pies mingled with giggles and chubby fingers furtively sampled the whipped cream.

Then, when we could wait no longer for the feast to begin, grandfather would disappear without a word. Each year this happened, and each year his absence seemed more prolonged to his impatient grandchildren.

Eventually, someone solved the mystery. A plate filled with hot turkey, oyster dressing, sweet potatoes and all the rest was wrapped and taken to Louie's home by our patriarch. Then grandfather returned to enjoy his own meal with his own family.

Years later, I asked grandfather about Louie. He produced a well-worn passbook from his desk. Louie's meager saving account, the acknowledgement of his citizenship in the land of freedom and prosperity, had been willed to the man who silently practiced the spirit of Thanksgiving. But the author will acknowledge the fact because his father related to him many times.

December 23, 2015, about 7:30 pm Patty and I were in the Community Building, (the old school band room), preparing boxes of food to be delivered to families in Haydenville for their Christmas dinners.

There was a loud knock on the door and a voice "can an old man come in" of course, Larry let him in. Neither of us had any idea who this old man could be, after a brief chat he introduced himself as one of Larry's ole Haydenville Grade School classmates Herb Moore from Vinton, Ohio. What a Christmas present! We had not seen each other for over 60 years.

We reminisced of days gone by and Louie Coleman (Hunkie Louie) became the subject of our conversation. Herb told me when Louie passed away Mr. Matheny called Herb's funeral home and ask Herb to make the arrangements for Louie's final resting place, "I picked up Louie's body and took it to the funeral home to prepare him for burial in Oak Grove Cemetery." Herb then commented that it" was dark outside and he had a long drive home." We shook hands and said a few words, I walked out to his car with him and meet his wife, we said goodbye and they drove away.

Paula's mystery is solved – Louie's last name is Coleman, but a new mystery has evolved; a man knocks on a door late at night, not knowing who will answer, an old classmate opens the door, they reminisce of days gone by. The man shares his life experience about one of the lost souls of Haydenville. He shakes hands with his classmate, and they drive away.

Death could not keep Haydenville from taking care of its own. The world now knows where Louie Coleman rests in eternal peace.

Chapter 24: Wolfe & Stiers Families

Wolfe and Stiers were two prominent families who lived at the East end of what is now Haydenville. Both families were active supporters of the growth of Haydenville and Southeastern Ohio.

Figure 52 Joseph D. and Mary V. (Rice) Wolf homestead at the East end of Haydenville (2018). The house was torn down in early 2021.

At the East end of Haydenville and close to the entrance to the Wolf Family Private Cemetery sits the last remaining physical structure of Joseph D. Wolfe (1822-1858). and Mary V. Rice Wolf (1823-1890) who were direct descents of the original settlers in the area of Haydenville Their home is now the permanent resident of the J. Colvin family and has the county house # of 17046.

- Joseph was killed while transporting, a load of farm products down the Hocking River, in a flat bottom boat, to an unloading port on the Ohio River. His body was brought back home and laid to rest in the Wolf Family Cemetery on August 19, 1858.

- He left behind his expectant wife and six children, Sarah M., Louis H., Mary M., Helena T., Andrew J., Fannie L., and Effie H. who was born a month after Joseph's death.

- Mary V. remarried to Jonathon Stirling in 1865; she passed away in 1890 and is laid to rest in the Wolf Family Cemetery.

- Helena T. married Samuel England; Samuel and their three children died in the "typhoid epidemic" of 1880. Helena T. remarried John Reuter both are laid to rest in the Wolf Family Cemetery.

- Sarah M. married George Fry.

- Louis H. became a farmer in Hocking County.

- Mary V. no information.

- Andrew J. moved out of the area.

- Effie H. lived at home and unmarried in 1883.

- Fannie L. (1856-1946) Married John Dougherty Sept. 19-1883 John was the bookkeeper and telegraph operator for Peter Hayden.

Grantor	*Grantee*	*Instrument*	*Date*	*Remarks*
Hocking County Records of Deeds Book "Z" page 268, November 23, 1871				
Mary V. Sterling	C&HVRR	Deed	May 28, 1868	Dowler Interest
Louis H. Wolf	C&HVRR	Deed	May 28, 1868	3/7 undivided interests
Helen T. England et. vir.	C&HVRR	Deed	July 2, 1868	1/7 undivided interests
Deed Book "5", page 47, January 14, 1870				
Jos. A. Wolf etal by Guardian	C&HVRR	Deed	August 9, 1869	3/7 undivided interests
Deed Book "Y" page 145-515 corrects width of the above R.R. Deeds to 60 feet.				

1876 Hocking County Maps, Starr Township, Section 18 identifies this property as Haydenville Station; the second Haydenville railroad depot is located on this property. Hocking Valley Scenic Railroad presently owns this section of the R.R. and the depot.

The additional width of the R.R. right of way was necessary to allow for a R.R. siding parallel the C&HVRR main line. Coal was loaded into railroad coal cars at the coal hopper in (Hopperville) and moved on Peter Hayden's standard gauge railroad to this RR this siding. The depot's station master via of the telegraph communication arrange for the loaded cars to be moved from this siding onto the main C&HVRR line and replace them with empty coal cars.

Stiers
Homestead & Family

The *Starr (Stiers) homestead was directly across the road from the drive way going up to the Wolfe Family Cemetery. Their *Starr (Stiers) driveway crossed the old canal and present railroad, their two-story frame house sat 150 yards out in the field on high ground above the flood zone of the Hocking River. Prior to the expansion of the factories there were three Indian mounds (Burial Sites) close to their house that overlooking the Hocking River.

The Stires family were basically farmers that grew and sold vast qualities of vegetables, apples, peaches, pears & plums. The remnant of their orchard is on top of the hill behind the houses on Red Row. My dad told me "He use to help them make sour kraut in large wooden vats, that were large enough to stand up in, and when the wind blew out of the East you could smell the sour kraut all over the valley."

Wolfe & Stiers

Family members directly associated with the growth of Haydenville, and buried in the Wolf Private Cemetery

- Joseph D. Wolfe, son of Christopher Wolf
- Mary V. Rice Wolfe, widow of Joseph D. Wolf. She sold the real estate needed for the expansion of the Haydenville factories.
- Wolfe, Kirby, Postmaster, Haydenville (1897)
- Harden, Superintendent of Haydenville Sunday school
- Thompson, Robert J., Postmaster, Haydenville(1904)
- McSherry Superintendent of Haydenville Sunday School Superintendent and mine boss Haydenville mines
- Fling Opera (Gip) Sharb purchase their farm on Greasy Ridge Road from Fling, statement as per Jack Sharb, (Opera's son)
- Haydenville Church supporters
- Granted railroad right of way to Coal Hoppers at Hopperville Hocking County Deeds Stiers to C& HVRR
- Dorr - She married a Wolf family member.
- The forgotten mining town of Dorr was named after her family. It had a one-room schoolhouse, the town was located northwest of Nelsonville, Ohio.
- Smoke, Henry, Superintendent and Haydenville Mine boss
- Chesher - Haydenville Mine boss
- Matheny, May - She married a Wolf family member, she was possible sister to C.S. Matheny, General Manager of the town of Haydenville, the factories, and mines.

Chapter 25: Wolf Family Private Cemetery

Situated in the North West 1/4 of section #12 Starr, Township,
Hocking County, Ohio assessable via County Road #25 at East end of Haydenville.

Figure 53 Wolf Family Cemetery

*Early families spelled their last name WOLF.
Headstone inscription were copied in the script as written, when legible

*The Wolf and Stiers Family were the original pioneer settlers to the area that in later years would become Haydenville. The Wolf Family Cemetery is on the top of a hill, at the East end of Haydenville. Many of today's local residents carry the last name of some of the families buried in the Wolf Family Cemetery.

Figure 54 Wolf Family Cemetery

Row #1
#1 Bessie
Dau. Of Vernnon & Leah Stiers
Original marker J.D.W.
Original marker I-I.T.W.

Row #2
#1 Headstone inscription not legible ??umd Daug of (?) (?) 182(?), (?)y. 15d.
Original marker C.M.W.
#2 Flora M. DAu of L.H. and M.A. Wolf – Died Dec 1 182(1?) 1y 1m.
Original marker C.M.W.
#3 Clarence L. Rolston Jan 12, 1904- Aug 25, 1905
Original Marker Rolston
#4 (?) A. Wolf 12,185, 7m 10d
Original Marker Rolston

Row #3

#1 Gertrude Pauline Wolfe Oct 5, 1903-May 1920
#2 WOLFE
Emma B. 1871-1960
Vance 1866-1949
#3 Donald E. Arnold 1917-1941 (veteran)
Soldier Rest, Thy Warfare O'er
#4 William Dow Arnold 1892-1918 (veteran)
#5 Wilford R. 1890-1918 (veteran) WWI
Edith L. 1889-19
Original Marker
Wilford Reeves Stires

Homer W. 1856-1929
Cora A. 1859-1922
Original Marker
Cora A. Stires
Homer W. Stires
STIRES

Row #4
#1 Charles C. Wolfe 1867-1934, Rachel his wife 1871-1915
#2 Leory M. Wolfe 1891-1918 (veteran) WWI
Joshua B. Wolfe 1893-1918 (veteran) WWI
Nobly they fell fighting for their country, buried in France.
#3 Helen Margaret Aug 17, 1917, July 26, 1919
Daughter of D.V. & Louise Fling
#4 Walter E. Drescher Oct. 14, 1895 – May 9, 1960 (veteran)
#5 Joseph F. Drescher 1900-1929
#6 Florence M. Aug 14, 1891-July 1900
Laura L. Jan 22, 1891- July 20, 1906
No last name on headstone
Original marker Laura L. Florence M.
#7 DRESCHER
Lewis Drescher Mar 22, 1816-Aug 13,1926
Ida M. Wolfe his wife Jan 29, 1863-Jan 4,1905
#8 Charles E. Aug 9, 1904 – Sept 9, 1904
No last name on headstone
#9 HELENA T. 1851-1903 Wife of J. Reuter
#10 Nellie Reuter 1892-1978
#11 John Reuter June 1853 – July 1931
#12 Henry Snoke (veteran) WWI 1854-1937, Sarah F. Snoke 1858-1939
Infant son Fredrick L. 1892-1892
#13 Wilson Patrick 1804-1872
#14 30"x60" flat stone 4" above ground level

In Memory of Christopher Wolf Who Died Sept 21, 1845, Age 65Yrs 7Months.

Farewell My Children & Friends So Dear
I am Not Dead But Sleeping Here
Wait in Hopes of that Blessed Day
When I Shall Rise & Leave My Bed of Clay

#15 14"x24" flat, broken stone ground level
Dau of J.D. & M., Died July 20, 1850, 0Yrs, 1 Mo, 7 Days

#16 27" x60" flat stone 4" above ground
In Memory of Ronda
Consort of Christopher Wolf
Who Died May 9th 1845 Age 61Yrs 9Mo
Friends Nor Physicians Could Save
Her Mortal Body from the Grave
Nor Can the Grave Confine Her Here
When CHRIST Doth Call She Must Appear

#17 24" x48" flat, broken stone, level
Joseph D. Wolf, Died Aug 10, 185(?), Age 35Yrs 7Mo 3Days
Go Home My Friends & Dry Your Tears
I Shall Rise When CHRIST Appears

#18 Father & Mother WOLF
Joseph D. Wolf, Died Aug 10, 1858, Age 35Yrs 7Mo 3Days
Mary V. Rice, Died June 15, 1890, Age 67Yrs 3Mo 14Days
Hester T. Wolf, July 19,1853-Sept 29, 1863
Original Marker J.D.W.

#19 EICHHORN
Ken 1904-1982 Kay 1904-1966

#20 Graham
Edith Ann 5/6/1880-10/10/1982 Mother
Pearl Albert 4/17/1876-4/19/1947 Father

#21 Dow
The beloved son of P.A. & Edith Graham
March 31, 1902 – Oct 21, 1909

#22 Wilford M. Stires 1866-1897

#23 Taylor
(Pete) Ralph June 28, 1915 – Dec 14, 1976
(Flo) Flora E. Feb 28, 1915 – July 6, 2001

#24 Campbell
Herbert E. 1892-1942

Nellie I. 1876-1971
#25 Mildred J. Campbell May 18, 1911-Aug 1, 2006
#26 Charles Campbell 1906-1963
#27 Harold E. Campbell Nov 3, 1913-July 31, 1941
#28 Vollmer
Vesper B. 1907-1948 Gerald 1905-1996
Infant son Robert L. 1926

Row#5
#1 Arminda J. Wolf 1858-1924
#2 Andrew J. Wolf 1855-1928
#3 Clifford G. 1882-1907
Pearl A. 1867-1897
Gone y blessed
Gone but not forgotten
#4 THOMPSON
Daughter of Mamie Marie 1891-1907
Father Wsley 1867-1902
#5 Christopher M. Wolf Dec 25, 1838, Age 66Yrs 1M 15D
Inscription on base of headstone is not legible
#6 ARA Wife of C. Wolf, Died Feb 2, 1880, 44Yrs 6M 28D
Inscription on base of headstone is not legible
Original Marker H.C.W.
#7 12"x30" flat stone ground level
Harlow C. Son of Edmond & Caroline Wolf
Died Sept 3, 1845 1M 8D
#8 12"x30" flat stone ground level
Emily Dau. Of J.&M. Wolf Sept 1, 1845 Age 4M
#9 12"X30" Christopher M. Son of J.D. & M.M. Wolf May 4, 1847 Age 12Y 13M 18D
#10 Arthur R. Stiers 3/30/1882 – 7/12/1961
Frederick W. Stiers 11/6/1878 – 8/6/1952
Father: Stephen Stiers 1852-1918 Mother: Kate Russell 1855-1950
Ward W. Stiers March 27, 1885-Feb 16, 1905
STIERS – a large headstone in addition to the above four headstones
#11 Getz
John Thomas 1940-1995
#12 Ralph Loren Taylor (veteran) June 29,1915 – Dec 14, 1976
#13 McElroy Madelene Carol, Marge, Dec 30, 1944

Donald Lee, Don, Oct 19, 1946
#14 Campbell
Ephraim 1851-1932 Adeliah 1854-1938
#15 Nellie B. Campbell - Wend 1872-1968
#16 Campbell Charles N. May 21, 1948 Teresa Feb 11, 1961
#17 Lester W. Lanning (veteran) Nov 2, 1919 – June 19, 1983
#18 Zoeta G. Lanning April 16, 1928 – March 18, 2003
In Loving Memory
#19 Beulah M. Vollmer (Moore) 1938-1962

Row #6
#1 WOLFE
Charles 1903-1982 Ethel 1908-1991
#2 Metal Brown's Funeral Home Marker
Ayla Clara Todarello 2008-2008

Row#7
#1 MC Sherry
Maria 1862-1945 John H. 1858-1939
#2 WOLF – At Rest
Father Charles C. Wolf Jan 2, 1826-Mar 16, 1897
Mother Emily Wolf May 1, 1929, May 21, 1918
#3 Robert F. Wolf Jan 18, 1850-Nov 24, 1920
Eliza A. Wolf Oct 8, 1848-May 1, 1900
Charles A. Wolf July 16, 1876 – Dec 27, 1880
Ruby E. Wolf Dec 15, 1837 – Oct 27, 1893
Original Marker RFW EAW
#4 Child headstone with lamb asleep on top of the stone
Charles A. Sone of B.E. & E.A. Wolf
Died Dec 28, 1880 3Y 3M 15D
Original marker not legible
#5 3chan-links inscribed
William H. Son of (?) & (?) Wolf
Died Mar 10, 1821 2Y 7M 7D
Original marker not legible
#6 Mary M. Matheny Wife of Wm. D. Wolf
Died Sept 6, 1876 Age 70Y 1M 2D
#7 W.D. Wolf Feb 7, 1886 – Nov 22, 1886
#8 Josiah H. Moore (veteran) Jan4,1885 Age 79Y 9M 18D

Lydia Moore Dec 27, 1881 Age 73Y 10M 14D
Original markers JHM & LM
#9 Rhoda, Eldest Daughter J.H. & L. Moore
Died June 4, 1880 Age 10Y 8M 22D
Nothing in my hand I bring. Simply to the cross I cling.
Original marker R M
#10 Thomas A. Huddy 1903-1985
#11 Nellie E. Huddy 1909-1975
#12 Alvira Wolfe Thompson 1869-1932
#13 Our Darling Flossie Thompson 1930-1942
#14 WALDRON
Gary L. Sept 28, 1949
Antoinette (Toni) S. May 15, 1948
Wed July 23, 2011

Row #8
#1 HARDEN
Ruth Miller 1919-1987
Larry J 1935-1990
#2 John E. Davis (veteran) Apr 19, 1930 – Sep 20, 2010
#3 Mable L. Allen Davis 1908-1930 Mother
#4 Ruth McSherry 1893-1973
Mae Hock 1920-2005
#5 John Charles (veteran) McSherry Dec 29, 1927
#6 Mary J - I & M Moore Died Feb 28, 1859 6Y 4M 2D
#7 MOORE
Mary A. Feb 17, 1831-Feb 22, 1912
Isaac Nov 25, 1823 – Sep 27 1881
#8 FORD
Steven J Feb 3, 1946
Linda I Oct 22, 1946-Jan25, 2008
#9 William F. Campbell (veteran) Feb 14, 1919-Jan 10, 1966
Margaret L. Campbell Drumm 1919-1999
Raymond F. Drumm 1921-1995
#10 Paul E. Campbell (veteran) Nov 15, 1917 – May 3, 1966
#11 Edward Lee Campbell 1952-1954

Row #9
#1 HOOVER

Mildred J. 1909-1999
Harland T. 1907-1971
#2 Father John Wesley Wolfe 1875-19674
#3 Loretta L. Wilson 1913-1999 Dau of Frank & Blanche Wolfe
#4 Blanche Wolfe 1892-1963
#5 Frank D. Wolfe 1883-1966
#6 Jonathan Wolfe (veteran) Nov 22, 1840
Sarah E. Wolf Sep 18,1841-Oct 4,1916
In GOD we trust.
#7 10'x18' concrete slab on Haydenville brick foundation, 8" above ground level. A 30" high metal decorative railing is secured to the outside edges of the concrete slab. Only one headstone sits on the top of the slab, it is 30" high, handmade of clay and fire glazed with the inscription…
Mimie F. Wolfe
Died September 12, 1877
Effie Wolfe Died July 3, 1878
Daughters of John and Sara Wolfe
Mimie 4 months 15 days
Effie 4 months
I'll take these little lambs He said
And hold them in My breast
Protection they shall find with Me
Sweet Blessed
#8 CW???
Son of CF & SE
George, Died Jan 3, 1894 21Yr
Inscription in base of headstone not legible
Clifford, Son of CE & SE, Died Aug 4, 1892 10 Mos
Sarah E. Wolfe, Daughter of CE George, Died Oct 8, 1891 Age 21Yrs 6M 21D
Buried on Earth, To Home in Heaven
#9 Large Tree with These Two Original Marker on Side of Tree
C G W H W
#10 HOYE
Husband, Noah A. June18,1900-Nov 4, 1923
Wife Mildred V. June 26, 1908-1983
#11 Original marker and possible child's marker sunk in ground unable to read
#12 CAMPBELL

Foster L. 'Rocky' Aug 22, 1942-Mar 7, 2011
Leslie A, March 6, 1956
Parents of Christy, Stone, Cody, Corey and Brooke
#13 Ronda E. Lonberger
Feb 28, 1930-July 17,1994
Go to the highest mountain shoutin'
Mother your work on Earth is done
#14 Gail G. Longberger (veteran)
1927-2005
#15 Flag and flowers, no headstone or marker

Row #10
#1 Robert D. Wolfe, July 17, 1927 – June 4, 1998
#2 Stephen L. Wolfe, Feb 7, 1960-Sept 30, 1961
We shall meet again.
#3 WOLFE
Josiah H. 1874-1946
Flossie Mae 1891-1951
God shall be my hope, my stay, my guide and a
Lantern to my feet
Boy Frances 1955-1955
#4 H.H. Wolfe, Dec 3,1843-Feb 22, 1917
Mary his wife, Mar 30, 1841-June 21, 190

Row #11
#1 HOYE
James 1870-1945
Mary L. 1872-1943
#2 Lawrence Hoye 1892-1918
#3 Sister, Minnie Hoye Robinson 1897-1924
#4 Mary Elizabeth Wolfe 1851-1929
#5 William T Wolf 1876-1922
#6 Amelia H Wolfe 1883-1950
#7 A Josephine Wolfe 1908-1929
#8 BYRN
Darline W 1930-20
Hubert C 1928-2009
It was never dull
#9 HAMMOND

Sue W 1939-20
Kenneth L (veteran) 1928-2011
#10 WILSON
Susan A, 1954-
Wilbur L. 1938-2014
Those you keep in memory are yours forever.

Row #12
#1 HARDEN
David (veteran) Aug 24, 1933
Estle Sept 24, 2009
Our chain is broken, and nothing seems the same
But as GOD calls us one by one, the chain will link again
#2 HARDEN
Lester Dec 13,1921-Feb 20, 2004
Ruth P. Nov 23, 1914
Married May 18, 1962
#3 Charles M Pyle 1939-1939 'monty'
#4 Charles W. Harden (veteran) 1923-1978
#5 HARDEN
Pearl K. 1901-1986
Estle O. 1898-1961
Joind in Holy Wedlock Feb 23, 1921
#6 Thomas
Elija Johnathan Andrew March 18, 2014-Dec 6, 2014
Blessed Son & Brother forever in our hearts
The greatest gift we can give
Those who have left us
Is to live fully in their place
#7 PYLE
Martha 1879-1962
Leonard 1972-1937
#8 TOOPS
Mary L, Dec 12, 1911-June 26, 1991
Roy Howard Toops (veteran) Sept 7, 1923-Oct 1, 1992
#9 Bonnie Lee Toops, Aug 7, 1947-Dec 25, 1996
Mother of Michael & Mary McCauley
#10 BAUER
Minnie B, 1876-1937

Lewis 1877-1966
#11 Myrta B. McManaway Church, 1878-19
#12 Frank McManaway (veteran) 1876-1933
#13 Beulah W. Bobo, 1905-1970
#14 Brooks
Florence 1911
Albert S. (veteran) Oct 1905-Sept 1978
Beyond the sunset

Chapter 26: Jim Moore Family

Jim gave me this copy of the letter he sent to Chuck and Margie he said " I might want to put it in this book. Jim passed away before I got this book published, and in 2019 a 'RARE' flash flood devasted his home on Route 595, Jim and Marge lost all their belongings and family keepsakes.

It was a blessing in disguise that I had copied this letter and his copy of the original 1957 Natco Labor Contract.

Author note:
I helped Jim unload the truck load of material for this house and have never seen the area around flood. Jim said, "the water came so fast down the hallow behind the school building that Marge couldn't get out of the house." He said, "the last measurement he had was 5 feet of water on the kitchen floor and still raising" The old grade school building also was flooded.

The Logan fire department had to rescue Jim and Marge plus two of their neighboring families.

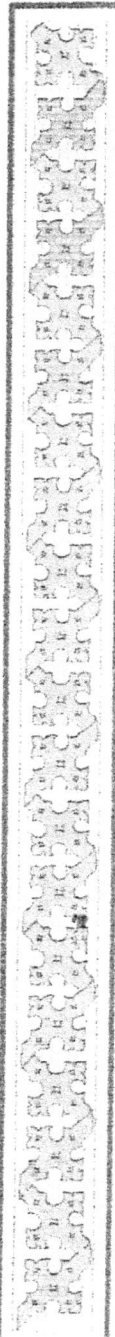

October 12, 2000

Dear Chuck and Marjie,

I just want you to know when you gave your talk about your dad and mom, it brought back memories. Your mom was our neighbor. She moved to Haydenville when we were in the 7th or 8th grade. She always had a smile on her face and had lots of friends.

Your dad was the nearest father that I had. Dad died in October 1933 when I was almost four. Your dad was 10 or 11, Lew was 16, Victor 14, Nancy was 12, Bill 8, Roger 6, Beulah 2 and Katie wasn't born until February 14, 1934.

Lew quit school and went to work for Natco until he was 17 or 18 when he went to CCC and spent two or three years. Nancy finished high school. When your dad reached 16 he quit school and went to work full-time. Before he reached 16 he worked for Mrs. Grubb and Charlie Moore, they were farmers, for $1.00 a day. The money he made

went to my mom to help raise the rest of us kids.
Your dad stayed at home just likea father to us.
He would see that the family needs were met.
He went into the army in late 1943 or early 1944.
He was in the infantry on the front lines in the Battle
of the Bulge and was shot several times.
Bill went to school until the day he was 17. and left
for the Navy in January 1943. Bill stayed away
from home the rest of his life. He was in the Navy
for 29 years.
Roger quit school when he was 16 and went into the
Army Air Force.
I was 16 in October 1945. In January 1946 I
went to work at Haydenville until I wa 18 and went
into the Army for four years. Your dad and mother
were married by the time I went into the Army so it
was my turn to supportr mom, Beulah and Katie.
Beulah quit school and got married to Ray in 1950
or 1951 and started a family. She died at the age

I thought you might like these letters and pictures.
The letters were called V-Mail and your dad sent
them to mom from Germany in 1944.
You will notice he sent money and asked about us kids.
The picutre is of you and your mom putting on a coat.
your dad and mom with Cathy. taken in 1949.
Your Grandma and Grandpa May . taken in 1949.

As you can see, I keep everything and I am glad I
did.

Love.
"Jim"

Chapter 27: Fannie McFadden Horn

The following is a handwritten letter from Fanny McFadden Horn. The letter is printed with permission from Carl Horn (1925-2019), Fannie's son. Carl and I spent several hours talking at his home in Ilesboro, Ohio. He said his mother's middle name was Gertrude. We discussed the strange coincidence that my dad and his dad were both named Bert (nicknames).

Fannie was born November 22, 1881 in Hocking County, Ohio, to Winfield Scott McFadden and Mary Nancy Wolf McFadden. She married Marion Albert Horn and had four children: Charles Albert, Ruth Alice, William Winfield, and Carl Edward. Fanny passed away on December 2, 1942 in Laurelville, Ohio.

"My first 90 years."

1- I was born Nov. 23rd 1881.
In a humble little shack, near.
Haydenville, Ohio, the second child
to Winfield and Mary (Wolf) McFadden.
I was a sickly little critter, I had a
bowel trouble, that was hard to
Controle my mother tried several
remedies, finally some one said
to dig Black berry root, and make tea.
with the first Couple doses, there
was quite a change for the better. so
she kept on, till I was cured.
my sister Nora was 5 yrs. older than
I was, she would rock me. but
if I kept crying, she would say
Oh! Baby! when I was about 2
years old. we moved to the Hoppers
where they dumped coal in large
Cars to go to Haydenville. some
was used to fire the kilns.
Bob McFall was engineer, and
my Dad was engineer on a much
smaller engine. "The Owl"
most people called it the little
Dinky, or narrow guage, he
went thru the light tunnel, and
the dark tunnell, then down
in the Cann entry. where he got
Cars of Coal to bring to the hoppers

2/
to be sent to Haydenville.
We had a much better house
and a large pasture field. we
had a horse, 2 Cows, Pigs and
Chickens. one time they sent the
little engine to Columbus to the
Car shop for repairs, Dad went
and stayed a week and helped
work on the repair. when they
brought it back. Frank Pickett
Came with several yoke of
Oxen to pull it up the hill.
they put planks down, and
got it up the hill and on the
track again. we always watched
that. we had real nice neighbors
Kate and Will Fisher, Clara & Nellie.
Ed Lehman, wife they had four
boys. Emett, John, Ramey & Noel.
John Reiders family. uncle John
and aunt Maria McSherry they
had Mabel, Bernice, and Freda.
Mr and Mrs Charlie Springer
and family. The Ohlinger family
lived there awhile then they moved
to Pomeroy. Henry stayed with his
sister Kate Fisher. he soon started
going with Nora. Will Fisher had a
nice Horse, and Buggy. and he let

3/

Henry have the horse + buggy and he and Yora would go to Haydenville to church, and I remember my first school days all the children in our neighborhood went to Coakley school it was a mile or more, over the hills. We had some bad snowy weather in those days. we wore high top shoes, but our artic over shoes was just one buckle, the snow would get down inside of them our Mother made us wear long black stockings to keep our feet dry. but when we got to school we took them off and hid them in an old stump, then put them on after school to go home they were froze stiff. but we got them on. they always had a picnic on the last day of school. my first teacher was Minnie Crow. then J. B. Mathias, he had a song and prayer each morning. after he quit teaching he studied for the Ministery, and I had the pleasure of meeting his son Joe at Camp meeting at Stoutsville, he said evry one I talk to spoke so well of him

4/

I wish he could have lived so
I could have known him.
But I was just 16 months old
when he died. my other teachers
were, Clara Hopkins, Joe nunemaker,
Will Stone, Seber Holcomb, Walt Risley.
one thing I recall. teacher would let
two of us get a bucket of water then
one would pass it up one isle and down
the other till evry body had a drink.
we used one tin cup for evry body.
think of the slobbers, the last Guy
would get. but I dont think any body got
sick. when Seber Holcomb was teacher. I
was putting on my over shoes, time to go
home, and he thought I was talking
to Mattie Worth that sat behind me and
he threw an eraser, at me. so I gathered
all my books, took them home, I was
quitting school for sure. this was
Friday. on Monday I had sore throat
and did not go for two days. but
Wednesday I took my books and went
back. later on they changed engines
they had Bob McFall do the switching
in yard at Haydenville. put the
narrow track for Dad to use the
little Dinky to haul coal to Haydenville
and used Mules to haul Coal out to

5/ the hoppers to be dumped in little
Cars. then we moved to Haydenville
I was about 10 or 11 then. we were
Close to Church and I think we
attended evry service. I was elected
Librarian, I gave out the song books
seen that each class had leaves.
and I helped Mrs Sarah Arnold
in the little Sunday school room
they had a little Organ in there and
I Kould play one song: Bring them
in from the fields of Sin- I soon
took a few music lessons and
soon could play several pieces. I
liked working with the Children.
some times Mrs Arlold Could not
be there, and I took full charge.
some times there was 40- little
ones. they were in the Big room
for opening service. then marched
in little room. after classes they
would march out again. I throught
I was Very important. later Ma
taught the Class of girls my age.
and Lidia Lemman taught the
Boys. we had class parties some
times, Cora and Kate Stiers bath
played the organ for Church.
after they quit Coming to Church

6/

Nora and Zona King played later on. Ida Allen Blanche Allen, and I played then Ida Moved to Logan. that left Blanche and I. we went to school at Haydenville. our teachers were Will Stone, Emett Kreider. he whipped one of John Boling's boys. dont think he hurt him but Boling was mad, and hid behind his fence. Kreider had a heavy long over Coat that Came to his ankles. Boling had knuckles on. jumped out knocked Kreider down and beat him awful. he had to serve a long time in the Pen for that. our Minister B. F. Evans taught school 2 weeks till they got another teacher and Porter Price Came, he was real good teacher. later on we had E. S. Monce, he was wonderful. he taught Vocal, and Piano lessons. Edith Nargrisney and I both took Piano lessons. We Marched down to the road. Willis Allen beat the bass drum and Nellis the tenor drum. While Rev Evans was Pastor. They had a 6 weeks revival. the Church was full evry night. my Mother was teacher of the girls class Liddy Lehman of the boys class. nearly all of both classes were saved during that meeting. I was 14 years old I'll never forget the change that came over me, when I joined in singing. "I've anchored my soul in the Haven of rest" we had a junior League for us younger ones. Aunt Mary Allen was our leader. Nora was of the older set that had Epworth League. later they wanted us to go into E. L. we did not want to but they tried to reason with us. so we were just pushed into it. Aunt Chat Lyman, was such a good old soul. whenever she said my soul says "Praise the Lord" she would start jumping. she bounced like a rubber ball. I have seen her fall across a couple seats, stiff as a board her face as white as snow. pretty soon she would say whooee. start jumping again. we had an Organ but traded to Frank Beck in Lancaster for a Piano. Kirby Wolf could play every thing he ever heard. Will Finkey was telegraph operator at Haydenville and roomed with Kirby they would come up some time and play a little duet. and some times, we would have cream and cake. when we lived where I was born. Nora went to her first term of school to Jennie Dollison. at Stiers school. later Charlie Cox taught Stiers school. several boys from Haydenville went there too Cox was very strict. on the last day, most of them spoke a piece Joshua Lehman, thot he would be cute. he spoke "Oh Lord of Love look from above" and pity us poor scholars. who hired a fool to teach our school and gave him $30.00 The crow flew north the crow flew south with Charlie Cox in his mouth but when he found he caught a fool he ~~[illegible]~~ dropped him down in Stiers school. then Cox jerked him out of his seat and gave him a hard whipping. I have heard Arlie McFadden laugh about that lots of times.

Moral is - dont try to beat your teacher.

Maude Mc Fadden would Come
to our house and stay a week
or more, and Nora and I would
go to Nelsonville and visit Maude
the neighbor kids would Come
over under Uncle Jims Grape
Harbor. we played store and
Pins for Money. Mulligan kids
pulled some green grapes. Uncle
Jim was so mad: aunt Dill told
him Maude and I did not do
it, he knew he did not dare to
whip the other kids, so he
whipped Maude & I both. Nora was
real sorry for us. but Could
not do any thing about it, we
both wished we were home. But
had to wait till our time was
up, and Dad Came after us. I
used to visit other Cousins and
they Came to our house, But I
was always glad to get back
home, Nolas gang played the
Peak Sisters. Haydenville had a
Band, they practiced in one of the
school rooms Nora & I would stand
outside and listen to them, The ladies
of the church would have ice cream
suppers and the band would always

10.

Play that evening, then in return they could have all the cream & cake they could eat. The people of the community would always donate milk, cream, eggs & sugar, and some of ladies would make custard and we made our own ice-cream. The Band boys were, George Smith Bass drum, Joshua Lehman played Tenor drum, Kin Poston, son Bert Todd Wolf, John, Bert Wolf, Asa Lehman Walter Bartholow, Frank Shaw, I think there was 15, but cannot remember any more names. I think about this time Nora and Henry got married in the Church by Rev B. F. Evans, and a reception at the house about 80 guests. Lowie allen & Sister Sarah helped Ma & I. we had Ham Sandwiches Baked beans, little sweet pickles Cake, pink & white ice cream. Lowie said Mary cut the pickles in two Ma said I have listened to you in every thing else, but I am not cutting these little pickles in two. Will Bartholow moved to Tarlton and we moved in their house. Walt was working at the store so he boarded with us. Ben Shrader was

11.

was meat cutter in Butcher
shops, he moved to Logan and
then they had Walt cut meat.
he bought some unbleached
Muslin, and we made him
several apron's. we starched
them. he was real proud of
his clean apron's. Kirby Wolf
got a Bicycle for me I paid
$26.00 for "The Clipper" Orange color
had Clincher tires. Walt always
kept it pumped up for me,
several girls had Bykes. Blanche
and Leah Allen, Mary and Kate
Thompson. Mae + Jessie Ruble
and Amanda Lehman. Amanda
and I went to Logan Decoration
day. went to aunt Kate Adkins
awhile. on Friday evening I went
on my Byke to Uncle Rob's and
gave Gertie a lesson. Sat morning
Came over to the Lock and gave
Carrie Cole and Lattie Campbell a
lesson, then drove horse over to
Laurel Run, up the big hill and
out on the Ridge gave Chloe Evans,
and Nellie Todd lesson's
Louise was born March 4th 1900.
aunt Lyde Wolf died May 1st 1900

12.

President William McKinley dies Sept 14th 1901 assassins Bullet in Buffalo, N.Y. they had Memorial services all over the U.S. I know we had to learn. "Lead kindly light" his favorite hymn. I think about this time Walt went to Columbus to work as traveling Salesman, and worked there till he retired, for Tracy Wells. When J. H. Westervelt was Pastor at Haydenville. my gang played the Peak sisters, Mrs Westervelt was our big sister. I was the one that giggled at every thing and still do. We were dressed, there were 12 of us in yellow Pink and Blue, 4 of each color, we had a hoop drill & they were covered with cheese cloth the color of our dresses. Mine was yellow.
Rev Westervelt preached a sermon, he said it was wrong for us to ride our Bicycles on Sunday. Mae Wolf was at our house that day, and I asked Ma if Mae & I could take a ride before supper & she said yes, I dont care Mae got Fannie Reuters Byke and I dont think we got father than the Church Mae caught her skirt, ~~tore~~ large 3 corner in it

13/

When I was about 19 yr old. I went to Indiana, on the train. I went some time in Nov and Came home just before Christmas. Uncle Sam let Omar have horse and buggy. and Omar, Pearl and I went to Craigville to revival services several nights. then one day Uncle Sam took Omar, Pearl, Eunice, Artie Shady and I to Bluffton and had our Pictures taken, and went to a Resturant for dinner, that was a treat, Uncle Ike, aunt Zelda had Blanche, I stayed there a lot Uncle Charlie and Aunt Rose, and Grandma Wolfe and Emily. we all went to Sunday school and Church in Tocsin. when I came home I stopped at Delaware, Uncle Lucius Alward Met me. it was real Cold snowy weather. aunt ann heated bricks put in buggy to keep our feet warm he had to drive 4 miles. I bet they wished I had went on home, but seemed to enjoy me being there, Ross Eckleberry worked for them and his Mother invited us down for supper. they

14

had an Organ, and wanted me to play Church songs so of Course I did. then I went down to Columbus and went to Uncle George McFaddens, Bertha, Ethel and I had a good time, one day Bertha + I were up street, she said Come in this drug store. I want to Indroduce you to Louie Smythizer he had real red hair. when we went out I said why did you say I was from Indiana. She said that sounds bigger. well you just Came from Indiana.
Soon after I Came home, I was Clerk in the Post Office for Kirby Stolf. I soon Could do all the work and I was appointed Post Mistress, my mother was my assistant, The office was in the front Corner of the store, with full glass window. Soon there were several Boys Came to work at the factory. Ed Calhoun from Columbus, was the youngest one Kirb always had some one room with him so he took Ed he got so much clay dust in his hair, and Kirb would wash his hair every night. he worked at the dry pan where they ground Clay.

15

There was a big chunk that had to be broke. instead of throwing the belt off. he took a pick to break it and it pulled him in and crushed him so bad. they carried him on stretcher past my window. he was turning his head from side to side just begging the boys to kill him. they got Dr. But all he could do was give him something to ease the pain, he lived about 2 hrs. Ed was a nice quiet Boy, evry body liked him. and felt very bad about his death. The other boys that came were, Charlie Sheldon from athens. Nate Cox, Sherman McDowell. Bill Milstead, Grant Phillips, Bert Horn. Birch Noble, Bill Hartzell. John Terry. Then they moved the Post Office in a Corner of Co. Office, a dark place I did not like, and I had the Phones to take care of.
George Finney was tellegraph Operator, we had 5 trains a day 7:15 A.M - 10 o'clock A.M - 12 noon, North 5:28 South and 6 o'clock north. There was no register ~~clerk~~ clerk on 12 noon I sent all registered mail on 6 o'clock North. one night George went up home

16.

and left Fred the boy who helped him to throw mail bag on, next morning for some reason he went to Station first on the track found mail bag. over he Came. Fannie did you have registered mail last night? Yes, $80.00 in Gold for goodness sake get this open. Oh! I said it is all right the Bag is not Cut. and it was 4 $20.00 Gold pieces. Well when you have register mail tell me I sure will. we talked about that lots time. I never will forget it. the Company wanted to get rid of thier Gold and I traded them paper money, not near so much writing, when you send coins. I was not in that dark Corner so long till they moved me down in the brick that used to be the Dr. Office and they moved the Phones down too. I had 2 room's that way. I could keep all the old records in there records from the first Post Office. I think Harvy Groce was P.M. and of Course my recordes are there now too. and now I think how we had to use Pen and ink - Nelsonville got new Post-office boxes, then they wanted to know if I Could use more, I think there were 17 boxes for $10.00 Dad thought I

17.

better get them and I did
aunt Maria had a Birthday
Party for Bernice. Blanche Allen
was working for Ma. George
said Fannie I will take you
and Dr. will take Blanche
It was rainy but Dad let us
go any way. Dr. Slipped + fell
going down hill. had to stand
in front of grate fire and get
dry. it rained so hard washed
foot log away. then we had to
go thru tunnel going home.
Dr told Blanche for his girls
to soak our feet in real warm water
and put some mustard in it
so we would not take cold.
Gertie Wolf and Gar Adcock were
married in church before this
some time, and lived on Gars
old home place, out from Logan
One Sunday Pa + Ma. Love and
I went on my Byke. Blanche allen
went with me as far as her Uncle
Jim allens, when we started
home, I stopped for Blanche, John
was working in Haydenville. so
he started with us, but when we
got to Postoria he said, I will ride.

faster than you girls so I am
going on, you two are getting wet.
we took our time, and got home
before it rained any way. after
Nora got married I wanted to stay
home, not go to school, I had to do
a little crying and a lot of begging
But promised to go on in music.
I went to Logan on afternoon train
took lessons of Mabel Hoyt, but I
only took a few till she married
Clarence McCray, and moved to
Columbus, Ma wanted me to take
lessons from Florence Bright but
I begged off again. Promised to do
what I could my self. which I did.
when I took lessons of Mr Monce
he said if I could work my fingers
as fast as I could read music
I would make a good musician
Ma and Mrs Reuter thot they would
like to learn to ride Bicycle, one
evening Ma + I went up as far as
the church. I got her on and she
was doing real good but when
she seen she was ahead of me
she started to wobble, and went
off the road and fell in the sharp
weeds, hurt her head that ended it

I always kept all my Postal supplies in the Co. safe. and after I moved in the brick office, I still took my money box up at night, and in the winter when it was dark. George always said you wait for me I'll go up with you. one night he said the freight will be a little late tonight, but you wait till I Come there are two tramps getting ready to stay in the warm Kilns, and they may be over in town after bit. George and I worked together so much, it was like being in the same office. George was big brother and Boy Friend, all Rolled into one. Willis allen. and George were special chums, and so was mayme Kizer and I. we had a lot of jolly times together. there were Birthday parties, Class Parties We played Flinch once in a while had taffy pulling. Nell King was my Clerk. sometimes the Post office Inspector would Come, I was a little nervous at first. he always said you have

20.

your office in good shape, and your book work done. Well I do that each morning and so does my clerk. "well that is fine." so Nell and I did not care at all after that. during Christmas season, the 5:28 or old 37 would be 1 or 2 hrs late. no matter how late it was we had to wait for the mail. Mr Thompson ask us to write a list of as many names as there were that got mail he sent them to a soap co, and soon every body got a bar of soap. another time it was a sample of medicine "666" there would always be a big mill sack full, so that kept us busy for awhile. Nellie Ohlinger was born, Oct 8th 1903. one year during Lancaster Camp meeting Mrs Ed Lehman and the boy's had a cottage and went to attend all services. Mr Lehman was Bank Boss. there was a place in the roof that did not look safe he gave it a tap, and it all fell crushing him, the men had a hard time getting the slate off him and had to put him in a little Coal Car.

21-

to bring him out of the mine-
sent for Mrs Lehman and the boys
they Came on late train. Pa + Henry
got little engine out took them
home. they made several trips to get
thing's for the undertaker. he had a
hard time getting his body to look
right. soon after that Bert started
going with me. he still wrote to his
girl Friend Ora Rickey for awhile, and
after a while decided to stay with the one
where he was working, but soon went
to Logan to work at Carpenter trade with
Uncle Bill Huggins, Walter Sanner was
going with Mae Ruble. by the next
year we were both planning to get
married. we were both Canning Peaches
Walter worked below Nelsonville and
started to jump a coal train to Come
to see Mae, but fell under wheels
and that cut both his leg's off.
he soon bled to death. Bert and
Uncle Bill have worked for Estella
Linton, they had a tent just below
her house close to a swamp- When
they started working at Mt Pleasant
school. Bert had my Byke and stayed
at his home. but both soon got sick
with Typhoid fever both were very

22.

sick- but got well. I was in the Post office
till Sept 1st. made my last postal report
then I was free. Bert and I married
Nov 23rd on my 23rd Birthday. It was
day before Thanksgiving. I got some
nice Gifts. Kirby Wolf and Effie Wolf
stood up with us. Dad + Mom gave us
$10.00 Nora + Henry a nice big rug. aunt
Maria's a pretty Picture. Uncle Rob and
Girls silver knives + forks. Kirby a
real nice stand. Mr Jones + Emma butter
knife and sugar shell. Jim Pearly - Dish
Dr and Mrs Wood Cream + sugar. Reuter
and Girls, silver fruit basket and
George Finney silver Pudding dish
Henry and Gertie Woodworth. Cream
and sugar, Carrie Sheldon a dish.
We went to Berts parents Thanksgiving
after dinner. Mother Horn gave us
Sheets, Pillows + Cases, quilt and Comfort
sister Bertha a nice lamp + glass pitcher
we went to Logan Saturday. went to aunt
Rachel Moore's and she told us that Uncle
Rob's house burned down while he and
the girls were over to Haydenville to
the Pathfinders Club. 2 boys that worked
for him got Mae's sewing machine out. Mae +
Uncle stayed at our house. They brought
Mae's machine over and she had a lot

23

of things to make. Bed clothes and evry thing, clothes to wear. Effie Came down Friday eve then Saturday morning Mac + Effie walked over to thier farm, they had another small house, and they cleaned that and got into that as soon as they could. then on Dec 15th Ma went to Logan to do her Christmas shopping, fell on the ice going over to the Depot and broke her left arm dislocated her shoulder. She had a basket with some dishes in and did not break any thing Louise still has one dish. she had that cast on for a long time. then in March Bert and I went to house keeping in Logan We rented of Ella Blosser $8.00 a month in advance, Bert worked at Carpenter for Charlie Stephenson $1.50 a day John Cramblit worked with Bert too. so his wife Ethel and I got acquanted we played Flinch a lot. Stevie paid the boys evry Saturday evening Ethel and I would go up st. after Charles was old enough to ride in his baby carriage the Boys would give us some money, we would get ice cream one got it one night

and the other the next time. we
lived at Blossers over 2 years. we
lived there when there was a flood.
Bert and George Wright was doing the
finishing in the ambrose hotel
when he came to dinner he said
why dont you & Lulu have Mrs Blosser
keep the babies and go and see
the water. he & George had took off and
seen how it was. so Lulu & I did
but the night before Kirb and Dr.
Little came up on evening train
and the train could not go any farther
so Kirb & Dr came to our house and
stayed all night they wanted Chub
Tucker to go with them, he said no
that will be too many to go in on
Bert. he had to climb up on a barrel
in the freight room & sit all night
then he said I wished I was over to
Bert Horn's too. the boys all walked
home next day. the Rail road bridge
above Logan washed out. when they
got word Rush Creek was coming
in soon. they knew that bridge
would not be safe. Nelsonville and
athens was awful hard hit too. we
moved up on North Mulberry st and
Blanche Mitchell helped us move.

25.

in Kesslers house, we lived there
little over 2 yrs, Ruth was born
there. Bertha Lehman lived on the
same st. a few houses below me
and she Came up and helped me a
good many times. one day she
Came up and said, I have nice
Clean water, so I am going to
wash your rug's for you, and
she would Come and do part of
my ironing for me. The termites
would swarm, each spring. They
Came out from under the door
Caseing in the dinning room. I
would get teakettle of boiling water
and killed most of them. when Ruth
when 4 months old, we moved to
Haydenville. there were no empty
houses so we moved in with Ma.
they were building new houses and
Jim White was Boss. Bert worked
for him, and he wanted his wife
and boy's to Come for summer &
he asked Bert if he would let them
have enough furniture to do them
for the summer. there was a little
white house empty. the Co moved
the things up. Nora & I Cleaned
and fixed evry thing to look nice

26.

even put a doily with vase of flowers on the table. we thought surely, as part of our furniture was there, we would get that house. Nora and I both talked to Herbert Elliott. we stayed with Ma till Ruth was 2 yrs old and then we moved to the Kreitz farm, we had a wonderful time there. a large Orchard with every kind of apple you could think of. Bert bought a lot in the Wright addition, and was going to build our own house, he asked Mr Elliott about building block, and he priced them to Bert, but when he asked where he was going to build, Bert said in the Wright addition he said well if you build there you wont have any more work there. "tough luck," I'm sure that it was. so we sold the lot to Levi Bond. we had a couple cows sold milk at Haydenville. one time Bert said why dont you take a few dozen corn too. when Harts came out to get thier milk, I said would you want roasting ears? yes, she took a dozen in, but when

27.

she asked how much they were, I said .20 she cam back with the corn, Mother said it was too much. I rember when the U. S. Battle Ship Maine Xploded in Feb, 16th, 1898. That started the Spanish War, Joushua Lehman, Frank Johnston & Arlie Mc Fadden all 3 went from Haydenville. Floyd Vore married Alice Sewenkie they moved to Haydenville, Floyd worked in the store. Alice was Pregnant he told Bert to keep her in fresh corn. he wanted her to have all she could eat. after Jim White left, Frank Lewis was Boss Carpenter, Lewis was real nice. Elliott was movingout and T. D. Brown was taking his place. Lewis laughed to Bert, they were working in the yard, right under Elliotts. Nose fixing up for Mr Brown to move in. then we got to move to Haydenville in a little Brick house next to Ed Cooley. when Ruth was 4 yrs old we went to Indiana on a two weeks visit. had a wonderful time. Charles was 6 yrs old and started to school. Georgia

Hickman from Nelsonville taught the Primary room. she came up on 7 o'clock train stayed at our house till school time, then school-out 3. P.M. and she waited with me till 5:28 train later Marie Mooney came with Georgia taught school & waited at our house. Alvira McCarty was Principal and she took her meals with us, and had a room at Ben Scharaders. another time, Mary Kreig from Logan taught and she boarded with us. she went home Friday evening and came back Sunday eve, on late train. and Bert would go over to meet her. she appreciated it. sometimes it was so dark and stormy. Mary was a real nice girl. When Ruth was 8 yrs. old, William was born. Nov 30th 1915. when he was 2 yrs old we bought a house of Uncle John Wolf, next to Oren and Jennie Patton. and close to Uncle Eli Patton. aunt Hester was gone, alf Woods stayed with him. and Ellen Smith his Grandauter kept house for them. Mary Zinn got sick and Ellen went to Columbus to take care of her. Uncle Eli asked me

29.

to milk morning and evening we were getting 1 qt of them each evening. but he had me take a quart each time I milked. While we lived there Ruth had the scarlet fever. Ben Biddle was our Dr. he had me bathe Ruth every day, then go over her body with Carbulated vaseline. and all the dishes she used to eat with, to scald them 15 Min kept the other two out of her room. we had 2 nice sour Cherry trees there Early Richmand and Montmorency in the front yard. when Bert picked them, one of the Jones boys was under the tree, Cherries was pretty ripe and shattered off. he kept eating them as fast as they would fall. Bert said if they boy dont have the Belly ache tonight it will be a wonder. while we lived at Haydenville Miss Hoover Came and organized a Lady Maccabee Lodge. I joined. we held our meetings in the I.O.O.F. hall. The Odd Fellows used to have family night once a year. and every body. took a basket of food. The Lodge would buy Oysters too.

30.

Elsie and artie moved from Union Furnace over. and did not live far from us. Paul was born there. we had a big garden, and a large lawn. had a Croquet set. that was quite an attraction for kids. Bert played with the Children but I never Cared much for it. before I was married the Church. had Pie socials and Box-suppers. Tom McFadden, Dick Reider, Joshua Lehman, George Smith and others I forget some of them had a play "Ten nights in the Bar room" Later, Noras bunch played the "Peake Sisters" after a few years my age groupe played the same. Nora and her girls and Hilda, Bert and I and our two used to go to "Buzzards Glory" up to the top of a real high hills among real large rocks and there was such lovely wild Columbine grew there, we went time after time, never seen a snake. artie + Elsie, Nora and Girls. Bert and I and our two, picked huckle berries one Sunday afternoon, we sure had some pies, but we all got so many giggers. it wasn't funny-

When William was 4 yrs old.
Bert got the farm fever. so
we traded our home to Harry
Heinline for the farm, he had
just bought from his Dad.
then we moved to Mt Pleasant.
was just one mile from church
we walked it lots of times. we
had a buggy, but Bert bought
a surry with the fringe on top.
They repaired the church, Bert,
albert Reddick and Oll Durbin.
did the work. when it was done.
They had a minister come to
Dedicate it. But they still owed
$100.00 This minister suggested
we go down to the hall, and
Organize a "Ladies aid" which
we did & went in as a Charter
member, and still pay my dues.
but now I seldom attend meetings
The neighbors all helped each
others, butchering, threshing
or whatever there was to do.
aunt Sallie gave us several cans
of Grape butter. she would come
when we butchered and clean
the tapes, and we would stuff
the sausage in the evening

32

Ruth went to school one term
Vance Griffith started that year.
The Ladies aid had suppers and
entertainments to raise money.
One time Gretha Schorr and I
made Oyster soup and fried
Oysters, I made each of us a
apron and cap out of the
unbleached muslin. the other
ladies served sandwiches
Pie, Cake and Coffee. we always
had a good sized crowd and
very seldom had any thing
left over. we had a play one time
"sewing for the heathen". I was
Mrs Judd-Ruth was my maid
she had just come from Germany.
and was dutcher than Sour
kraut. I was to serve lunch.
Ruth said over in germany.
ve had veniers. we had to
practice a lot, so the ladies
kidded me about refrestments
so I said all right, I will
bake a Chocolate Cake and
and bring ½ gal of Cold tea.
so when it was time to serve
She gave each one Cake and
tea, there were 12 or 14 ladies

3B

then we pulled the curtain, and the
audience, said awwwe, we had
hired an Orcharstra and they played.
We did evry thing we could to raise
money. ~~Once we had an Oyster
supper Iretha Shorr & I made soup
and fried Oysters. I made aprons
and Caps out of unbleached muslin
for us 2 to wear. the other ladies
served, Sandwich, Cake, & Pie then~~ one
time we had a supper, and Program
Bill Shorr, Bert, Charles, Dwight and
Ken Huggins, Joe Sain, Vern Stalker
and Clyde Johnston, had colored false
faces, sang. "Who broke dat lock
on de hen house door." then one
time we had a "kitchen Cabinet"
Orcharstra. we had a man's coat on
and we sewed those little tin ~~spoo~~
spoons two rows of them up the
front. each had a jazz blow.
and used kitchen utensels, Clarence
allen had the store, he let Ruth have
a new galvanised tub for bass drum
we took wodin Potato masher and
wrapped it heavy. Dessie allen had a
dish pan for tenor drum. Ruth and
I could play several nice duets.
and we played them for church too.

34

I really liked it at the farm.
Ruth and I did a lot of outside
work, but Ruth did not like to
pick berries, or wash the cream
seperator. but we cultivated with
old Charlie horse. and helped
with the hay too. we moved to
the Heinlien farm at close of
World war 1- soon after my Dad
had a stroke. was parlized from
his hips down. Henry and Nora
had to help Ma. soon the I.O.O.F
sent a day nurse. he came at 8-
or 8:30 By that time she had
Dad up + breakfast over. he was
there for dinner and supper
that left Ma to get Pa to bed
after awhile she said he is not
helping and I have him to
Cook for. the Co wanted them
to take a smaller house. We
all talked it over. Pa said Bert
I will give you $100.00 if you will
build another room on and
we will Come over there. We all
sorta had our Irish up. so
William and I went over and
I said we came to help pack up
he was real glad. I said we will

35.

stay all week. Sat you will be
ready to go to Nora's, and we
will go back home. The tears
ran down his face, and he
said that will be fine. Ma
Nora and I really got busy
ma sold a few things, gave
several things to friends, and
we put in one little room
the things they wanted to bring
to our house for thier room.
on Saturday they were ready
to go to Nora's. William and I
went home. They stayed one
month with Nora. they came
to our house. Bert got the room
built. Dad enjoyed being there
on the farm and watch threshing.
after they were done, he said
Fannie I can tell you how much
wheat you had - we had lattice
work around the porch - evry
time they put ½ bu in grainry
he put a mark down. Joe Sain
was a little late, so he had to
carry 1 bushel his first trip.
Pa lived 18 months after he came
to our house. died in October 24
1923. after Pa was gone Ma

36

stayed with Nora in the winter
and with me in the summer.
We had a sale in Feb, we had stock
to sell and farm equipments, so
we moved to East 2nd St Logan O.
and Carl was born May 8th 1925.
Charles worked for Gabriel in lunch
Counter. Bert had a sick spell. Dr
was afraid he was taking typhoid
again but soon got over it. that
was in august, and Charles left
Logan then with a picture agent,
But he soon found out he was not
honest and left him. he was in
York Pennsylvania. Met Roy Lewis
and they both enlisted in the
U. S. Marines for 4 years, they
trained at Paris Island, he earned
enough Credits that he could take
a Course in an armory school.
in Pennsylvania. from there he
went to San Diego California.
from there he went over sea on
Transport ship "The Henderson".
They landed in Shanghai China
the day Grandpa Horn was buried
the first of May then he soon went on
up to Tiensin, went in barges at night
I think there is where they had to

37-

Carry, John D. Rockefeller's oil out of a burning building, The Chinese are no fire fighters, but had hose and kept water on the boy's while they worked, next morning there was oil on the river. The boy's again were called out they worked in water waist deep to put sand bags on the keep oil from spreading, and this was Christmas day 1928. in the mean time, we had moved to East Main st was there two years, then moved to Corner of Furnace & Church st. next to Ed and Ottie Keller, then I got so tired living in town, with other children coming to play & getting to fuss and having trouble I wanted take children and spend the summer on our farm. But Grandma Horn's house was empty there by Danes, so he told Bert why dont you move out here, and we did, lived there about 3 years, we had a large melon patch and had bushels of melon's did not sell any we give every body all they wanted. When Charles was out of the

36.

Marines, he worked in a clothing store in California, but soon started ~~loving~~ driving a team for Barnum and Bailey Circus when they got to Wenatchee Washington. there were people working in the apple Orchard and he decided he would stop and work there too. Mrs Fleming Started keeping boarders and Charles boarded with them. he soon chose Ida Mae, for his wife. they were married on New Years day then the following Nov. They Came to Ohio. we were living at Mother Horns home. Charles wanted to work the coal, so we moved back to our farm. then Charles Jr was born June 22nd 1932. When Charles was 2 yrs old they went to work in the Oil field Mich Then Feb 27th 1936. Patty was born. then on Christmas, 1936 I had all of our family home. this was the last time we were all together. January 27th 1937. William and Arthur Kalklosch, left for arkansas to visit Arthur's aunt Mamie Reed. on March 4th William had to be rushed to hospital for appendicitis Operation on March 6th he passed

39

away. Blood clot on his heart, he was sent home and funeral on Wednesday March 10 th 1937 soon after that Ida had a severe sick spell nearly took her life but Thank the Lord she is still here. after she got well she and children went to Washington Charles went to South America to work. when he came home stopped at Ruth's. was sick with that tropical fever. Don soon came to Ruth's and they got him in a hospital. soon as he got better came down home to see us. when he felt able to travel. he went to Washington and joined the family, and got work. I think Ruth and Don were married soon and Ruth still worked at Lazarus for awhile. Ma and I would take the sled and old Charlie get 3 bushel of apples, Peel and core them to make apple butter the next day. Bert always enjoyed helping with that, he worked in

40

Logan. But would be up early and built the fire and get a kettle of apples on before going to work. that was the year we made one kettle full for Elsie. and 2 or 3 more kettles full. all together we made 26 gal. Nora got some she came and stayed all night and we helped her make a kettle full. Henry liked it so well. he used to help his Mother make it they called it "Pomeroy salve" Nora and Henry had a filling station down by Stiers Crossing Nora and Girls Came on Sunday afternoon and lots of times brought a big piece of ice. Carl and I would not be long getting a freezer of Cream made. Later on Bert was out of work nothing he could get. he said why dont you write your sister ask her if they would loan us $10.00 or bring groceries and we would pay soon as we Can. so over Come Nora and Nellie with box of Groceries and $10.00 said Henry sent Groceries dont want any thing for them.

41.

Nora helped Henry at the filling station. he liked to have her down there with him, and on Nov 8th 1939. Henry went hunting with Jim Farley. when ready to go back to Station, they parted on the hill Farley went down in Haydenville and Henry started to the station, a boy Came running down, said Henry Ohlinger is up on the hill dead. several rushed up where was got him home Called the Dr. and he really had passed away. supposed it was a heart attack. that was a terrible blow for Nora and the girls. Freda Matheny and Mary Fisher Came over the next morning and told us. after they got thier business straightened up. they hired some one in the filling station for a while. then Nellie and Nora took it over. But they soon Changed the high way. that cut a lot of the traffic off. then they Closed it because it did not pay them to keep it open. Ma was with me Bert had bought me a rug loom. Paid $15.00 got of Mr archer, we

42.

liked it very much this was 1938.
Carl made the first rug. Bert made
rug's too. and Ma made a couple.
I made lots of rugs. people brought
sewd rag's for me to make. and I
Charged 40 a yard for weaving and
furnished the warp. but prices
Continued to rise on every thing so
I had to Charge more for weaving
I had to pay more for the warp
I have made an awful lot of rugs.
I do not take custom work any
more. But I have a lot of ~~[illegible]~~
nice rags sewed. and I am making
some rugs for some of the family
Bert bought a John Deere tractor
of Delbert Davis. he and Carl did
quite a lot of farming put out
Corn, made Hay. they soon traded
the first Tractor and got a larger
one. I remember riding the hay
rake and tripping it every little
bit. I liked to work outside. We
always had Chicken's and pigs. and
Cows. I made a lot of cottage cheese
most always had some ready to put
the Cream in on Sunday. there would
be some one Come I wanted to give
some too. they were always glad to get.

Then we went to the Heinleine
farm, I wanted to raise turkeys
Uncle Ike Wolfe in Indiana
got me 2 white Holland hen's
and a Gobler, and I really
enjoyed raising them, they
were so tame. the little poults
would jump on your hand, or
in your lap when you ~~stoped~~
stoop down, to feed them, when
they were half grown, and you
would call. peep, peep, peep- they
would fly all over you. I fed
them cottage cheese with lots
of pepper, cut up green onion
tops, and small am't of sand.
I had 9 or 10 to sell besides a
couple we ate, I sold them
to Ed Ohlinger who had a
grocery store in Logan. got
\$30.00 for them. then later we
raised Bronze turkeys, Charles
and Ida was there, Charles and
William teased the old Gobler
he was cross, he jumped up
at Charles, struck a match he
had in his pocket Carl was
afraid of him. Bert said get
a stick and give him a whack.

44

he sure did give him a whack
he fell down. Carl was afraid
he had killed him but he
soon got up. when I would
be at the grainry and start to
the house, if he started with me,
I took hold of his neck and
lead him clear up to the
steps, then he would go back
down. he really expected me to
lead him up, the Bronze grew
fast and got real big but were
not so tame. I got so many
eggs of the white ones. Maynard
Stone and Lena Griffith both
got a setting 11-eggs a setting. 2.50
Lena had a good hatch. and
they were doing fine, but the
foxes got some, you cant
hardly pen them up. we raised
Chickens too. we had white Rocks
there was one little rooster
it was so sassy always, pick you
just wanted its fight we called
it Hitler. we had Cows. had a
Cream seperator. "The Butter Fly" real nice
we sold Cream to Pickerington Creamry.
I think we all enjoyed being on the
farm. had lot of Chestnuts at first.

45

Bert bought a John Deere tractor of Delbert Davis, they did a lot of work with it. Carl ploughed with it. we had a large truck patch, one year we had sweet Corn. Potatoes, sweet Potatoes. I had several rows of broom Corn. we planted musk Melon's and water Melon's had a Dixie queen that weighed 26 lbs. Bert helped Carl pull the ripe ones at night and Carry them to the top of the hill. next morning Carl and I would put them in the cellar. they traded the small tractor for a larger one. on Dec, 7th 1941 - The Japs bombed Pearl Harbor. shot down the plane that Colon Kelley was flying. killed him. then that started World war II. Bert worked on the high way the following summer. he boarded at Charlie Millers on Main st. one evening he took real sick, had Dr. he said you have the Flu, and will have to stay in bed, well I want to go home. well get Heinlein and wrap up warm. so at

46

8 o'clock he got home. we had Dr.
ever so many times, but he
kept getting worse. then Dr said
he had Pneumonia. Carl and I
stayed up evry night. he was
Chokeing up so I thot may be
he had asthma. Carl went in
town on his Bicycle got more
medicine then we had Dr out
again. but on Thursday he was
worse. Carl called aunt Elsie and
uncle artie to come to stay
with us that night. he passed
away just before they got there.
then Artie went up and called
Heinlein and got Dane. Harry
said he was filled with poison
from his abdomen to his heart.
Nellie came and stayed with
us. Ruth came and stayed
with us till Wednesday after the
funeral - Bert died Nov 19th 1942.
The funeral was, Nov. 22nd just
the day before my Birthday and
our 38. wedding aniversary.
Carl and I stayed on the farm
that winter. I had raised such
nice Giant Pascal celery that year
I kept banking it up. then one day

Bert said mom I am going
to bank your Celery real good
for you. he put boards on each
side, and filled in nearly to the
top. but we had so much on
our minds, we forgot it, and
the tops froze a little, but we
put it in the cellar, had all
we could use, and gave every
body celery that wanted it. then
in March we moved to Ewing.
Carl still had the tractor. and did
work for several over there. we had
a big garden he ploughed, we
had a nice Jersey Cow. there
was a big pasture field and a
creek for water. on Mothers
day Nora and Girls brought
Ma over. they said Ma is not
very good, she seems so restless
at night. so on Tuesday I seen
she was sick. I sent for the Dr
and Nora. Dr said I dont think
she will be here very long. she lived
13 weeks. Carl was 18 the 8th of May
and went in the service aug 12th
Ma died aug 26th then on Labor
day. Nora and girls helped me
move to Mt Pleasant Nora

48

stayed till Wednesday, after she went home. I realized how lonely it was not to have any body with you. I tried to be brave, but was a little afraid any way. I was close to Church and Cemetary. that helped. Pauline and Ralph Wadsworth aunt Sallie, Lottie Engle, and Fred and Ruby Davis. Carl trained at Fort McCellan Alabama. there is where he broke his collar bone. he was home a couple days, then went to Fort Ord California from there was sent over Seas. Bert's sister Alice came and she helped me finish up my Canning. then in October I went to Washington and stayed with Charles and Ida that winter. Ida was working and buying a house. at the beginning of world war II. Charles was welder in Todd ship yard. they soon decided to buy a small farm Near Renton had cows, but had to haul water for stock. they had a chance to work on a Dairy ranch for Mr Newby. they took cows

49

and moved up there the spring
of 1944. I went out there in
October 44. and spent the winter
they had an awful bad house
to move into. Newby was
building a new one. Floyd
Fletcher, and Ray Willkes were
Carpenter and Electritison. We
were sure glad to get
moved into the new one.
Charles and Ida got up at
4 o'clock. went down to milk
I got up later got breakfast
for the children, helped to get
them off to school. then they
Came from the barn. I fried
pancakes and eggs for them.
Charles, Ida, Mr Newby and
sometimes his son Jim.
We were there till January 1st
Newby did not live up to
his Contract. so Charles quit.
But he did take the cows.
Charles went up to diablo
and got work that very day.
then we moved to "Concrete".
rented of Nell Quackenbush
and her Brother Cliff. Charles
had to batch at Diablo

he came down home evry two
weeks. then some times Ida
would go up there. once we all
went. Ida and I went way up
the mountain. Crossed sour
dough, and Damnation Creek.
we made snow balls and we
said hope we dont see any
bears. when we got back, the
neighbors said, you were lucky.
there has been bears down all
ready, getting into peoples
garbage cans. one time, I want
you to go up this week, with
Charles. you will soon go home
we baked an angel food cake got
a dressed chicken. Charles had an
Electric stove. I had chicken done.
but noticed something on top
of oven. I thot maybe I had
better pull that, I should left it
alone, he had to have some one
fix- but he also had a hot-
plate, so I cooked potatoes
made gravy, and Coffee. I
was starting home on Saturday
before Easter Sunday. Ida and
Children were going up to be with
Charles. I had my Easter on the

51.

train. I sure enjoyed the
trip. you always meet nice
people. a lady and her daughter
got on at Wilmer, Minesota
were going to Portland. Oregon.
the Mother said so many people
are going to get off 10 min. at
Spokane, Irma wants to get
off but I dont want too. I'll
get off with her, no, I wont
let you two get off by yourself.
so she got off with us. we all
went in the depot when we all
got off the tracks, they closed the
big iron gates, now see where we
are, we laughed, they wont leave
us. The engine went on up and
got water, when they came back
and opened the gates I think she
was the first one out. Ida and
Children Beulah + Joe. met me at
Seattle, we went to Ida's Mothers
then she went with us. stopped
some place on the way and ate
dinner. then I spent a week
with Ida's Mother 2 different
times, she was working in the
Salvation Army store. I liked being
there with her some times

52.

I am not getting this written
the way I should. I write
something down. then think
of something happened long
before that. But I do want to
record this. when we first
moved down to Haydenville
the old Canal run thru the
town. it was not long till
I took Maliria fever. I had a
Chill evry other day. my fever
would be 104- two times it
was 106- we always had Dr
he got fever down in a hurry.
aunt Sarah Matheny told Ma
to give me 1 tablespoon of
water before breakfast and
each morning increase it one
till the 9 the morning I took 9-
and I never had a chill after
that- this sounds like a fairy tale
But it is true. I should know
"I was the victim." I was still
in a weak Condition. Dr gave
me medicine and said she
will be alright. but let her have
her way as much as you can.
they never told me till a long
time after that. or I might

53.

have did more things I wanted too. I remember having Scarlet Fever, Whooping Cough, Mumps, the old fashioned measles, and the 3 day measles. my hair Came out in bunches & Dad took me two different times and had it cut and I remember he was a colored Barber, "Old Dick Ramsey." then one time in January I was in bed 3 or 4 days with La Grippe had a terrible pain in my head. Dr had me start at 4 o'clock in morning taking quinine. and he said you will still have that pain each morning even after you go back to the Office but it did not last so long and it was less severe.

I will try and start where I left off. Rouna was born april 10th 1943. I went up and stayed one week Glen Huggins stayed with Carl in Ewing- then in May was when Ma Came over. Carl left Aug 12th for the service. Ma died aug 26th. then Una and Girls helped me move over to

54.

Mt. Pleasant. I had a large garden there and enjoyed working in it. I canned a lot of vegtables. had a few Raspberries, had some good pies and jelly. I spent a lot of time with Ruth and Nora and Girls. The W.S.C.S. bought the old School House and we had meetings out there Lottie Engle and I would go out on Tuesday and sweep and clean up then the members would each fix something, and we had dinner, regular meeting after that. Lucy Stone was President for a long time. Viola Smith Secy and I was Treas. for 4 years. We had lot of fun doing our work together. but we were ~~always~~ always .02 ahead. Lottie and I kept the building clean, built fire in the winter. some of the members thot we aught to be paid 50 apiece we got that for awhile then some one kicked on that, and we said forget it. we will do that any way. later on Lottie was not able to help. Ethel Rimmer moved by me so Ethel and I kept it clean. Ethel was President for a good while and so

\

55.

many times, when there was a
sale, our society served lunch
that sure was a lot of work,
I went with Nora and Girls up to
Perrysburg to Nellie & Bertha Lehman
50th Wedding aniversary, and also
one other time. then I have
gone with Louise and Cousins
a couple times since Nora & Nellie
is gone. I am just 5 days older
than Bertha. She has had arithitis
fell down basement steps and
broke her hip. got over that and
around again. then one day
not long ago, her right leg just
gave way, broke half way between
hip and knee, Dr put plate & screws
on the outside. but her bones are
so thin and brittle, 4 screws have
come out. Dr told nurses to not
get her up any. I do feel so bad
for her. she wont ever be able
to go back home any more. I
finally sold our farm to the
Central States Coal Co. before Carl
came home from the army. after
he was home awhile he started
going with Frances Bone, after awhile
they were married, and lived with

56.

me for awhile. Carl was working on Construction work. then got work with "Ohio Pipe Line" and soon learned welding, and is an extra good welder now. Barbara was born Dec 2nd 1947 Frances wanted to live at Bloomingville, so they moved there, things did not work out too good. so Carl came back home got a divorce. pretty soon we got Barbara. I must add Tom Liles was born before Barbara 1946 Frances married Bud Swackhamer after awhile they were divorced, and then remarried lived at Lancaster then Laurelville, on to Bloomingville then back to Lancaster. Barbara was changed around so much it was pity full she lived with Carl and I till She was in 8th grade, then her Mother took her they moved to Lancaster and she Graduated from High school there. we were all happy over that after 9 years Carl married Geraldine Gamble. They bought a farm near Illesboro, they had a cow. horse, and pigs, raised pigs for quite a while, Carl tried to farm some but that is up hill business. so

58.

any more. I stay with Carl and Jerry in the winter, and Ruth and Don in the summer. Charles married Ida Mae Fleming they have Charles Jr. + Patty, Orseth Charles Jr married Marylin King. they have Marcia Charles III Doug Lisa + Nancy Jo. Patty has Susie Cherry, Jerry and David. Ruth married Don Liles, they have Donna and Tom A. Donna married Leonard Heim they have Judy and Roger. Tom married Judy Miller they have Donnie. Carl married Frances Bone. have Barbara. she married Jim Iles and have Jodi + Jimmie They all have nice homes and doing fine. I have a nice room at Ruths a T.V. just 2 steps to Bath room and 2 steps to kitchen I do not know of any body that has it as nice as I do. and the Lord has blessed me with good health all these years. I am so Thankfull. there are so many real sick people. and a good many of them are much younger than I am. I almost forgot to mention that I have one great, great Gran Daughter

59.

April 26th 1969 Louise and I went to Tocsin Indiana to Ray and Nettie Wolf 50th wedding anniversary. visited Cousin Minnie Thompsons that evening then on Sunday went to church. then the reception in the afternoon. We stayed Sunday night, left at 8 o'clock Monday - got home about 3.00 P.M. We sure did enjoy our trip. I went over to Louise for Decoration day. and we went to athens to see Georgia Nida - found she was in a Presbyterian home in Columbus. after I came to Ruth's I wrote to her. she answered real soon. she likes it there and I know she is lots better off, than living alone. I am glad for her. she has 2 neices + 1 - nephew left. Charles Smith he took over and got her in this Presbyterian Home and she is very Thankfull.
This is Friday June 22nd Charles Jr Birthday 41 yrs old. we watched the Skylab astronauts splash down. + get on the ship. Charles "Pete" Conrad Joseph P Kerwin + Paul J Weitz. The U.S.S Ticonderoga.

60.

Saturday morning June 30th/73
Frances, Barbara and Children,
Came up after me, and I spent
the weekend with them. I
sure had a wonderful visit,
with them. we went down to
Lancaster sales in the evening.
Sunday a real nice day Jim
did some work for Frances.
then they had to do thier mowing
Monday July 2nd. Frances, Barbara
and Children brought me home.
Frances gave me 2 jigg saw
Puzzles. Monday July 23rd - 1973.
Capt-Eddie Rickenbacker died world
no 1- Flying ace, Heart failure in a
Zurich hospital Switzerland. he
was 82. he was Cremated and
his ashes will be brought to Cols
for burial he was a Columbus Boy.
Roger Heim has been playing
Base Ball. his team beat, they were
all given a trophy. he sure is
proud of his. here is something
that happened. when Barbara
was in the sixth grade she broke
her left elbow. at Enderles walking
on a barrel, she only missed a few
days of school. got along fine.

62

Donna has a good job she is accountant for the Kroger Co. Len is taking a Course in Electronics and will soon have a good job too. the Children are doing real well in school. Judy is sewing making her slacks for school. she has baked cookies for Ruth several times. you dont need ask what kind they are always Chocolate Chips. Saturday aug 25-1973 Charles Jr Horn and family drove in had station wagon + their Campers. we sure enjoyed them. Well. = =

Mike Gabor gives the weather on T.V. sometimes. but. "Poor Mike fell off his Byke and hurt himself Severely. He broke his hip + Cut his lip now he will pay for it quite Dearly In the Hospital 3 weeks. (Poor mike this is true

62.

on saturday Sept 15th a cousin Mabel Sonnenberg and husband Bob drove in from Uniondale Indiana just to see me. we had a nice visit. we did not get down to Haydenville for Home Coming at Church or over to Mt Pleasant either. Ruth did not feel able to drive. I guess evry one knows I am a jigg-saw Crank. Judy Liles and Tom sent me a extra pretty one flowers and Cactus, and it is so nice to work with. and they sent pictures of thier home and several pictures of the mountains and they certainly have a very pretty place to live. But they have rattle snakes out there. we do have a few here too. I surely rember the one I saw on our farm when I was picking Raspberry's. there was such nice big berries by a big log I started to pick I heard a rattle looked over top of bush there was a large "diamond back" it rattled again. I went over another place I only had bucket half full. I had our Sheapard dog. I waited a little then said take em out Bruno he went over a little and sniffed a little then Came back. I said all right Bruno Come on we are going back home. Bert said dont ever go over there again. we told Billie Schorr and he said I would like to have it to make a belt. Bert said that whole Corner is Yours berries + all he went up ever so many times with shot gun. never saw it. here is something else I want to mention the fall of 1915. just a short time before William was born. one Sunday afternoon. Bert said I will hitch Nellie horse up and take a ride you need some fresh air- so we got as far as the church when Nell started to stumble; and she had her head down just turned a somersault in the shaffs. we all got out Frank Wolf Came just then. helped Bert get her out of harness. She was just trembling. Ruth and I walked

64.

back home. This is Oct 4th 1973
Carl has been working in Mich
was home for a few days and
he and Jerry Came up a while
yesterday morning and this
morning Don Ruth got thier new
refrigerator very nice. I think of
something to Record. my Dad had
3 brothers, Isaac, Bill, and Joe. in
the civil war. all came home. and
Grandpa Tom had one brother Bert in the
army. he took measles and died.
my Mother remembers about
"Morgans Raid" they took evry thing
they Could get as they went. they
would leave thier tired worn out
horses + take farmers good horses.
Mr Washburn lived in Nelsonville
he had a grocery. his son Arthur
had a fine horse, they heard that
Morgan was Coming thru Nelso
Arthur rode his horse above
Nelsonville and into the woods
quite a way. they came to the
Store. Mr Washburn said take
any thing you want Boys but
for God sake dont make any
noise. I have a child at the
Point of death, with Small-Pox.

they sure left there in a
hurry. that was one time a
lie, was better than the truth.
I should tell about our boys
from Haydenville that went to
World war I - Dal Smart, Ralph
Walker, Irvin Matheny, Raymond
Auchauer, Guess Boy, and Skiver
Wesley King, Roy and Joshua Wolf Brothers
Clarence ~~went~~ Thompson and
Wilber Kreyseig went first in the
Rain bow, division, and from Logan
Raymond Hess and Claude Petitt.
Roy and Joshua Wolf and Raymond
Hess. were killed. the rest got home.
Raymond Auchauer drove the
amunition truck to the front then
after getting home, met a violent
death at Clay mine. Wilbur Kreyseig.
met his death in the Pentinsary fire
of Johnie Mc Sherry - was a sailor
on a Transport Ship - made 7 trips
across the Ocean, during the
war. then took his own life,
When Nora and I were kids - 7 and 12
on Christmas eve, we put four
plates out, in the morning, there
would be Candy, and nuts on
each plate, and a present for Nora & I.

66.

I think those were the good old
days, The children now would not
be satisfied with that. Nora and I
were all ways up before day light.
we would light the lantern and
go over to aunt Maria's and see
what they got. then on New years
we always got Candy and nuts.
when my Dad and Mother Came to
the farm to live with us. we saw
an advertisement in a magazine for
a knitter to knit socks it was $15.00
I had a heifer Calf, Bert said he did
not think it would make a good
Cow why dont you sell that to Hill
Sain & Marsh Steele to butcher they
will pay you $30.00 that will be
$15.00 for you $15.00 for Ruth and Ma
was going to put $15.00 so that will
get the knitter. so we did. and soon
were making nice wool socks. we
sent a bunch of socks to the Company
They paid us for some & returned
some they said were not perfect so
we soon seen, we were not making
money, but we make socks for the
family, but now I wonder what we
ever done with the knitter, I still
have a bunch of the needles.

67

Pa lived to be 74. he died in 1923 then Ma stayed with me in the summer. and Nora in the winter. Ma lived to be 89, died Aug 26th. Carl went in the Service in Aug. I moved to Mt Pleasant Close to church and Cemetary then when Carl was over Seas I went to Washington, and stayed that winter with Charles and Ida. when I came home, I spent a lot of time with Ruth, Nora and the girls. one time when Carl was 9 or 10. he hurt his finger. I put Merthiolate on. but it hurt, I kept dofeing it up. his finger started to swell. then I looked at the bottle and I had been putting red cake coloring on. "how dumb" I was up to Ruths all summer of 1973. she she had my Birthday dinner on Thanksgiving day. Donna's family were there. Carl and Jerry came up. then I came home with them then on Dec 4th, Carl went to Warren Ohio to work. Jerry started getting things ready for Christmas, got a tree in town and Ronie helped her Put it up. and trim it, then on Monday

68.

Dec 17th. the water pipes were froze up. so on Tuesday 18th Jerry took me over to Louise's. they were getting ready for thier class Christmas Party. and I went to that which I enjoyed very much. they had sandwiches and Coffee, and a lot of Christmas Cookies. 5 different kinds of Jello salad. Jerry Came after me Wednesday. said water Pump froze and bursted a piece out she got the piece and got it fixed. Carl was snowed out so he Came home. will be here till after Christmas. We went to Barbaras in the morning. Children were having a nice time with thier toys. Carl was home till New Years day. then back to work. Don and Ruth went to Arizona by Plane Jan 4th, home Jan 11th. had a grand time, altho it either rained or snowed evry day they were there. Ruth enjoyed the mountains and Catcus better than Don. I enjoyed the Mountains, and snow capped ones in the distance. and I still like the hills in old Ohio too.

69.

March 5th 1974. I started to throw up blood, about 3 or more pints, It scared Jerry, and she called the Dr. he said bring her to the hospital, I will call for a bed to be ready, and I will be there. in about 20 minutes the ambulance was at the door and we were soon there. EX showed, I had a bleeding ulcer. I was in the hospital till the 17th of March. when I got home, I was in bed one week, had to be quiet so ulcer would heal, I was on a special diet but am doing real well. as there are still plenty of good nurishing food. I can have, at the hospital I got 3 pts of good blood back, drop by drop drop. I am O.K. now and wash the dishes again, which I really enjoy. I think of things I have left out. Nora fell in Bathroom and broke her hip was in Nelsonville hospital but finally got so she could walk with a walker for a while then soon, did not need walker. then

70.

Nellie got real sick was at River-
side hospital, finally got home and
back to office to work. then Nora had
a stroke, soon passed away. Nellie
got to feeling bad, not able to
work. soon had to go to Hospial
again, her trouble was malignant
and she did not live very long
after she went to hospital. Nora
passed away Jan 1963, Nellie in
June 1963. So Louise is all I have
left of my sisters family.

Chapter 28: Diamond Brick Factory – Mrs. Kapple's Story

Figure 55 Diamond Plant early 1950s

In 1911 Martin Olinger, John Reiter, Hud Price, and James Pealey purchased a large parcel of land from the Wolfe family. They constructed the Ohio Fireproofing Company factory in the valley north of the Canal Locks and began the production of clay tile.

Mrs. Kapple's history of the Diamond School brings to light a lost piece of history on the town called Diamond. September 5, 1912, the Ohio Fireproofing Company sold one acre of land to the Starr Township Board of Education.

A few years later, the company discontinued the tile production and began the exclusive production of clay brick. The name DIAMOND appears on all their clay manufactured products.

Company owned houses were built for the factory employees, a church and a school was built for the benefit of the Diamond community.

I share this story with the permission of Mrs. Kapple's son, Ronnie.

Mrs. Kapple's Story

Dedicated to
Ruth Tucker Poppenhaeger
Her parents and siblings
Who call Diamond "Home"

Sources of information
Old deeds and records
Ruth Lewis Ringhiser
Ruth Tucker Poppenhaeger
Lolita Jeffrey Allen
Ada Smith Ralph
Ralph Hess

The History of The Diamond School
Chapter 1

The beginning of the twentieth century was a "boom" era for the Hocking Valley, not only for the coal mining industry but also for the manufacturing of clay products.

The clay soil in the rugged hills of the area was suitable for the making of bricks, various types of tiles and pottery. There were factories in Logan, Greendale, New Straitsville, Corning, New Cadiz (Union Furnace), East Clayton (Nelsonville), and Diamon, all within approximately fifty miles radius.

Each of the companies would build houses for their employees, would have a company-owned general store and also would generously help support churches and schools in the vicinity. The company wanted to provide good living conditions for the workers, who migrated to the area from all part of the United States and foreign countries.

Peter Hayden, Pittsburg, Pennsylvania, formed Haydenville Mining and Manufacturing Company (Natco), which purchased several hundred acres of land in Green, Ward and Starr Township, Hocking County, Ohio.

On March 22, 1902 the company sold sections five and six of Starr Township 12, located west of the Hocking-

Athens County line to the National (Ohio) Fireproofing Company.

A tile factory and a small hamlet (Diamond) were established. Research has failed to reveal how the name for the community originated.

Throughout the years the factory changed ownership several times. Presently, it is under the management of General Clay Products Corporation who, with the modern technology of ceramics, combine wood sawdust and chemicals with the clay in the production of bricks which are trucked to all the eastern states.

Like other companies they provided housing for their workers at the rental price of nine dollars a month. With the passing of time all the residences were demolished except for one. The current population is fourteen.

The children of the area had to walk approximately two miles up the road to attend the Stires School, Starr Township. As the population of Diamond increased there were enough children to have a local school.

On September 5, 1912, the Ohio Fireproofing Company President M.P. Ohlinger and Secretary L.H. Price sold one acre of land in section six to the Starr Township Board of Education. The school board president, Charles H. Patton and clerk, John R. McClain negotiated the transaction.

The acreage lies easterly to westerly parallel to the United States Highway Route 33, formerly Ohio State Route 31. Prior to that it was described as the Hocking County Road running from Haydenville to Nelsonville. The land is bounded on the south by the Hocking Canal. The Hocking Valley Railroad (Chessie System) is adjacent to the canal. Opposite the railroad flows the Hocking River formerly named, "Hockhocking" by the Delaware Indians who roamed the area. In their language "Hockhocking" meant "Bottle River". At some points the stream is very narrow and straight forming a neck then widens on each side into the appearance of a bottle. According to the archeology class of the Hocking Technical College, Nelsonville, Ohio, and Indian settlement had been located in the field between the railroad and river.

The Diamond portion of the Hocking Canal was completed in 1840. It was four feet deep with sloping earth banks which extended out to forty feet. The actual bottom of the canal was only twenty eight feet wide.

The remnants of the canal bed and tow paths are presently visible. Horses and mules would trudge along the tow paths pulling the heavy barges loaded with coal to market to the Ohio River or Lake Erie. Fast packet boats carried mail and passengers in and out of the valley at the speed of four miles an hour. The trip from Diamond to Columbus would take four to five days.

The canal was abandoned in favor of a faster method of transportation for both passengers and freight. The National Fireproofing Company leased the canal from the State of Ohio for a period of ninety-nine years.

The Hocking Valley Railroad was built in the 1870's. For more than a century it was extensively traveled. The Diamond factory continued shipping brick by rail until 1987. At the present time the only use for the tracks is when the Hocking Valley Scenic Railway provides rides to the tourists from Nelsonville to Logan during the summer and autumn months.

Chapter II

During 1914 and 1915 a one room schoolhouse was constructed near the Diamond Chapel. The dilapidated structure of the church remains. If only it could talk, what interesting stories it would tell. After church services were terminated for more than three years, the property was converted back to the original land owner - The National Fireproofing Company.

The school had brick walls that were a foot thick covered with a multi-colored slate roof. The inside dimensions were twenty-four feed wide, thirty-five long and the height of fourteen feet. It was believed that the higher the ceilings, the more healthy it would be. The prevention of air-pollution began many decades ago. On the southeast side of the building, near the back door, stood a coal-house. Beyond it was a boys' privy and on the west side was a girls' privy where the scrap paper was recycled. Behind the school was a water well with a long-handle pump. The water was carried inside in a two-gallon tin bucket for drinking from a dipper or poured into a granite was basin for washing hands. The Diamond ladies would come to the well for water to cook beans as they believed it was better for that purpose than any other water.

Ralphy (Hammy or Ham-bone) Hass, Columbus, Ohio recalls that during his seventh and eighth grades he was the school janitor for "the handsome sum of five dollars a month". The custodial position consisted of scrubbing the out-houses, sweeping the wood floors, dusting all the desks, cleaning the blackboards, pounding dust from the erasers, carrying water and coal, taking out the ashes and kindling a fire in the huge iron pot belly stove that was in the middle of the east wall.

Mr. Hass has vivid memories of his boyhood days while living with his Aunt Cora and Uncle Nate Ellis at Diamond. After sixty plus years he can related the names of each household, the exact property lines and numerous land-marks.

The three R's were taught to the first eight grades in the one room with one teacher.

The standard procedure to begin the school day was for the children to stand with bowed heads to recite the Lord's Prayer. It was followed by pledging allegiance to the large United States flag that stood in the corner in front of the room.

The school hours were from eight o'clock in the morning to four o'clock in the afternoon with an hour intermission at noon. A few pupils would run home for lunch. The rest would eat from tin pails containing their mother's home-made goodies. The two half-hour recesses were the best part of the day. Ruth Lewis Ringhiser remembers the pleasurable times she had with her class-mates when they crossed the road in front of the school to play in the woods around a rock cave. They would make believe that Indians lived there.

There were very few toys on the market and very little money to buy them so it was necessary to create imaginary activities to fill the leisure time. For example, the girls would draw eyes, nose and a mouth on acorns, give each a name and pretend they were people in the home, church or school. The entertainment would continue for several hours. An ancient sport for the boys was rolling a rim from an old wagon wheel with a wire, it was a challenge to keep "the hoop" balanced. The games at school included hide and seek, hop-scotch,

London Bridge, drop the handkerchief, ring around the rosie, skip the rope, tug of war, shooting marbles and the ever popular baseball.

It was a pleasant interlude from the everyday school work when Martha Smith, Creola, Ohio arrived at the school one afternoon a week to teach vocal music. After she was transferred to the Union Furnace School, Mary Elizabeth Kessinger, Nelsonville, Ohio, continued the singing instructions. Miss Kessinger also proceeded to Union Furnace.

It was a common practice for a student to "skip" a grade or two. Bernice Lewis Dalton was a year older than her sister, Ruth Lewis Ringhiser and had been in school a year when Ruth started. To make it easier for the teacher, Walter Ruttan, they were taught equally which continued all through high school, as a result they graduated the same year, 1937.

Children were permitted to begin school at the age of five years. Ruth Tucker Poppenhaeger was six years old and her younger sister, Helen Tucker Hilton, was five when they entered the first grade together. They had an unique ambition - to attend school for twelve years without missing a day. Ruth had the misfortune of contacting the scarlet fever which forced her to remain at home until recovered. Helen successfully accomplished the praise-worthy feat.

Florence Woolery was the teacher for the seven years the Tucker sisters attended the Diamond School.

More frequently than omitting a grade was the failing to pass a grade to force the scholar to repeat the same work the following year.

The down-fall of many students was the memorizing of the tricky multiplication tables, the soon-to-be-forgotten history dates and the mountain of poetry.

At times the pupil would be in the eighth grade two or even three years and be the size of the teacher before dropping out. The truant officers strictly enforced the laws of the State of Ohio which requires a citizen to remain in school until the legal age of sixteen years.

The teachers not only taught form the few available textbooks but also good manners, personal hygiene and moral conduct. Most of them were stern disciplinarians. It has been said, "They have eyes in the back of their heads". Often, very often, a wood paddle or hickory stick was whacked across the posterior for committing the slightest provocation. The school-master received full cooperation from the parents who constantly warned their off-spring if they got a "threshing" at school they would get a more severe one at home.

Rhea Evens Barber remembers quite well that when she was in the first grade, she was cracked on a hand with a ruler (for whispering) by her mentor, Nita

Powers. Miss Powers was the last teacher at the school. She lived with her parents, Clarence and Mary Powers at the Locks - a half mile from Diamond.

Other educators were: Irene Sate Murtha, Walter Haas, Arlie White, Miss Carpenter, Porter Heinlein, George Christian and Edna Patton.

The school term was in session eight months a year with it ending during the last week of April. "The last day of school" was a much anticipated event. The teacher would plan a celebration. Some would have a picnic, others would have a program with the entire student body participating with recitations, reading and singing. The teacher would give a certificate to the scholars who had achieved their goal of perfect attendance. The room would be decorated with sweet Williams, mayapples and other wild flowers that had been collected on a field trip. The parents and friends were invited to attend the auspicious affair.

Some teachers would have an eighth grade commencement. A diploma would be presented to each student who had successfully completed all eight grades. This was prestigious honor.

For many of the pupils, elementary school was the only formal education they ever received. Often the fathers would persuade the foremen to hire their sons to work at the factory and the daughters would become the "hired girl" for the more affluent families in the nearby cities.

May day (May 1) was another special day in a child's life as it was the official day to begin going barefoot. The rest of the summer shoes were worn only to Sunday School in order to conserve them.

When the enrollment increased at the school, another room measuring twenty five feet wide and thirty feet long was added to the east wall of the first room. The classes were divided with four grades in each room. Both rooms were used only four or five years then the classes were combined into the original room.

One September a kindergarten for the pre-school age children was started. Due to the lack of interest and low attendance it closed in December. Thereafter, the new room or "little room" acted as a gymnasium.

The enrollment at the Diamond School decreased as rapidly as it had increased. The older inhabitants remained in the community and most of the younger generation moved to other localities. Therefore, the birth rate declined.

According to one of the former residents, Grace Jeffery, she, her husband, Alfred and five children moved to house number nine in the row of newly built four room company houses. She swept out the saw dust and remained in the community the rest of their lives which was more than ninety years.

After Mr. Jeffery's retirement from the factory, they spent their "golden years" at the home of their eldest son, Joubert, who was a very sentimental person. He insisted the residence and its contents to be just as his parents left them at the time of their deaths, as a monument to their memory. Mr. And Mrs. Jeffery were granted their one request - to be allowed to die at home instead of a hospital. The domain located at Diamond on a high hill overlooking the valley is gradually deteriorating including the contents.

Gerald (Chub) and Bertha Tucker were among the early settlers at Diamond. They had many joyful memories but also of the many hardships they endured while raising a family of eight children on his pay of one dollar a day while loading the clay cars. Most of the workers would start in the clay mine then advance to the better positions paying two to three dollars a day.

Bertha was an ambitious lady who dedicated her life to "do unto others". She would help any of her neighbors in every way she could, especially the new mothers. She would assist with the housework and care for the infant; she gave many former inhabitants their first bath. She would hang wallpaper for one dollar a room. Her happiest days were when her children and grandchildren gathered at her home for holidays and Sunday dinners.

Donna Tucker Sullivan remembers when her father, Lowell (Snake) was elected the village constable but in the by-gone days it was a needless position in the peaceful little municipality. Just about the only excitement was occasional altercation among the young people which the parents would soon remedy as they did not "spare the rod".

Another first family was Eugene (Gene-Dad) and Jennie Lehman. He was a justice of peace and performed weddings in his home. Gene-Dad was a religious individual who tried to persuade his neighbors to attend the local church but was not very successful.

A book could have been written containing the countless stories told by William Buttermore and his siter, Janie Buttermore Cullison Goody concerning their (and their predecessors) struggles for survival which were a familiar part of Early American History.

Four members (Jack, Phillmon, St. Clair, and sister Maxine Leffler Stump) of the large family of Edward and Mary Leffler returned to work and live at Diamond.

Other than the previously mentioned surnames associated with Diamond are: Allen, Joy, Wolfe, Campbell, Hankison, Mahaffey, Fisher, Ohlinger, Skiver, Fox, Williams, Reider, Thompson, Heading, Keplar, Arbaugh, Bacus, Shaw, Gastin, Hull, Connor, Warren, Welch, Spillman, Wilson, Mathena, Keels, Norman, Cassells, Avis, Malone, Smathers, Winchell and Kapple.

The year Mary Tucker Burd was in the eighth grade, the Diamond classroom was overcrowded. To eliminate the situation, she and her counterparts joined the high schoolers to walk three miles to the Haydenville School, Green Township. Occasionally one of the fathers would car-pool the students but there were very few family automobiles in the locality.

During the period of time the Greyhound Bus System maintained an hourly schedule from Columbus to Pomeroy. As Diamond was not a regular stop the patrons would stand by the roadside to flag the bus. ON the return trip home they would pull the overhead cord for the vehicle to stop. The cost of the ticket was ten cents from Diamond to Nelsonville. On the west side of the Diamond "city limits" was Wolfe Basin from where the bus fare was fifteen cents. The prospective passengers would cross the dividing line into Diamond or vice versa to save the difference of a nickel.

The residents would travel the distance of four miles to Nelsonville to buy groceries and other necessities. The Ohlinger and Wolfe store served as the Diamond Company store where the employer would charge their purchases then the amount would be deducted from their paycheck every two weeks.

Each family would grow a garden during the summer and preserve the vegetables for the winter months. They would have a few chickens for eggs and to eat.

Sometimes there would be an extra dozen eggs to sell to a neighbor or take to market in a basket. Each household aimed to have a pig or two to butcher for meat. Only a few would have a cow buy they would share the milk with whoever wanted it. The cream would be churned into butter for the family table and to sell. It would be molded into one pound rolls with a design of a flower imprinted in the center on the top. The stores had a policy pf paying more for the farm products if the amount was "traded out" instead of accepting cash.

Harold Smith, a Diamond native, said, "At one time the place was overflowing with cats, dogs and kids."

As there weren't any natural gas lines in the area, the residents would heat their homes with coal. They were very excited when the pretty brown "heatrolas" replaced the ugly black monstrosities. They would have a coal and wood range in the kitchen for cooking and heating water. Some folks used a more modern method of cooking which was stove operated by kerosene (coal-oil). It was purchase in town for fifteen cents a gallon and brought home on the bus in one to five gallon tin cans.

Before electricity was available, kerosene was used in lamps to light the homes.

The only telephone in the vicinity was at the company office which the personnel was welcome to sue in an emergency.

The Diamondites journeyed to Nelsonville for professional assistance. There were several family doctors where the patients would go into the office to wait "their turn" instead of a "necessary appointment". The examinations and medication in either a glass bottle or a neat little envelope bearing the instructions cost three dollars. The amount was considered "excessively high" as there was an elderly practitioner who charge one dollar for "lending a sympathetic ear" and issuing a packet of tablets. It was rumored that he purchased those little red pills by the barrel and prescribed them for every ailment. He would extract an aching tooth without any fee while those licensed in dentistry would charge one dollar a tooth.

The physicians would make house calls to Diamond for five dollars, including the medicine. They would deliver a baby for the price of twenty-five dollars. When the expectant parents did not have the available cash for a qualifying obstetrician, a neighboring mid-wife would perform the birthing ritual.

After the Haydenville High School closed in 1933, the Starr Township pupils were transferred to the Union Furnace High School by a bus owned and operated by John Norris and sons, John Jr. and Stanley, Laurel Run.

Around 1930 the Laurel Run School, Starr Township consolidated with the Diamond School. The fourteen pupils were transferred to Diamond for almost two years. Due to the protests of the parents the Laurel Run School reopened for two years then closed permanently in 1934. The children of Wolfe Basin and Locks also attended the Diamond School.

In the fall of 1932, the community was informed that Diamond School would close at the end of the year and in January 1935 the pupils would be bussed to the Union Furnace Elementary along with the high school youth.

The little brick school by the side of the road was filled to its capacity with an emotional audience at the last Christmas program. This writer witnessed this grand finale of twenty years.

Contrary to the educational statistics everyone who attended a one room school claims they learned more than the youngsters do today with the modern sophisticated system.

The following is a partial list of the Diamond School alumni: Joubert, Gladys, Lolita, Gerald and David Jeffery; Lawrence, Letha, Lowell, Emma, Mary, Ray, Ruth, and Helen Tucker; Ralph Hass, Vivian, Roger and Ralph Campbell; Eugene and Helen Evans; Jack Jov; Ivan and Melvin Wolfe; Joe Cullison; Kenneth Good; Bernice, Ruth and Bill Lewis; Ada Willard and Harold Smith; Frank, Eugene, Ruth and Kathryn Cheshire; Wavelene and Buddy Shiver; Fred Willis; Bonnie, Bill and Clarence Bacus; Rhea Evans; Gerald Karns; Dwight and Nellie Evans;

Charles, Nellie, Ronald, Flora, Paul and Foster Campbell; Minnie, Fred and Louise Tucker; Emma Loomis; Marian Lehman; Maxine, Bob and Kathryn Fox; Virginia Hankison; and Mary Louse Watkins.

Chapter III

On December 15, 1934, the Starr Township Board of Education sold the Diamond School property to William Evans (grandfather of Rhea, Myrtle and Bill Evans) who was "born and raised" at Diamond. At the present time the fifth generation of the Evans Family resides on the same plot of land. William's younger brother, Clifford (Pete) was brutally murdered at the location. The catastrophe occurred around six o'clock in the evening when Pete was home alone while the remaining populace of the valley were in Nelsonville for the annual Parade of the Hills in the early 1970's. Approximately twenty years later the crime remains unsolved.

Another tragedy that saddened the community was when Hardie Smith was fatally injured by a car while crossing Route 33 on his way home (house number seven) at the end of a day's work at the Diamond factory.

The entire country sympathized with the Ivan (Boy) and Bessie Wolfe family when their youngest son,

Melvin (Wimpy) lost his life in combat during World War II.

Bill Bacus, Columbus, Ohio, a former "hometown boy" tells the following story: Once upon a time the Smith family, Herdie, Cora and children Ada, Willard and Harold invited the entire burg to their backyard in the row for a wiener roast. The hot dogs cost one cent each. Bill, a mischievous lad of eleven or twelve years of age, "did not have a penny to his name" but went to the party anyway. Kindhearted Cora gave him a hot dog. He admired the lady from the day forward.

For the past forty-nine years the former Diamond School has provided shelter for Sidney and Madeline Kapple and their two children, Ronald Dean Kapple and Ruth Ann Kapple until they reached adulthood.

"It's not what you've got but what you do with what you've got that counts."

Madeline Bacus Kapple

December 5, 1989

Chapter 29: New Beginning 2008

Haydenville started as a Company owned town in the late 1800's. When the company closed its doors forever in the late1950's, the town was left to fend for itself. We had no central government or law enforcement protection, the residents had no one to turn to for guidance or help. Within a few years, deterioration and physical decay was beginning to overcome the town. Thanks to the tireless efforts of the Haydenville Preservation Committee the physical appearance of the community began to improve. During this time frame I was self-appointed and recognized by the elected Hocking County Commissioners and Green Township Trustees as the advocate for the residents and community of Haydenville.

When the company owned the town we had no street lights or sidewalks. My first major project was to work with John S. of the American Electric Company (AEP) and the State of Ohio Public Utilities Commission (PUCO) to get the numerous electric safety violations corrected. I appealed to the Green Township Trustees for street lights through the community. They suggested that I work with John S. of AEP to determine the most critical and economical locations for street lights. The Township Trustees agreed to the installation of 17 street lights and assumed the monthly utility bill for the lights. AEP installed and maintained the street lights at the locations John S. and I had chosen. Efforts to improve the community had not gone unnoticed. Tri-County Community Action (TCCA) applied for the very competitive Community Development Block Grant (CDBG). Jessica S. of TCCA and I gathered volumes of needed paper work and held meetings with the local residents to get their impute on improvement for the community. We used the recently install street lights as our contribution requirement for a CDBG grant.

Our efforts were rewarded, we received the full $486,000 grant. With that money in hand we purchased the land and removed the remnants of the old school building to prepare the site for the first-ever community park. We solicited bids for concrete sidewalks, improvements to the interior of the old school band room, shelter house and playground equipment, a 30" drain from the old canal to the Hocking River, and numerous storm drains through the town.

Figure 56 March 8, 2008
Thelma Avenue, the first of 17 streetlights

Figure 57 September 17, 2008
Patty and Larry breaking ground for the Community Park.

Figure 58 Larry Horn, Sr. standing at the entrance to the Haydenville Community Park.

Figure 59 Larry Horn Sr. standing by the old band room, now the community building.

Chapter 30: Christmas Eve 1984

Figure 60 Christmas Eve 1984: Avenelle, Shirley, and Dad

Christmas Eve at Dad's house has been a family tradition since early 1960. Dad would slow-bake a ham all day, make a big bowl of fruit salad with a lot of fresh fruit and bake several pies from scratch.

All five of his children, their husbands and wives, and all of his grandchildren would gather for a Christmas Eve dinner and gift exchange. I have seen over 20 people in Dad's house at one time. Dad would say, "There is always room for one more."

After dinner, Dad would set down on the floor beside the Christmas tree and hand out the gifts. The evening started out in the usual way. Dad was handing out gifts when someone knocked at the door. I don't remember who answered the door, but Santa Clause came in. Everyone was dumbfounded, and the little kid creamed with joy, "Santa Clause is here!"

Santa called each one by their name, including Avenelle, and gave each one a lollipop. He said, "It was time to go, I have a lot of work to do tonight!"

Figure 61 Larry, Santa Claus, and Dad

Santa Claus agreed to have his picture taken with Dad and me before he went on his mission of joy to the world. Our family still talks about that very special Christmas Eve at Dad's house.

That year, in 1984, my siblings and I sat down and wrote a poem about Christmas…

It Happened

Have you ever known a Christmas
When your secret dreams come true
We had that luck in '84
And the joy I'll share with you

Now our family, as we gathered
And numbered twenty-seven
Experienced the kind of love
That only comes from Heaven

My Dad and Avenelle
Had called us all together
The night was clear, the air was fresh
And gentle was the weather

But the strangest thing did happen
What could result from thunderbolts
The lights went out, 'twas oh so dark
Gave all our senses curious jolts!

There appeared no obvious reason
The lights would not be glowing
It was the Christmas season
All electric brilliance showing

But, not to be in Haydenville
The darkness had to be
The modernism was not God's will
Now we can clearly see

As we opened gifts by candlelight
Danny's inner wish came true
He wanted an old-fashioned Christmas
And it's basic trimmings, too

Connie wanted Plum Pudding
And Plum Pudding it would be
Ann made the dish fulfilling her wish
A coincidence, you see

Ann wished for home-made gravy
The kind her daddy made
And he made it without recipe
His memory didn't fade

It was simple fare to many
But not to this fine bunch
Bread 'n gravy served in childhood
Was this family's favorite lunch!

The music box that Avenelle got
Played "Here Comes Santa Claus"
Its tinkling was sweet to the ears it did meet
But did cause our hearts to pause...

A tap at the door and who should arrive
But the jolly character himself
What a splendid treat for the children
The coveted Christmas Elf!

Larry had arranged for Santa
To appear in his warm red suit
He called kids by name, wished them well
And promised to leave them some loot!

Chrissy had to take a peek
To see the reindeer trail
But they were gone
Without a glimpse, his magic couldn't fail!

Sister Shirley is the link
That makes the circle whole
Having us all together
Was her one and only goal

Oil lights and candles
Togetherness and love
Homemade gravy, dinner
But no dirty dishes of

Without the modern pleasures
Of electricity
We *had* to be together
My family and me

We huddled, talked and listened
To each other, side by side
The obvious joy did glisten
On my father and his bride

Dad's little house did glow that night
Though lights were scant and dim
We knew the Lord was with us
As we praised and honored Him

More Christmas memories…

Walter and Doris C. and their family have been close friends with my family for over 30 years. When their daughter Kim gave birth to a little girl, they named her Savanna. Savanna was only a few hours old when I held her in my arms for the first time, her tiny hand clasping my little finger, and a special bond formed. I became her Godfather. The bond between us has never faltered – her PapPaw Larry has always been there, be it good times or hard times.

Christmas 2020 was no exception. Every year, I gather with Savanna and her family on Christmas Eve for a big dinner and gift exchange. That year, Savanna's youngest daughter was old enough to open her presents, one little strip of wrapping at a time. It was a slow process, but we enjoyed watching her. From Savanna's very first Christmas, I always give her a gift wrapped in bright blue paper.

This past summer, Addie, Savanna's oldest daughter, made a special book for me (see below). Addie and I talked about my book *Haydenville* in detail. She told me she had written a book once, but had a hard time holding the pencil. I asked her how old she was when she wrote her first book, and she said, "Six, but I'm older now. I'm in the 3rd Grade and can hold my pencil better."

Addie said she was going to put my name in her book and ask me if I would put her name in my book. Of course, the answer is obvious, I'm her Grampa. Her name in my book has become the subject of conversation among her family and friends.

Grampa has kept his word. The world knows Addie is a very special part of my life. This book is closed, but not finished. Memories are a never-ending story.

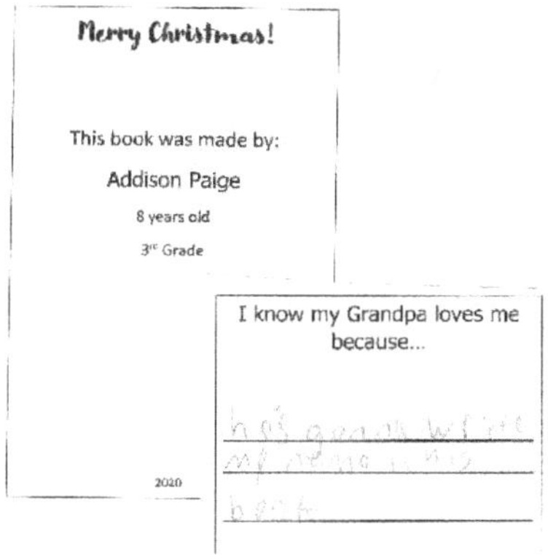

From the Author

This book has become a passion, a challenge, a dream. Why? Why have I spent untold hours compiling this book? I have never written a book before let alone have one published.

What are the odds so many people would share with me information of their families, their life experiences and precious memories of days gone by?

What are the odds I would discover that the S. S. Mills Stone Quarry was close to the coal hoppers at Hopperville, that I am a direct decedent of the Mills family, and that the forgotten community of Hopperville was in existence several years before Haydenville was founded?

This book is the foundation for the recognition of Hopperville and the installation of a Historical marker on the site of its large company employee boarding house.

What are the odds that the I would be conducting in-depth research on Louis Coleman (Hunkie Louie) on October 30, 2020, exactly forty-four years after the date of his burial?

What are the odds that I observed the ghosts of three children watching me while I was doing the physical history of the Haydenville Cemetery? That a few years later I would see the same little girl (ghost) in the backyard at house #16876 Haydenville Road? She was watching the children playing in the backyard next door.

My experience with the three (ghost) children is proof we are not alone. Is the ole adage true, everything happen for a reason?

Larry A. Horn, Sr.

Larry Horn 1958 and in 2014

About the Author

Larry A. Horn is the oldest son of Arthur Ethelbert and Ruth May (Mills) Horn, born July 19, 1939. Larry's dad said he was born in the Greendale Hotel, Greendale, Ohio. His grandfather Harry C. Mills was superintendent at the now abandoned Greendale Brick Company.

In the early 40's Larry's parents wanted to be closer to their friends and relatives in Haydenville. The family moved to the 6th house north of the Church. A few years later they moved down the street to house #25 (now #16866) and were living in that house on that sad day in, July 1957, when my mother passed away at the young age of 42. The family had grown to a total of five children; Shirley, Larry, Danny, Connie and Ruth Ann.

Larry has many fond memories of those childhood days, playing on the hills around the town, working on the farm for Mr. Grubb, picking strawberries for 5-cents a quart, planting acres of gladiolas for 25-cents per hour, delivering *The Logan Daily News* when it cost 4-cents a copy to his 39 customers with a commission of 5-cents per week per customer. As years went by Mr. Matheny and his wife (Freda) took a liking to Larry, and in the early 50s Mr. Matheny offered him the job as stock boy in the Company Store for 35-cents an hour. Ward Phillips, store manager; Libby Phillips, clerk; Bernice Carter, clerk; Gertie Aucher, clerk; John Clouston and Homer Carter, meat cutters.

When word leaked out to the factory workers that Mr. Matheny had personally given me the job in the Company Store, it became the unwritten rule amongst all the factory workers "that's Matheny's boy, don't stop him, and let him go wherever he wants to go in the factory." I never abused that special privileged but made friends with many of the men and thus the history I have recorded is from events and conversations with many of those workers of days gone by.

Figure 62 Larry A. Horn, Sr. at work.

www.ingramcontent.com/pod-product-compliance
Lightning Source LLC
Chambersburg PA
CBHW062036090426
42740CB00016B/2928